The Center for Democracy and Technology and Internet Privacy in the U.S.

Lessons of the Last Five Years

Joyce H-S Li

The Scarecrow Press, Inc.
Lanham, Maryland, and Oxford
2003

SCARECROW PRESS, INC.

Published in the United States of America
by Scarecrow Press, Inc.
A Member of the Rowman & Littlefield Publishing Group
4501 Forbes Boulevard, Suite 200, Lanham, Maryland 20706
www.scarecrowpress.com

P.O. Box 317
Oxford
OX2 9RU, UK

This book is based on a dissertation written for the School of Information Sciences, University of Pittsburgh, April 2001, dissertation advisor Dr. Toni Carbo.

British Library Cataloging in Publication Information Available

Library of Congress Cataloging-in-Publication Data

Li, Joyce H.-S., 1972–
    The center for democracy and technology and internet privacy in the U.S. : lessons of the last five years / Joyce H-S Li.
        p. cm.
    ISBN 0-8108-4442-7 (hardcover : alk. paper)
        1. Privacy, Right of—United States. 2. Internet. 3. Center for Democracy and Technology. I. Title.
    JC596.2.U5 L54 2002
    323.44′8—dc21

                                                        2002007280

♾™ The paper used in this publication meets the minimum requirements of American National Standard for Information Sciences—Permanence of Paper for Printed Library Materials, ANSI/NISO Z39.48-1992.
Manufactured in the United States of America

To my family.
I am most grateful to my parents for instilling in
me the value of education from time immemorial.
Thank you for giving me the opportunity to be the first
in our family to attend university, let alone obtain a Ph.D.

Contents

Appendixes

Figures and Tables

Acronyms and Abbreviations

ABA	American Bar Association
ACLU	American Civil Liberties Union
AICPA	American Institute of Certified Public Accounts
AOL	America Online
BBB	Better Business Bureau
BBS	Bulletin Board Service
CALEA	Communications Assistance Law Enforcement Act
CDA	Communications Decency Act
CDT	Center for Democracy and Technology
CFA	Consumer Federation of America
CIA	Central Intelligence Agency
CICA	Canadian Institute of Chartered Accountants
CIEC	Citizens Internet Empowerment Coalition
COPA	Child Online Protection Act
COPPA	Children's Online Privacy Protection Act
CPA	Certified Public Account
CPSR	Computer Professionals for Social Responsibility
CTIA	Cellular Telecommunications Industry Association
DMV	Department of Motor Vehicles
DoJ	Department of Justice
DPWG	Digital Privacy Working Group
DSF	Delivery Sequence File
EBB	Electronic Bulletin Board
ECPA	Electronic Communications Privacy Act
EFF	Electronic Frontier Foundation
EPIC	Electronic Privacy Information Center
FBI	Federal Bureau of Investigation
FCC	Federal Communications Commission
FCRA	Fair Credit Reporting Act
FTC	Federal Trade Commission

GLAAD	Gay & Lesbian Alliance against Defamation
HEW	Department of Health, Education, and Welfare
IBM	International Business Machine
IC	[Congressional] Internet Caucus
IP	Internet Protocol
ISP	Internet Service Provider
IT	Information Technology
IWT	Interactive Working Group
LAN	Local Area Network
LEAs	Law Enforcement Agencies
NCOA	National Change of Address [Office]
NPR	National Public Radio
NRC	National Research Council
NSA	National Security Agency
NSF	National Science Foundation
OMB	Office of Management and Budget
OTA	Office of Technology Assessment
P3	Pentium III
P3P	Platform for Privacy Preferences
PFAW	People for the American Way
PGP	Pretty Good Privacy
PICA	Public Interest Computer Association
PPA	Privacy Protection Act
PPSC	Privacy Protection Study Commission
PRC	Privacy Rights Clearinghouse
PSN	Processor Serial Number
ROM	Read Only Memory
SAFE Act	Security and Freedom through Encryption Act
TACD	Trans Atlantic Consumer Dialogue
TCPA	Telephone Consumer Protection Act
TET	Telecommunications Education Trust
UCAN	Utility Consumers' Action Network
UCE	Unsolicited Commercial Email
USPS	United States Postal Service
VTW	Voters Telecommunications Watch
W3C	World Wide Web Consortium
WWW	World Wide Web

Foreword

When Joyce Li met with me to discuss the ideas she had for her dissertation and to ask me to chair her committee, I was impressed by her intelligence, broad understanding of the issues, and enthusiasm for the topic. It was clear that she had read extensively about privacy and had thought carefully about the approach she wanted to take with her research. Over the months, she and I spent considerable time exploring the topic, discussing the research questions and methodologies, and the subjects of privacy and the Center for Democracy and Technology (CDT). Of course, as the chair of the Board for CDT, I immediately told Dr. Li that we needed to make this involvement clear to the full committee and to determine whether anyone thought this would be a conflict of interest or might affect the research oversight in any way. The committee determined that they did not see any potential conflict or problem and suggested that the connection might actually be positive in providing improved access to CDT.

The dissertation on which this book is based is a very significant contribution to knowledge in the information sciences field, particularly information policy. The chapters on privacy provide an excellent overview of privacy: its historical role in the United States, the high value placed on the protection of privacy in America, definitions and characteristics of it, issues related to the ownership of personal data, and the means of protecting privacy. These chapters can stand alone in their own right and provide a fine "primer" on privacy, illuminating this complex subject.

The selection of the Center for Democracy and Technology for the case study was appropriate because CDT began with a focus on privacy protection as part of its concerns for the protection of civil liberties in the Digital Age. In addition, Jerry Berman, who founded CDT, is widely considered to be one of the leading privacy experts in the United States. This is the first study of the CDT and, as such, it provides both new knowledge about the organization and a model for the examination of the many other public interest organizations established to protect civil liberties, as well as other not-for-profit groups in other areas.

Dr. Li's research provides a useful conceptual model for other research projects in the future; she has effectively used triangulation to explore her subject. This book is a highly readable story of the evolution of privacy protection and of one of the leading U.S. civil liberty organizations. I expect that it will be read and quoted widely, and it is likely to become a classic study in the years to come. The School of Information Sciences at the University of Pittsburgh is fortunate to have Dr. Li as a graduate of the program, and it was a personal privilege for me to have the opportunity to work with Dr. Li. I am confident that she will be a very successful information professional and scholar in the years ahead.

Dr. Toni Carbo
Dean of the School of Information Sciences
University of Pittsburgh

Preface

The first half of this book serves as a general introduction to the issue of privacy in the United States. Chapter 1 describes the emergence of privacy as an issue in this country; here, we will discover why privacy has been so valued by Americans throughout the nation's history. Chapter 2 deals with the different aspects of privacy, namely its definitions, characteristics, criteria, and functions. Chapter 3 discusses the ownership of personal data, specifically one's name, address, telephone number, and electronic mail. Chapter 4 examines the means of protecting privacy, from technological to governmental and from individual to industry.

The second half of this book contains the first ever case study of the social impact of the Center for Democracy and Technology (CDT), or any privacy advocacy group, for that matter. The CDT's work on Internet privacy from January 1995 through March 2000 forms the focus of the investigation.[1] Three research questions guided this project:

1. What have been the major results of the CDT in terms of its work on Internet privacy?
2. How has the CDT been perceived by the American public as reflected in the mass media?
3. What has been the social impact of the CDT according to its funders?

It is important to study these questions for several reasons. First, privacy is much valued by Americans as a result of episodes of privacy invasion throughout our history. This value for individual privacy is so strong that the Founding Fathers created clauses in the Constitution that would uphold this right. Second, the creators of the Constitution were correct in protecting our right to privacy because it is essential in a democracy where citizens need to be autonomous and freethinking to ensure self-government. Third, and probably the most important reason, is that with concern about the loss in individual privacy on the rise, it is crucial to examine how an organization that advocates and defends the right to personal privacy functions, and what kind of reception it has received from the public. As Patricia Strum wrote:

> Groups like the American Civil Liberties Union, the Electronic Frontier Foundation, the Electronic Privacy Information Center, Computer Professionals for Social Responsibility, the United States Privacy Council, the Privacy Rights Clearinghouse . . . are responsible for much of the privacy that still exists in the United States. These are the institutions that monitor encroachments on privacy, lobby against them, and maintain a network to alert the public about new developments.[2]

Chapter 5 describes the major achievements of the CDT. Chapter 6 turns to the American public's perceptions on the CDT as reflected in the mass media. Chapter 7 examines CDT funders' perceptions on the social impact of this organization. The final chapter summarizes the research findings and includes several suggestions for future research.

This book is a revision of my dissertation for a doctoral degree in Library and Information Science at the University of Pittsburgh. I have restyled and added new materials to make this book more appealing to the general reader. For those interested in the methodology behind the study, please consult appendix A.

There are a number of people I would like to thank for making this book possible: Dr. Sue Easun, my editor at Scarecrow Press, for giving me the opportunity to publish my work; members of my dissertation committee—Professors Toni Carbo, Stephen Almagno, Ellen Detlefsen, Thomas Schott, and Martin Weiss—for their guidance and support; staff at the Center for Democracy and Technology, particularly Jerry Berman and Danielle Kolb, for their time and help; past and present funders of the Center for Democracy and Technology who took time to answer the questionnaire; and reference and interlibrary-loan librarians at the University of Pittsburgh and beyond for their help in locating materials for my research.

It should be noted that the chair of my dissertation committee, Dr. Toni Carbo, is also the chair of the Center for Democracy and Technology's board of directors. Professor Carbo's affiliation with both committees does not pose any conflicts of interest. In fact, her connection with the CDT has opened up doors for me in my research that would otherwise have been closed.

NOTES

1. It should be noted that the Clinton administration was in power during this period, and that the Republican Party had control of the United States Congress.
2. Philippa Strum, *Privacy: The Debate in the United States Since 1945* (Fort Worth, Tex.: Harcourt Brace College Publishers, 1998), 201.

1

The Emergence of Privacy as an Issue in the United States

As a concept, privacy has existed throughout American history. In the 18th and early 19th centuries, concerns about privacy are probably best exemplified by mail communications, the census, and the Bill of Rights. In early colonial America, no formal postal service existed. Letters were usually transported in an ad hoc fashion and without fixed charges by ship captains, friends, or people hired for the sole purpose of delivering specific items.[1] From the outset, the privacy of written communications could not be guaranteed for it was in the hands of strangers who had to be implicitly trusted. Moreover, even if the carriers themselves were honest, problems could occur in the delivery process. For instance, mail from England, if unclaimed from a ship captain on arrival, was left in a tavern or coffee house until finally collected.[2] The same applied to letters sent within the colonies.[3] Thus, local gossips could ransack unattended letter bags when news, especially from overseas, was scarce; likewise, businessmen could intercept "the correspondences and secrets of Merchants" in order to gain a competitive edge over their rivals.[4] When the British government took over the colonial American post in 1710, they quickly imposed regulation on the system. The Post Office Act of the same year prohibited all mail tampering except when authorized by a secretary of state. Still, some colonists boycotted the new government postal system due to the high postage that subsidized official communications of the Empire: this subsidy was considered by many to be yet another form of illegal taxation. Consequently, many colonists continued to risk losing privacy in their mail and to take advantage of occasional travelers and merchant sea captains even though private carrying of letters was now forbidden.

Having said this, the greater problem before Independence seemed to have been official rather than local tampering with private correspondence. For example, Governor Bradford of the Pilgrim colony at Plymouth Plantation seized and opened the letters of two disgruntled emigrants on their way back to England. He observed that the letters were "full of slanders, and false accusations, tending not only to their prejudice, but to their ruine and utter subversion."[5] Colonial postmasters, who began the first newspapers in America and delivered them free, were suspected of using mail entrusted to them as a source of news matter.[6] However, interception of private correspondence by upper British government officials was probably both more common and more pernicious than that by governors and postmasters.

As the 18th century progressed into the 19th century, post office regulations and procedures improved to enhance the confidentiality and security of mail. Such examples are (1) special locks on bags of "through mail" that inquisitive postmasters in smaller mail transit towns did not have keys to open; (2) the introduction of cheap postage meant that more people could afford to send letters, which in turn provided protection through sheer numbers; (3) prepayment by the sender insured that privacy no longer depended on "the whims of a clerk who willingly delivered letters to anyone who would pay for them, without taking the trouble to find out whether or not they belonged to him"; and (4) the Postal Act of 1825, which still remains in effect, imposed a fine

> if any person shall take any letter, or packet, not containing any article of value, or evidence thereof, out of a post office, or shall open any letter, or packet which shall have been in a post office, or in custody of a mail carrier, before it shall have been delivered to the person to whom it is directed, with a design to obstruct the correspondence, to pry into another's business or secrets.[7,8]

"Any person" meant literally what it stated; the prohibition extended from postal employees to government officials with no specific exemptions. The penalty for opening other people's mail was a fine of $500 with a year's imprisonment. However, the penalty for postal larceny was flogging, a more lenient sentence than death, which was the original punishment for mail theft.

Via the census, the authorities overtly gathered personal information from the public. The United States of America established the first periodic national census in its federal Constitution of 1787. The debut of this instrument was met with misgivings such as that expressed by Representative Livermore of New Hampshire. He had opposed any government demands for additional information for fear that

> it would excite the jealousy of the people; they would suspect that Government was too particular, in order to learn their ability to bear the burden of direct or other taxes; and, under this idea, they may refuse to give the officer such a particular account as the law requires, by which means you expose him to great inconvenience and delay in the performance of his duty.[9]

Another congressman urged moderation in the inquiries of their avowedly political census. Representative Page believed that "this particular method of describing the people"

> would occasion an alarm among them; they would suppose the Government intended something, by putting the Union to this additional expense, besides gratifying an idle curiosity; their purposes cannot be supposed the same as the historian's or philosopher's—they are statesmen, and all their measures are suspected of policy.[10]

Indeed, these misgivings seemed to have been warranted. Although the 1790 census was very limited in scope, it ran up against state loyalties disputing its federal authority, suspicions that the returns would be used for some new tax, and objections on religious grounds.[11] Nine years later when the federal government tried to register the number and size of windows for a house tax, people in the northeastern counties of Pennsylvania protested to such an extent that President Adams had to order military occupation to quell the disturbance.[12]

From the beginning, census administrators placed accuracy above confidentiality. From 1790 onward, two copies of the enumerators' lists were posted in public places in every district so that citizens could check for errors. This practice continued, in one form or another, until 1870.[13] "As originally conducted, the system was harmless, since only the names of heads of families were given and only the number of persons constituting the family reported."[14] In succeeding decades, however, the returns posted included more and more personal information such as physical defects (1830), insanity (1840), and the value of real property (1850). Also, from 1850 onward, returns were no longer aggregated under the name of the head of the household but under each individual within the household.[15]

Another invasion of privacy pertaining to the census was that every person over the age of sixteen was required to "render a true account, to the best of his knowledge, of every person belonging to the family in which he usually resided."[16] Enumerators were obligated to make an inquiry in person at every house or gather information from neighbors. Naturally, suspicions were aroused that "an occasional enumerator, clothed in a little brief authority, should seek to gratify his curiosity concerning his neighbors under the pretense of carrying out instructions."[17]

Not only was there the population census, but also the economic and manufacturer census. Statistics relating to occupation, agricultural holdings, and slaves were collected for the economic census, whereas raw materials, machinery type, capital invested, market value of products, contingent expenses, wages, and composition of the labor force were gathered for the manufacturer census. The very incompleteness of the 1810 and 1820 returns reveals evidence of resistance in suspending the economic questions. Proof of noncompliance can be seen in the manufacturing schedules for the 1840 census: rural counties of several Southern states (i.e., Virginia, Georgia, Alabama, and Louisiana) refused altogether to reply.[18] By 1850, it was necessary to append an assurance of confidentiality to the manufacturers' census schedule:

> Should anyone object on the ground of *not wishing to expose* the nature of his business, the assistant marshal should state that it is not desired to elicit any information which will be used or published concerning the operations of any individual or concern. The individual facts are confidentially imparted and received, and will only be published, if at

all, in connection with and as part of a great body of similar facts, from which it will be impossible to abstract or distinguish those of individual firms or corporations.[19]

Still, this assurance was limited; it made no mention of other uses—judicial or regulatory—to which such information could be put further by those in government who gained access to it.

As shown here, the authorities abused their power in order to access personal information. The United States Constitution is essentially a limitation of this kind of power. It was written in an effort to strike a balance between the need for greater governmental authority in the thirteen newly independent colonies and the fear that government represents the greatest threat to individual liberty. The Founding Fathers based their apprehensions on several hundred years of British history during which the Crown fought intensively to retain its political and economic prerogative.[20]

Most historians believe that the main catalyst for the Bill of Rights was the Stamp Act of 1765, which imposed taxes on the American colonists for the purposes of maintaining the British army. Every type of document was taxed, from liquor licenses and playing cards, to books, advertisements, and pamphlets. The colonists deeply resented not only the taxes themselves, but also the fact that they had been imposed by a far-off legislature where they were not represented. Mistrust also accompanied resentment due to the methods used to enforce the act. For example, customs inspectors in search of contraband had the authority to enter people's homes at will—even without evidence of violation—and ransack citizens' belongings.[21] Thus, the drafters of the Bill of Rights looked to the British experience and the abuses of the Crown to determine what kind of governmental conduct should be prohibited, or conversely, what kind of rights should be granted to citizens. One such right is that of privacy as implied in the First, Third, Fourth, Fifth, and Ninth Amendments.[22]

The First Amendment guarantees the freedom of religion,[23] speech,[24] press,[25] "the right of the people peaceably to assemble," and "to petition the Government for a redress of grievances."[26] The Third Amendment states that "no soldier shall, in the time of peace, be quartered in any house, without the consent of the owner, or in the time of war, but in a manner to be prescribed by law." Thus, the objective of this amendment is to secure the enjoyment of that great right of the common law, that "a man's house shall be his own castle." The Fourth Amendment protects people from "unreasonable searches and seizures" of "their persons, houses, papers, and effects." Thus, the Fourth Amendment is indispensable to the full enjoyment of the rights of personal security, personal liberty, and private property. The Fifth Amendment proclaims that "no person . . . shall be compelled in any criminal case to be a witness against himself, nor be deprived of life, liberty, or property, without due process of law."[27] The Ninth Amendment states that "the enumeration in the Constitution of certain rights shall not be construed to deny or disparage others retained by the people." This implies that there are additional rights that Americans should enjoy; rights not listed in the Constitution or the first eight amendments. Since none of these "additional rights" were named, it would be left for later Americans to both discover and protect them. Some courts have interpreted "the right of privacy" to be among these unlisted rights.[28, 29]

As the 19th century drew to a close, new pressures on and threats to privacy emerged as a result of social and economic transformations. One such change was the population boom following the Civil War. Immigrants, especially from Eastern Europe, flocked to the New World in hope that employment in American factories would enable them to live better. Almost all newcomers settled in cities. Consequently, people crowded together in tenements and, thus, had little privacy.[30] Not only was physical density reducing privacy, but so was technology. People acquired devices with which they could enter homes without physically being present. With the invention of the telephone, for example, one did not have to go to people's houses in order to talk with them. Other technological advances such as inexpensive portable cameras, window glass, and even primitive recording devices all enabled people to pry into others' affairs if they were so inclined.[31]

Another characteristic of privacy at the end of the 19th century is that the idea was distinctly class-based. The public hungered for information about other persons, particularly those in privileged positions.[32] The relatively new mass media became an ally of the lower classes and an enemy of the upper class; the media provided the former news and gossip, and to the latter, it threatened to shift the source of identity by making it into a social construct rather than a choice governed by oneself and one's intimate associations.[33]

Having said this, it is not possible to locate unanimous concern for the values of privacy in any single class of late 19th century America; it seems that various individual temperaments and motives converge in a public outcry.[34] Nor was privacy an issue unto itself; rather, it was a feature among other issues. For example, slavery in America was considered inherently wrong in the sense that it was a deprivation of liberty and a repudiation of Christian principle. Servitude was never considered wrong as a violation of privacy, which was precisely what made it so evil, according to Deckle McLean. The owner or overseer could torture or intimidate his slaves to reveal the content of intimate communications; a master could maintain surveillance with impunity through informers, or enter a slave's house at anytime.[35]

As the United States entered the Cold War, increased urbanization, the ability of the government to monitor citizens' lives with advanced technology, and concerns about national security, all combined to propel privacy to the top of the public agenda from 1945 onward.[36] In the 1960s, several factors further heightened the public's awareness of privacy: first was the debut of the earliest commercially successful computer (IBM 360); second was the proliferate adoption of the Social Security Number as a personal identifier; third was a general societal mistrust of the government due to the Vietnam War; and last was the proposal for a National Data Center to centralize various federal agencies' databases.[37] In the mid-1970s, privacy problems mainly derived from the use of personal information that organizations such as credit reporting agencies and direct mail marketing firms collected in the course of normal business.[38, 39] Society had tacitly acknowledged the legitimacy of companies' and agencies' use of personal information for organizational purposes. However, complaints surfaced because data subjects were treated unfairly and abusively, not informed in advance of the use, and rarely had a mechanism for voicing their objections.[40]

In the 1990s, part of the concern about privacy was the unlimited potential for disclosure from numerous sources for multiple and unknown uses.[41] This unease is known due to the fact that "since the 1970s, Americans have been surveyed repeatedly about their attitudes toward privacy, especially in light of technical changes."[42] Most of these polls have been privately sponsored, often by credit reporting agencies, telephone or insurance companies, and at times, major public opinion research organizations.[43] The most cited privacy polls were conducted by Louis Harris & Associates, Inc., for Equifax.[44, 45, 46] According to the results of their 1979 survey, 64 percent of respondents said they had a "real concern" about the loss of personal privacy in recent years. Eighty-one percent believed they had been unfairly penalized because private information about their lives remained too long in government and private businesses' databanks and computers. Seventy-two percent thought government and private sector investigators asked for data that should remain strictly private. Seventy-six percent agreed with the statement, "Americans begin surrendering their privacy the day they open their first charge account, take out a loan, buy something on the installment plan, or apply for a credit card." Seventy-six percent agreed that the right of privacy should be added to the list of traditional rights enjoyed by American citizens (i.e., rights to life, liberty, and the pursuit of happiness). Thirty-four percent felt the United States was "very close" to a realization of the world depicted in George Orwell's *1984*, whereas 39 percent thought we were somewhat close to *1984*. In fact, most Americans seemed to believe that "we might arrive in *1984* right on time."[47]

Eleven years later, the situation remained much the same, if not worse, than before. According to the 1990 Harris-Equifax poll, the public, again, believed that privacy ranks with "life, liberty, and the pursuit of happiness" as a fundamental right. Just under half of the 2,254 polled (45 percent) agreed with the statement that "technology has almost gotten out of control." Seventy-one percent feel they have lost all control over how personal information about them is circulated and used by businesses.[48, 49]

In a 1998 survey sponsored by Privacy & American Business and Price Waterhouse LLP, Louis Harris & Associates and Alan F. Westin[50] found that

1. Eighty-one percent of Net users and 79 percent of Net users who buy products and services on the Net are concerned about threats to their personal privacy while online. However, only 6 percent of Net users and 9 percent of users who buy products and services on the Net report that they have actually been victims of online privacy invasion.
2. Net users and computer users want businesses to strengthen privacy online in specific ways. Ninety-one percent of Net users and 96 percent of Net users who buy products and serv-

Table 1.1 Degree of Public Concern toward Privacy as Reflected in Harris-Equifax Privacy Polls from 1978 to 1993[51]

	1978	1983	1990	1991	1992	1993
Number of responses	1,511	1,256	2,254	1,255	1,254	1,000
Very concerned	31%	48%	46%	48%	47%	49%
Somewhat concerned	33%	29%	33%	31%	31%	30%
Not very concerned	17%	15%	14%	12%	13%	11%
Not concerned at all	19%	7%	6%	7%	8%	6%
Not sure	1%	< 0.5%	1%	1%	2%	3%

ices online say that it is important for business websites to post notices explaining how they will use the personal information customers provide when buying products or services on the web. Similar majorities of those not yet online say this would be important to them if they were online: ninety-four percent of computer users and 79 percent of noncomputer users say this would be important; and 81 percent of computer users and 63 percent of noncomputer users say it is "very important."

3. Computer users are more concerned about the confidentiality of e-mail than they are about other widely used forms of communication. This concern is greatest among computer users who do not actually use e-mail: they are more than twice as likely as e-mail users to be concerned about this form of communication.

4. With regard to the handling of confidential information, computer users have less confidence in online companies than they do in other institutions.

5. Computer users' privacy concerns translate into privacy-sensitive behaviors. Of those who have been asked by a website to provide personal information, the majority have, at some point, declined. The majority of those who did not provide the information say they would have provided it if they were aware of, or were comfortable with, the site's information use policies or if they were more familiar with those sites. Nevertheless, privacy online behaviors are practiced among a small proportion of Internet users.

The *Business Week*/Harris Poll seems to corroborate the rising concern with online privacy.[52] According to the data, almost two-thirds of non-Internet users would be more likely to start using the Net if the privacy of their personal information and communications were protected. Respondents cite privacy as the top reason for not going online; this came well ahead of cost concerns, complicated technology, and spam (unsolicited commercial e-mail). Eighty percent are "very" or "somewhat" concerned with giving out credit card details for cyber purchases. Over half of the respondents believe the government should regulate the collection of personal information on the Internet.

According to the survey results of the Center for Democracy and Technology[53]

1. An overwhelming majority of respondents avoid registering at websites and giving out personal information for fear of losing privacy.
2. While over half of the respondents did not inquire about the information practices of their online service providers, 95 percent said they were interested in the privacy policies of websites.
3. Although less than a quarter of the respondents reported experiencing a violation of their online privacy, a majority were concerned about others collecting information about them, as well as the potential harm from the misuse of that information.
4. Of those respondents actively taking measures to protect their online privacy, relatively few use devices such as the "anonymizer" or an anonymous re-mailer.[54] Slightly more reported encrypting their e-mail, disabling the cookie function in their web browser, or providing false information when asked to register at a website. Using multiple e-mail addresses and turning on the "cookie prompt" are the most common technical solutions.
5. When faced with protecting their children's privacy online, most parents who responded use "low-tech" approaches such as instructing kids not to give out personal information, or limiting their children's access to the Internet or the web.
6. Tracking people's use of the web, and the sale of personal information, were cited as the most pressing privacy issue on

the Internet. While junk e-mail rated third in terms of overall privacy concern, it generated the largest number of anecdotal complaints.

Like the results from the Privacy & American Business, and the CDT studies, the Graphics, Visualization, & Usability Center's Survey Team found that security is the chief reason web users do no online purchasing.[55] Much of the population is unaware of what cookies are and what they do. However, those who are familiar with the device consistently dislike cookies along with other identifiers that label users through multiple sessions at a site. In order to protect their privacy, a significant number of people falsify information for online registration. The most common reason for not registering is the lack of statement on how the information would be used by website owners. Respondents would rather forego accessing a site than reveal information. Most participants strongly agree (39 percent) or somewhat agree (33 percent) that there should be new laws to protect Internet privacy. European respondents agree less strongly (somewhat agree 39 percent) and are more neutral on this issue (18 percent); women agree slightly more strongly than men (strongly agree: 41 percent female, 37 percent male) in this case; novices agree most strongly that there should be new laws, as do experts except that more of them disagree than novices; and those over age 50 disagree more strongly than the other age groups.

While many studies have provided evidence of people's concern for privacy, few have explored the nature of the concern in detail. The AT&T study endeavored to look beyond the fact that people are concerned and to understand why they are concerned.[56] The research team found that[57]

1. Internet users are more likely to provide information when they are not identified.
2. Some types of data are more sensitive than others, e.g., preference information is less sensitive than credit card numbers or social security numbers. They also observed that there are significant differences in sensitivity to seemingly similar kinds of data. For instance, while postal mail address, telephone number, and e-mail address can all be used to contact someone, most of the respondents said they would never or

rarely feel comfortable providing their telephone number, but would usually or always feel comfortable providing their e-mail address.

3. Many factors are important in decisions about information disclosure, the most important of which is whether or not information will be shared with other companies and organizations. Other highly important factors include whether information is used in an identifiable way, and the kind of and purpose for which information is collected. Whether a site posts a privacy policy, whether a site has a privacy seal of approval, and whether a site discloses a data retention policy are also viewed as important, but considerably less so than the other factors asked in the questionnaire.

4. Acceptance of the use of persistent identifiers varies according to their purpose. Fifty-two percent of the respondents indicated they are concerned about web cookies, and another 12 percent said they are uncertain about what the device is. Of those who knew what cookies are, 56 percent said they had changed their cookie settings to something other than accepting all cookies without warning. However, 78 percent say they would definitely or probably agree to websites using persistent identifiers to provide a customized service. Sixty percent would consent to the use of such an identifier for customized advertising, and 44 percent would accede to using the identifier to provide customized advertising across many websites.

5. Internet users dislike automatic data transfer. When asked about several possible browser features that would make it easier to provide information to websites, 86 percent of respondents reported no interest in features that would automatically transfer their data to websites without any user intervention.

6. Internet users dislike unsolicited communications.

7. A joint program of privacy policies and privacy seals seemingly provides a comparable level of user confidence as that provided by privacy laws.

To conclude, generally people believe privacy protection is not accidental, but that it has something to do with distinctive qualities of the times in which we live. Most would probably identify technological change (in particular, the development of computers) as the main culprit of privacy erosion.[58] Many feel that the new technologies motivate the collection, storage, and use of all sorts of personal information that previously could not be treated in these ways.[59] In the next chapter, the different facets of privacy will be examined, specifically, its definitions, characteristics, criteria, and functions.

NOTES

1. For more information, see David H. Flaherty, *Privacy in Colonial New England* (Charlottesville: University Press of Virginia, 1976), 115–27.

2. Flaherty, *Privacy in Colonial New England*, 31.

3. Karl Baarslag, *Robbery By Mail: The Story of the U.S. Postal Inspectors* (New York: Farrar & Rinehart, 1938), 294.

4. Massachusetts Historical Society, Collections, 3d serv., v. 7: 83, quoted in David J. Seipp, *The Right to Privacy in American History* (Cambridge: Harvard University Program on Information Resources Policy, 1978), 8.

5. William Bradford, *History of Plymouth Plantation, 1620–1627* (Boston: Massachusetts Historical Society, 1912), 383.

6. Gardiner G. Hubbard, "Our Post Office," *Atlantic Monthly* 35 (1875): 90, quoted in Seipp, *The Right to Privacy in American History,* 9.

7. Moreau de St. Mery, *American Journey, 1793–1798,* trans. Kenneth Roberts and Anna M. Roberts (Garden City, N.Y.: Doubleday, 1947), 62.

8. Simon Greenleaf, *A Treatise on the Law of Evidence,* 3d ed. (Boston: Little and Brown, 1846), 367, quoted in Seipp, *The Right to Privacy in American History,* 12.

9. Joseph Gales, comp., "Census of the Union," *Annals of the Congress of the United States* (2 February 1790): 1107, quoted in Seipp, *The Right to Privacy in American History,* 18.

10. Gales, "Census of the Union," 1107, quoted in Seipp, *The Right to Privacy in American History,* 18.

11. W. R. Merriam, "The Evolution of American Census-Taking," *Century* 65 (1903): 834, quoted in Seipp, *The Right to Privacy in American History,* 19.

12. John Fries and Thomas Carpenter, *The Two Trials of John Fries, On an Indictment for Treason* (Philadelphia, Penn.: William Wallis Woodward, 1800), 2, quoted in Seipp, *The Right to Privacy in American History,* 19.

13. Carroll D. Wright and William C. Hunt, *The History and Growth of the United States Census, Prepared for the Senate Committee on the Census* (Washington, D.C.: Government Printing Office, 1900), 30 and 35, quoted in Seipp, *The Right to Privacy in American History,* 19.

14. Henry Stone, "The Census of 1880," *Lippincott's* 22 (1878): 109, quoted in Seipp, *The Right to Privacy in America History,* 20.

15. Wright and Hunt, *History and Growth,* 85, quoted in Seipp, *The Right to Privacy in American History,* 20.

16. Wright and Hunt, *History and Growth,* 85, quoted in Seipp, *The Right to Privacy in American History,* 20.

17. *New York Times* (19 July 1875): 4, quoted in Seipp, *The Right to Privacy in American History*, 20.

18. Robert C. Davis, "Confidentiality and the Census, 1790–1929," in *U.S. Department of Health, Education, and Welfare, Records, Computers, and the Rights of Citizens* (Washington, D.C.: Government Printing Office, 1973): 186, quoted in Seipp, *The Right to Privacy in American History*, 23.

19. William and Hunt, *History and Growth*, 312, quoted in Seipp, *The Right to Privacy in American History*, 24.

20. Frank M. Tuerkheimer, "The Understandings of Privacy Protection," *Communications of the ACM* 36 (1993): 69–73.

21. Ira Glasser, *Visions of Liberty: The Bill of Rights for All Americans* (New York: Arcade Press, 1991), 29–31.

22. Jean Slemmons Stratford and Juri Stratford, "Computerized and Network Government Information," *Journal of Government Information: An International Review of Policy Issues and Resources* 25 (1998): 299–303.

23. For further details, see Paul L. Murphy, ed., *Religious Freedom: Separation and Free Exercise* (New York: Garland Press, 1990).

24. For further details, see Paul L. Murphy, ed., *Free Speech* (New York: Garland Press, 1990).

25. For further details, see Paul L. Murphy, ed., *Free Press* (New York: Garland Press, 1990).

26. For further details, see Paul L. Murphy, ed., *Rights of Assembly, Petition, Arms and Just Compensation* (New York: Garland Press, 1990).

27. For further details, see Paul L. Murphy, ed., *Criminal Procedure* (New York: Garland Press, 1990).

28. Stephen Goode, *The Right to Privacy* (New York: Franklin Watts, 1983), 17–18.

29. For further details, see Paul L. Murphy, ed., *The Right to Privacy and the Ninth Amendment* (New York: Garland Press, 1990).

30. Philippa Strum, *Privacy: The Debate in the United States Since 1945* (Fort Worth, Tex.: Harcourt Brace College Publishers, 1998), 14.

31. Strum, *Privacy*, 15.

32. Randall P. Bezanson, "The Right to Privacy Revisited: Privacy, News, and Social Change, 1890–1990," *California Law Review* 80 (1992): 1139.

33. Bezanson, "Right to Privacy," 1140.

34. Seipp, *The Right to Privacy in American History*, 90.

35. Deckle McLean, *Privacy and Its Invasion* (Westport, Conn.: Praeger, 1995), 1–2.

36. Strum, *Privacy*, 20–21.

37. Stephen A. Smith, "Communication and the Constitution in Cyberspace," *Communication Education* 43 (1994): 10.

38. Besides credit reporting, there was little or no "information industry" in the early 1970s whose commodity-in-trade was personal information and whose economic viability depended on exploiting such information for profit gain (Willis H. Ware, "The New Faces of Privacy," *The Information Society* 9 [1993]: 199–200).

39. These are what Edward Shils called the "centers of power," that is, powerful, but more or less distant social entities that demand for personal information, and that include private and government agencies alike (James B. Rule, *The Politics of Privacy* [New York: Elsevier, 1980], 23).

40. Ware, "The New Faces of Privacy," 199–200.

41. Bezanson, "Right to Privacy Revisited," 1140–41.

42. Priscilla M. Regan, *Legislating Privacy: Technology, Social Values, and Public Policy* (Chapel Hill: University of North Carolina Press, 1995), 43.

43. A caveat should be issued: these polls present three major problems in accurately gauging the concern about privacy. First, those who are most concerned about privacy probably will not respond to surveys. As Oscar Gandy observed, "any survey that is concerned about opinions related to privacy and personal information will be nonrandom and systematically biased" (Oscar Gandy, *The Panoptic Sort: A Political Economy of Personal Information* [Boulder, Colo.: Westview, 1993], 125). Therefore, survey results would tend to underestimate the level and intensity of concern. Nevertheless, "there is little practical way to surmount this weakness since standard practices of estimating nonrespondent characteristics would not work well for this dimension of nonresponse" (James E. Katz and Annette R. Tassone, "Public Opinion Trends: Privacy and Information Technology," *Public Opinion Quarterly* 54 [1990]: 126). The second problem involves not underestimating, but overestimating, privacy concerns. Privacy surveys, or for that matter, any attempt to measure peoples' attitudes about a particular issue, may exaggerate respondents' concerns. It may be that respondents do not have a genuine opinion on the issue to begin with. In such case, the survey may be measuring a nonattitude. The subject of the poll may be one that is somewhat remote from the respondents' concerns, but not one for which they have developed real views. However, once the respondents know what the survey is about, they may express views on that subject even if they did not have any before, and may answer in the way they think pollsters want. The question then becomes whether the survey is measuring or creating attitudes (Regan, *Legislating Privacy*, 49–50). The third difficulty in interpreting results of privacy survey data is that "there are no universal definitions of privacy, and individuals are likely to be responding to quite different things when they indicate the presence or absence of concerns" (Gandy, *Panoptic Sort*, 127). Therefore, the different perceptions of privacy would make it problematic to compare or aggregate responses.

44. Regan, *Legislating Privacy*, 48–49.

45. These surveys are: *Harris-Equifax Information Privacy Survey 1993; Harris-Equifax Consumer Privacy Survey 1992; Harris-Equifax Consumer Privacy Survey 1991; The Equifax Report on Consumers in the Information Age; The Dimensions of Privacy: A National Opinion Research Survey of Attitudes Toward Privacy; The Road After 1984: A Nationwide Survey of the Public and Its Leaders on the New Technology and Its Consequences for American Life.*

46. Polls conducted by major public opinion research organizations such as Louis Harris & Associates, are essentially "special interest group polls" (Irving Crespi, *Public Opinion, Polls, and Democracy* [Boulder Colo.: Westview, 1989], 39–40), that is, they are conducted to identify the public's preconceptions about the issue of privacy and to determine how knowledgeable the public is about the issues. Moreover, these surveys are not "advocacy polls" which are released only if the results support the position of the organization sponsoring the survey.

47. Goode, *Right to Privacy,* 3–4.

48. Paige Amidon, "Widening Privacy Concerns," *Online* (July 1992): 64.

49. As James Rule observed (*The Politics of Privacy,* 6):

> Public anxieties about large scale personal record keeping have been well-founded, not in the sense that everyone's most outlandish fears on these subjects have reflected actual record keeping practice, but in a broader sense of pointing to authentic and enduring issues in modern societies. Documentary information on otherwise obscure and anonymous people now provides a source of strength to organizations of all kinds. These powers of organizational action may serve the most beneficent social purposes or the most dreadful. Whether any particular use of these systems is desired or not, their cumulative growth changes something fundamental about the relationship between powerful institutions and their publics.

50. Louis Harris and Alan F. Westin, *E-commerce & Privacy: What Net Users Want* (Hackensack, N. J.: Privacy & American Business, 1998).

51. Sources for table 1.1 are Louis Harris and Equifax, *Health Information Privacy Survey 1993* (Atlanta, Georgia: Equifax, Inc., 1993), 23, Table I-I; and Louis Harris and Alan Westin, *Harris-Equifax Consumer Privacy Survey 1992* (Atlanta, Georgia: Equifax, 1992), 15, Table 1.

52. Louis Harris and Alan F. Westin, "BW/Harris Poll: Online Insecurity," *Businessweek* 1998, http://businessweek.com/1998/11/b3569107.htm (29 Jan. 2000).

53. Center for Democracy and Technology, *Survey,* 2000, http://www.cdt.org /privacy/survey/findings/cdtbody.html (29 Jan. 2000).

54. Among the few respondents who reported using the anonymizer, only two use it regularly, whereas most use the program only occasionally.

55. Graphics, Visualization & Usability Center, *Graphics, Visualization & Usability Center's 8th WWW User Survey,* 1997, http://www.gvu.gatech.edu /user_survey/survey-1997-10 (29 Jan. 2000).

56. Lorrie Faith Cranor, Joseph Reagle, and Mark S. Ackerman, *Beyond Concern: Understanding Net Users' Attitudes About Online Privacy,* 1999, http://www.research.att.com/library/trs/TRs/99/99.4/99.4.3/report.htm (28 Jan. 2000).

57. For details, see "Appendix: Survey Questions and Frequency of Responses" at http://www.research.att.com/~lorrie/pickup/tr/appendix. htm.

58. For example, McLean, *Privacy and Its Invasion.*

59. However, Rule believes this view only as far as it goes (*Politics of Privacy*). New technologies do, indeed, make possible many of the treatments of personal information that have led to present-day privacy controversies; elsewhere, however, the controversies stem from uses of technologies which have been with us for a long time. He feels that the key condition for the emergence of the privacy issue in the 1960s and 1970s was not any particular technology so much as new social relationships. The social structures of advanced industrial society give rise to distinctive demands (often not always abetted by new technologies) for personal information. For instance, we expect, even demand, that distant agencies, from the Social Security Administration to credit card firms, deal with us "personally." In other words, we expect such organizations to fully take into account our unique needs, backgrounds, qualifica-

tions, and special circumstances. We assume as much about the agencies that assess tax liabilities, determine insurance rates, issue driving licenses, or process security clearances. However, organizations can only fulfill our expectations through documentary record keeping on the people concerned. Thus, these bodies may come to rival the importance in traditional settings of neighbors, family, and other face-to-face intimates in their effects on our lives. And in thoroughness, the cold intimacy of their bureaucratic attentions may rival the intrusiveness of the small town or extended family. Thus, Rule suggests that we take a closer look at the origins of these demands to better understand the phenomenon.

2

Definitions, Characteristics, Criteria, and Functions of Privacy

DEFINITIONS OF PRIVACY

For most, privacy (or lack thereof) is easy to identify when experienced, but difficult to define because it can refer to so many things.[1] For instance, privacy protects the solitude necessary for creative thought. It allows us the independence that is part of raising a family. It protects our right to be secure in our own homes and possessions without government interference. Privacy also encompasses our right to self-determination and self-definition. It allows us to retain certain facts to ourselves if we so choose.[2] Privacy may also cover forbidden knowledge and experience, ideas of group membership, and the separation of spheres of activity.[3] Thus, no single, universal definition of privacy captures all nuances of this dimension of social reality even though there have been various attempts to create a synthesis of existing literature such as the works of W. A. Parent and Ferdinand Schoeman.[4, 5]

Privacy as Control of Personal Information[6]

Even though privacy is a concept related to solitude, secrecy, and autonomy, it is not synonymous with these terms; for beyond the purely descriptive aspects of privacy as isolation from the company, the curiosity, and the influence of others, it implies a normative element—the right to exclusive control of access to private realms. Sisela Bok, W. H. Foddy and W. R. Finighan, Hyman Gross, Stephen Margulis, and Marc Rotenberg all concur.[7, 8, 9, 10, 11] Margulis further points out that the ultimate aim of privacy is to enhance autonomy and/or to minimize vulnerability.[12] Rotenberg expands the definition of privacy as control by including accountability for those who misuse other's personal information, who profit from the sale of information without prior consent from the individual(s) concerned, or who breach another's confidence.[13]

However, H. J. McCloskey argues that there are problems with defining privacy as information access control in relation to marking off the self and its real extensions from the non self, and to showing very inclusive claims to privacy that commonly embrace much more.[14] His basic objection to this account is that it fails to acknowledge that we can show a lack of respect for our own privacy, that we can improperly forgo our own privacy. People who bare their souls to all are commonly thought not to have proper respect for their own privacy; we think they give it up too readily, and lack decent reticence. Thus, self-disclosure can involve neither invasions nor loss of privacy.[15]

Along the same vein, Schoeman points out the vulnerability of such a definition of privacy with counter-examples. He writes:

> We can easily imagine a person living in a state of complete privacy, but lacking control over who has access to information about him. For instance, a man shipwrecked on a deserted island or lost in a dense forest has unfortunately lost control over who has information about him, but we would not want to say that he has no privacy. Indeed, ironically, his problem is that he has too much privacy. To take another example, a person who chose to exercise his discretionary control over information about himself by divulging everything cannot be said to have lost control, although he surely cannot be said to have any privacy.[16]

In Schoeman's opinion, the only defensible definition of privacy is the identification of privacy with a state of limited access to a person: "A person has privacy to the extent that others have limited access to information about him, limited access to the intimacies of his life, or limited access to his thoughts or body."[17]

Privacy as a Zone of Exclusion

In *The System of Freedom of Expression*, Thomas Emmerson wrote that

> generally speaking, the concept of a right to privacy attempts to draw a line between the individual and the collective, between self and society. It seeks to assure the individual a zone in which to be an individual, not a member of the community. In that zone, he can think his own thoughts, have his own secrets, live his own life, reveal only what he wants to the outside world. The right of privacy, in short, establishes an area excluded from the collective life, not governed by the rules of collective living.[18]

In other words, "privacy is the right to live at least part of one's life divorced from public interest and the public eye, to live according to one's own individual choice and free from the probing of other people."[19]

Privacy as a Phenomenal State or Condition of the Person

Within this category, privacy has been viewed from different perspectives. George Bailey's examination of privacy and mental phenomena evaluates what is known as the *epistemic superiority thesis.* The competing theses claim that either some or all mental phenomena and only mental phenomena are such that, when they exist, there are some people whose experienced knowledge of them is superior in some way to that of other people. Bailey rejects both of these: "it is logically impossible that [mental phenomena] should exist without there existing some being capable of experience who has them."[20]

C. T. Fischer sees privacy as a sense of being in that it occurs

> when the watching self and the world fall away, along with geometric space, clock time, and other contingencies, leaving an intensified relationship with the intentional object . . . it is not necessarily a defensive escape, it is a state of relative openness which allows phenomena to unfold in new ways, thus facilitating personal growth and development.[21]

L. C. Velecky believes that "any concept of privacy is a concept of a state in which persons may find themselves."[22] He also considers that being alone is the closest to his own concept of privacy. However, he emphasizes that while the concept of privacy implies that the state is regarded as valuable, the concept of being alone bore no such implications.

Michael Weinstein asserts that the confusion regarding privacy is due to the fact that it is a condition of being that is neither moral nor valuable in itself.[23] While requiring that the *concept* of privacy be regarded as neutral to facilitate questions on loss of privacy, Ruth Gavison stresses that the *state* of privacy is a desirable and balanced condition of the individual which has a central value.[24] F. S. Chapin sees privacy as a value to be by oneself and free from the pressures of others.[25]

In summary, the perspectives above all place the definition of privacy squarely in the domain of the individual's psyche or condition. There are different emphases which, when added together, give a coherent *gestalt*. Despite their differences, there is a consistency of approach: for example, Bailey's notion of necessary ownership is totally compatible with Fischer's active openness which implies that privacy is beneficial, and that it involves or facilitates accountability, responsibility, personal development, and self-realization. Hardly any disagreement lies in the meaning of privacy, but much disagreement rests on whether the condition should be regarded as neutral in value, or of value in it. It would seem that the majority are strongly in favor of placing a positive value on the condition of privacy.[26]

Privacy as Solitude

From the phenomenological perspective, solitude, or "aloneness," is regarded as invaluable in providing the intellectual space needed for reflection and for making sense of the world.[27] Alan Westin, who believes that solitude is the most complete state of privacy that individuals can achieve, views it as a type of privacy in which the individual is alone and unobserved.[28]

For Leon Pastalan the distinguishing characteristics of solitude are solitariness and physical isolation. In his study of institutionalized elderly people, the results show that patients who possessed strategies for obtaining solitude had a higher life expectancy than patients without such strategies.[29]

Nancy Marshall in her factor analysis of neighboring and privacy found that a factor identified as *being alone* is one of two major divisions.[30] Darhl Pedersen's two factor analytic studies of privacy—one concerning the dimensions of privacy, the other regarding personality correlates of privacy—also identify solitude as one of six separate factors of the privacy domain.[31]

As evidenced, the great majority of authors cited here discussing solitude regard it as either a desirable or neutral condition. However, scholars such as Paul Halmos dissent due to the belief that solitude is an undesirable move toward isolation.[32]

Privacy as Isolation

Peter Kelvin views isolation as an imposition rather than a product of choice. He notes that the everyday meaning of isolation denotes the negative aspects of separateness and the positive ones of privacy.[33] Isolation occurs when an individual seeks relationships with others, but is physically or psychologically restricted from doing so. William Ittelson and colleagues view isolation as a case in which individuals have reduced options and less freedom of choice.[34] Pastalan sees it as a part of solitude which may be achieved through spacing distance and/or screening.[35]

Privacy as Anonymity

Gavison claims that anonymity is the second independent and irreducible element which, together with secrecy and solitude, comprise the complex of privacy. She points out that individuals always lose privacy when they become the object of attention—be it conscious, deliberate, or inadvertent—because attention is a primary way of gathering information.[36]

Privacy as Reserve

Reserve is regarded by Ittelson and colleagues as the type of privacy that is most complex and least dependent on the physical setting.[37] Pastalan feels that it is the most subtle form of privacy because of its reciprocal nature and the willing discretion of significant others.[38] In the empirical literature, a factor identified as "not neighboring" by Marshall is associated with items that emphasize attitudes toward having friends and neighbors drop in unannounced, and general involvement with others.[39] Ellen Bersheid suggests that reliable individual differences on a need for privacy dimension should be examined in relation to Eysenck and Eysenck's measure of social introversion-extroversion.[40, 41]

Privacy as Intimacy

Schoeman considers intimacy as a criterion of the private, but one that is nonnormative.[42] Charles Fried notes that intimate relationships require the voluntary relinquishment of parts of one's inner self, and according to Robert Gerstein, they also include a lack of self-observation:

> It is prima facie wrong to observe a person against his will at any time, because it violates his autonomous right to decide whether he will be observed or not. But the wrong is far greater where the victim of the invasion was submerged in an intimate relationship and therefore did not intend to be observed at all, even by himself.[43, 44]

Ittelson and colleagues believe that sought privacy of this type goes beyond freedom of observation to include a preference for minimizing all sensory input from outside the boundaries of an appropriate setting. According to them, intimacy simply cannot exist unless people have an opportunity for privacy.[45]

Privacy as Secrecy

There seems to be no consensus as to whether secrecy is a type of privacy.[46] For example, Edward Shils points out that privacy is voluntary and secrecy is mandatory.[47] Carol Warren and Barbara Laslett, too, believe privacy and secrecy are two separate and distinct entities. According to them, privacy protects behavior which is either morally neutral or valued by society as well as by the perpetrators, whereas secrecy implies the concealment of something which is negatively valued by the excluded audience, and in some instances, by the perpetrator as well. Privacy has a consensual basis in society, but secrecy does not—it is considered a means to escape being stigmatized.[48] Privacy implies the legitimate denial of access, and it is legitimate because most people believe that private behavior does not affect those to whom access is denied or restricted. Secrecy, in general, implies that the denial of access is illegal. Also, it appears to be an even more extreme form of denial of access to others than privacy, for not only is access denied when secrecy is maintained, but the most successful secrecy occurs when knowledge of denial of access (the secret's very existence) is also withheld. The irony here lies in the fact that information restricted by secrecy is more likely to be regarded as legitimate public property which must be hidden illegitimately through secrecy.[49] Thus, Warren and Laslett believe that privacy and secrecy are differentiated by the moral dimension of the behaviors to which they refer.[50]

Privacy as Territoriality

The term "territoriality," or the control of space, originated from the field of animal behavior, and has now branched out into the study of human interactions. In human societies, it was historically the affluent who had the means to demarcate areas of privacy. Privacy was a treasured possession and a mark of status in many early civilizations. To protect themselves from unwanted intrusion, affluent Egyptians had vine-hung gardens, Greeks used porticoes, Romans had various enclosures, and the wealthy British had country homes guarded by stone walls and parks.[51, 52] In poorer homes no such privacy existed.

In a laboratory situation, J. J. Edney and M. A. Buda found that territoriality and privacy could be differentiated experimentally by humans. Privacy led to enhanced feelings of freedom, and privacy plus territoriality encouraged feelings of security.[53]

Privacy as Behavior

Privacy as behavior involves both actions taken to acquire privacy and behaviors during privacy.[54] Much of this literature developed from studies of density and crowding in the environment, as well as territoriality and personal space. However, studies on privacy as behavior is frequently more on the social interaction itself rather than on individual behavior or person-object interactions. Thus, a consideration of behavioral factors is strongly involved in territorial matters, in boundary control—both physical and social—and in discussions on the mechanics of obtaining privacy. One of the strongest proponents of the behavioral perspective is Irvin Altman who mainly concentrated on the mechanics of obtaining and maintaining privacy. Altman is best known for his suggestion that different levels of behavior are used to achieve privacy.[55]

Privacy as a Process

Shils, like Altman, views privacy as a process; he believes that the main issue is control of information.[56] In particular, he is interested in the movement of data across a boundary from person to person, group to group, or group to individual, and thinks that privacy involves a zero-relationship between these elements. Westin, even though he does not regard privacy itself as a process, believes that the condition of privacy depends on an internal personal adjustment process in which individuals "balance the desire for privacy with the desire for disclosure and communication."[57] All of the above indicate that privacy regulation processes should not be thought of in purely cognitive terms as the need for privacy may arise at the affective, rather than cognitive, level.[58]

To summarize, many definitions of privacy have been offered over the centuries. Despite their differences, they can still be sorted under twelve major categories: (1) privacy as control of personal information; (2) privacy as a zone of exclusion; (3) privacy as a phenomenal state or condition of the person; (4) privacy as solitude; (5) privacy as isolation; (6) privacy as anonymity; (7) privacy as reserve; (8) privacy as intimacy; (9) privacy as secrecy; (10) privacy as territoriality; (11) privacy as behavior; and (12) privacy as a process. These classifications are by no means exhaustive nor are they mutually exclusive. However, they do provide a framework for a better understanding of the complex issues in pinpointing what exactly is privacy.

CHARACTERISTICS OF AND CRITERIA FOR PRIVACY

Characteristics of Privacy

According to Seumas Miller, privacy comprises of seven characteristics:[59]

1. The notion of privacy has both a *descriptive* and a *normative* dimension. On the one hand, privacy consists of being in some condition of not being interfered with or having some wider

power to exclude. On the other hand, privacy is held to be a moral right, or at least an important one. Most accounts of privacy acknowledge this much.

2. Privacy is a desirable condition, power, or moral right that a person has in relation to other people, and with respect to the possession of information by others about him-/herself or the observation/perception of him-/herself by others.

3. The range of matters regarded as private embraces much of what could be referred to as a person's innerself.

4. A person's intimate personal relations with other people are regarded as private.

5. Ownership appears to confer the right not to disclose information concerning a thing owned; or at least there is a presumption in favor of nondisclosure which can be overridden.

6. Certain facts pertaining to a person's various public roles and practices (e.g., voting decisions) are regarded as private because if disclosed, they can undermine the capacity of the person to function or fairly compete in these public roles and practices.

7. Privacy is necessary simply for a person to pursue his or her projects (e.g., planning). Authority requires a measure of privacy.

Likewise, according to Willis Ware there are five fundamental attributes of privacy as a concept that amount to axioms:[60]

1. Privacy cannot be achieved at zero cost. Like freedom, privacy comes at a premium to society collectively and to citizens individually. Sometimes the price will be monetary and at other times it will be an inconvenience or a limitation on one's ability to maneuver in society. For example, it may require larger or more complex automated systems; it may mean inefficiency in systems; or it may mean denial of a service that might otherwise be desirable to much of society.

2. However, privacy *at any cost* is a myth. Society is not likely to pay unlimited costs to achieve near-absolute privacy. To channel unlimited funds to privacy would amount to a bad compromise, a bad engineering decision, and a bad cost–trade-off analysis. The value of privacy declines a society's aspiration to have more and more rigid controls to as-

sure it. At some point, the cost of taking the next step exceeds the value to be derived or the harm to be avoided.

3. Privacy must not be used as a means to hide or escape from the consequences of illegal behavior.

4. In addition to threatening privacy, the use and/or exploitation of information about people will also tend to tighten the process of society. An example would be the automation of check clearing in the banking world. As a convenience to managing personal cash flow, one is no longer able to exploit the seven day cash float that was inherent in the slower old manual procedures.

5. If a nation drifts to an unattainable position in regard to privacy, it will be the cumulative effect of many individual decisions, probably made over a long period of time. Each decision at the time it was made, was seen as a reasonable and desirable position. It is probably the most insidious force working to detract from privacy of the individual and the most difficult to detect and control.

CRITERIA FOR PRIVACY

From perusal of the literature, David Flaherty compiled a list of information-related criteria in order for privacy to occur:[61]

1. The right to individual autonomy
2. The right to be left alone
3. The right to a private life
4. The right to control information about oneself
5. The right to limit accessibility
6. The right to exclusive control of access to private realms
7. The right to minimize intrusiveness
8. The right to expect confidentiality
9. The right to enjoy intimacy
10. The right to enjoy anonymity
11. The right to enjoy reserve
12. The right to enjoy secrecy

Flaherty argues that these are the kinds of privacy interests for which individuals ought to be able to claim protection with respect to personal information. They form an inventory of the ultimate values that should serve as the premise for the more detailed information-control principles and practices included in data protection activities.

FUNCTIONS OF PRIVACY

Functions of Privacy Serving the Individual

Personal Autonomy/Individuality

Privacy offers a space in which an individual might develop more fully into a person and accomplish important human tasks that are otherwise thwarted.[62] Not only does privacy enable autonomy and individuality, but it also provides room to evaluate oneself, others, and new situations.[63] Privacy allows the individual an opportunity to "assess the flood of information received, to consider alternatives and possible consequences so that he may then act as consistently and appropriately as possible."[64] It also recognizes the interest of the individual "in the proper timing of the decision to move from private reflection or intimate conversation to a more general publication of acts and thoughts. This is the process by which one tests his own evaluations against the responses of his peers."[65]

The need for private space to develop, and to reflect on ideas and opinions is critical in a democracy. Independent judgment

> requires time for sheltered experimentation and testing of ideas for preparation, and practice in thought and conduct, without fear of ridicule or penalty, and for the opportunity to alter opinions before making them publicly. . . . Without such time for incubation and growth through privacy, many ideas and positions would be launched into the world with dangerous prematurity.[66]

For the more confident individual, privacy assures space to reflect on one's choices and to determine the direction of one's life before one is ready to act.[67]

According to Westin:

> the most serious threat to the individual's autonomy is the possibility that someone may penetrate the inner zone and learn his ultimate secrets, either by physical or psychological means. This deliberate pene-

tration of the individual's protective shell, his psychological armor, would leave him naked to ridicule and shame and would put him under the control of those who knew his secrets.[68]

Therefore, the contribution of privacy to personal autonomy involves the protection of the inner core self which is the ultimate resource of the individual. A person seeks protection from the manipulation and dominance of others in defense of his or her uniqueness and dignity as a person.[69] The autonomy of the self depends upon the maintenance of wells of reserve. Under normal conditions, the ultimate sanctuary of the personality is never breached. The last resource of the individual is that no one can force him or her to bare his or her personality and expose his or her naked self to the shame of total understanding.[70] Or as Bloustein remarked:

> The man who is compelled to live every minute of his life among others and whose every need, thought, desire, fancy, or gratification is subject to public scrutiny, has been deprived of his individuality and human dignity. [He] merges with the mass. . . . Such a being, although sentient, is fungible; he is not an individual.[71]

In order to receive dignity, one must depend on respect from others for "to respect someone as a person is to concede that one ought to take into account the way in which his enterprise might be affected by one's own decisions."[72] By the principle of respect for persons, then, Stanley Benn means the principle that every human being, insofar as he or she is qualified as a person, is entitled to this minimal degree of consideration.[73] Thus, the content of the principle of privacy is to protect against interference with the person's way of realizing and developing his or her own interests.

Emotional Release

Privacy is necessary for individuals because it provides an opportunity for emotional release—the chance to be out of the public eye, to forget about social conventions, to express our opinions, vent our emotions, and so on, without fear of repercussion.[74, 75] For example, such moments may occur in solitude in the anonymity of a park, in the bathroom of one's own home, or among a select group of family, peers, or close friends. The consequences of denying privacy can be severe, ranging from stress to mental collapse, and even suicide.[76]

Not only does privacy as emotional release benefit the individual, but also organizations. Organizations require time out of the public eye to facilitate candid, relaxed communication, experimentation, and individual risk taking within organizational governance. As Westin observes:

> Given [the] penchant of society for idealized models and the far different realities of organizational life, privacy is necessary so that organizations may do the divergent part of their work out of public view. The adage that one should not visit the kitchen of a restaurant if one wants to enjoy the food is applied daily in the grant of privacy to organizations for their staging processes.[77]

Promotion of Human Relationships

It has been argued that a variety of personal relations is valuable and necessary, and that privacy enables us to engage in relationships by sharing our confidences with family, friends, and close associates.[78, 79, 80, 81] The variety lies in the assortment of people with whom we associate, and the different levels of intimacies we have with them. Consequently, it is necessary for one to be able to control the closeness of one's personal relationships.

Fried argues that love and friendship require "the voluntary and spontaneous relinquishment of something between friend and friend, lover and lover."[82] That "something" is the private self, according to David Bazelon. Privacy bestows on each individual title to information about him-/herself which becomes the "moral capital" that he or she spends in friendship and love. On the other hand, there will be secrets—thoughts that an individual finally does not ratify or adopt, personal history he or she cannot put behind—even between the closest of friends or lovers. Privacy protects these secrets that might wound if they were revealed. It also serves love and friendship insofar as it is an acting out of the respect an individual feels for another person's mental and physical territory. Privacy is vital, not only between two friends or lovers, but around them as well. Without faith in confidentiality, most people cannot share themselves with others. The relationship promoting function of privacy requires that individuals feel free of observation when with close acquaintances and that they have control over information about themselves and information which is passed between them.[83]

Withdrawal into privacy is also a means of making life with an unbearable (or sporadically unbearable) person possible. If the distraction and relief of privacy were not available in such case, the relationship would have to be terminated in order to avoid conflicts.[84]

In conclusion, without the ability to control the disclosure of intimate facts, individuals lose the ability to shape identity, establish trust, and form smaller communities within the larger community.[85]

Functions of Privacy Serving Society

Promotion of Democracy

Democracy is sometimes said to be superior to despotism for the following two reasons: (1) it is more responsive to the collective desires of the governed, and therefore, assures the greatest good for the greatest number more successfully than other forms of government; (2) it taps the talents and energies of more members of society than other forms of government, and therefore, tends to be more vital, more creative, and more adaptable than its paternalistic and totalitarian counterparts.[86] However, democracy does neither of these if its citizens do not have minds of their own. Therefore, respect for the broad principle of privacy which "attempts to draw a line between the individual and the collective, between self and society," is essential to the development of independently-minded citizens. Also, by allowing the citizen control over private information and communications, freedom from surveillance, and some spheres of action free of societal interference, privacy fosters the growth of autonomous, free-thinking individuals necessary for self-government.[87]

However, a conflict exists between society's need for an assortment of information (e.g., for provision of services, collection of taxes, protection against crime, and the maintenance of a free press) and the individual's right to privacy. For example, most governmental systems require information to operate efficiently; in order to do so, the information must be reliable, accurate, and timely. Thus, a citizen is divided between protecting his or her own privacy and partaking in the benefits reaped from an open society.[88]

In summary, privacy serves both the individual and society as a whole. To the individual, privacy offers an opportunity for personal development, emotional release, and the development of human relationships. To society, privacy provides an environment in which democracy can thrive. However, even in a democracy, privacy is not an absolute for there are times when society's need for information outweighs the individual's right to privacy such as when the president becomes too ill to properly perform his or her duties as the leader of a nation, or when a child tells a teacher that he or she is being abused at home.[89, 90, 91, 92, 93]

The following chapter examines the question of who really owns, and thus, has exclusive rights to personal data such as your name, address, telephone number, and electronic mail.

NOTES

1. Lucas D. Introna, "Privacy and the Computer: Why We Need Privacy in the Information Society," *Metaphilosophy* 28 (1997): 261.

2. Ellen Alderman and Caroline Kennedy, *The Right to Privacy* (New York: Vintage Books, 1997), xiii.

3. Judith W. Decew, "Defending the 'Private' in Constitutional Privacy," *Journal of Value Inquiry* 21 (1987): 13.

4. W. A. Parent, "Recent Work on the Concept of Privacy," *American Philosophical Quarterly* 20 (1983): 341–55.

5. Ferdinand Schoeman, "Privacy: Philosophical Dimensions," *American Philosophical Quarterly* 20 (1984): 199–213.

6. Personal information consists of facts, communications, or options that relate to the individual and which would be reasonable to expect him or her to regard as intimate or sensitive enough to want to withhold, or at least, to restrict their collection, use, or circulation (Raymond Wacks, *Personal Information: Privacy and the Law* [Oxford: Clarendon, 1989], 26).

7. Sisela Bok, *Secrets: On the Ethics of Concealment and Revelation* (New York: Pantheon, 1982).

8. W. H. Foddy and W. R. Finighan, "The Concepts of Privacy from a Symbolic Interaction Perspective," *Journal for the Theory of Social Behavior* 10 (1981): 1–17.

9. Hyman Gross, "Privacy and Autonomy," in *Privacy*, ed. J. Roland Pennock and John W. Chapman (New York: Atherton, 1971).

10. Stephen T. Margulis, "Conceptions of Privacy: Current Status and Next Steps," *Journal of Social Issues* 33 (1977): 5–21.

11. Marc Rotenberg, "In Support of a Data Protection Board in the United States," *Government Information Quarterly* 8 (1991): 79–93.

12. Margulis, "Conceptions of Privacy," 10.

13. Rotenberg, "Data Protection Board," 80.

14. H. J. McCloskey, "Privacy and the Right to Privacy," *Philosophy* 55 (1980): 23.

15. McCloskey, "Privacy and the Right to Privacy," 23.

16. Ferdinand David Schoeman, "Privacy: Philosophical Dimensions of the Literature," in *Philosophical Dimensions of Privacy: An Anthology*, ed. Ferdinand David Schoeman (Cambridge: Cambridge University Press, 1984), 3.

17. Schoeman, "Privacy," 3.

18. Thomas Emmerson, *The System of Freedom of Expression* (New York: Random House, 1970), 545.

19. M. C. Slough, "The Roots of Privacy," in *Privacy, Freedom and Responsibility* (Springfield, Ill.: Charles C. Thomas, 1969), 3.
20. George W. S. Bailey, *Privacy and the Mental* (Amsterdam: Rodopi, 1979), 46.
21. C. T. Fischer, "Toward the Structure of Privacy: Implications for Psychological Assessment," in *Duquesne Studies in Phenomenological Psychology*, ed. A. Giorgi, W. G. Fischer, and R. von Eckartsberg (Pittsburgh, Penn.: Duquesne University Press, 1971), 154.
22. L. C. Velecky, "The Concepts of Privacy," in *Privacy*, ed. John B. Young (Chichester, UK: Wiley, 1978), 18.
23. Michael A. Weinstein, "The Uses of Privacy in the Good Life," in *Privacy*, ed. J. Roland Pennock and John W. Chapman (New York: Atherton, 1971).
24. Ruth Gavison, "Privacy and the Limits of the Law," in *Philosophical Dimensions of Privacy: An Anthology*, ed. Ferdinand David Schoeman (Cambridge: Cambridge University Press, 1984).
25. F. S. Chapin, "Some Housing Factors Related to Mental Hygiene," *Journal of Social Issues* 7 (1951): 164–71.
26. Patricia Brierley Newell, "Perspectives on Privacy," *Journal of Environmental Psychology* 15 (1995): 90.
27. Charles A. Reich, *The Greening of America: How the Youth Revolution is Trying to Make America Livable* (New York: Random House, 1970).
28. Alan F. Westin, *Privacy and Freedom* (New York: Atheneum, 1967).
29. Leon A. Pastalan, "Privacy as an Expression of Human Territoriality," in *Spatial Behavior of Older People*, ed. Leon A. Pastalan and Daniel H. Carson (Ann Arbor: University of Michigan Press, 1975).
30. Nancy J. Marshall, "Dimensions of Privacy Preferences," *Multivariate Behavioral Research* 9 (1974): 255–71.
31. Darhl Pedersen, "Dimensions of Privacy," *Perceptual and Motor Skills* 48 (1979): 1291–97.
32. Paul Halmos, *Solitude and Privacy: A Study of Social Isolation, Its Causes and Therapy* (London: Routledge & Kegan Paul, 1952).
33. Peter Kelvin, "A Social-Psychological Examination of Privacy," *British Journal of Social and Clinical Psychology* 12 (1973): 248–61.
34. William H. Ittelson et al., *An Introduction to Environmental Psychology* (New York: Holt, Rinehart, and Winston, 1974).
35. Pastalan, "Privacy as an Expression of Human Territoriality."
36. Gavison, "Privacy and the Limits of Law."
37. Ittelson et al., *Environmental Psychology*.
38. Pastalan, "Privacy as an Expression."
39. Marshall, "Dimensions of Privacy Preferences."
40. Ellen Bersheid, "Privacy: A Hidden Variable in Experimental Social Psychology," *Journal of Social Issues* 33 (1977): 85–101.
41. Hans Jurgen Eysenck and Sybil B. J. Eysenck, *Personality Structure and Measurement* (London: Routledge & Kegan Paul, 1969).
42. Schoeman, "Privacy: Philosophical Dimensions."
43. Charles Fried, *An Anatomy of Values: Problems of Personal and Social Choice* (Cambridge: Harvard University Press, 1970).
44. Robert S. Gerstein, "Intimacy and Privacy," in *Philosophical Dimensions of Privacy: An Anthology*, ed. Ferdinand David Schoeman (Cambridge: Cambridge University Press, 1984), 267.

45. Ittelsen et al., *Environmental Psychology.*
46. Newell, "Perspectives on Privacy," 92.
47. Edward Shils, "Privacy: Its Constitution and Vicissitudes," *Law & Contemporary Problems* 31 (1966): 281–306.
48. For instance, George Simmel considers that the secret society lives in an area to which the norms of society do not extend ("Knowledge and Ignorance," in *Sociological Theory: Present-Day Sociology From the Past,* ed. E. F. Borgatta and H. J. Meyers [New York: Knopf, 1956]).
49. Carol Warren and Barbara Laslett, "Privacy and Secrecy: A Conceptual Comparison," *Journal of Social Issues* 33 (1977): 44–45.
50. Warren and Laslett, "Privacy and Secrecy," 44.
51. Phyllis McGinley, *Province of the Heart* (New York: Viking, 1959), 56.
52. Donald J. Olsen, "Victorian London: Specialization, Segregation, and Privacy," *Victorian Studies* 17 (1974): 272–73.
53. J. J. Edney and M. A. Buda, "Distinguishing Territoriality and Privacy: Two Studies," *Human Ecology* 4 (1976): 283–96.
54. Newell, "Perspectives on Privacy," 94.
55. Irwin Altman, *The Environment and Social Behavior: Privacy, Personal Space, Territory, and Crowding* (Monterey, Calif.: Brooks/Cole, 1975).
56. Shils, "Privacy: Its Constitution and Vicissitudes."
57. Westin, *Privacy and Freedom,* 7.
58. Newell, "Perspectives on Privacy," 95.
59. Seumas Miller, "Privacy, Data Bases, and Computers," *Journal of Information Ethics* 7 (1998): 43.
60. Willis H. Ware, "The New Faces of Privacy," *The Information Society* 9 (1993): 196.
61. David Flaherty, *Protecting Privacy in Surveillance Societies* (Chapel Hill: University of North Carolina Press, 1989), 8.
62. Janna Malamud Smith, *Private Matters* (Reading, Mass.: Addison-Wesley, 1997), 11.
63. Altman, *Environment and Social Behavior.*
64. Alan P. Bates, "Privacy—A Useful Concept?" *Social Forces* 42 (1964): 25–26.
65. Westin, *Privacy and Freedom,* 37.
66. Westin, *Privacy and Freedom,* 34.
67. David L. Bazelon, "Probing Privacy," *Gonzaga Law Review* 12 (1977): 590.
68. Westin, *Privacy and Freedom,* 33.
69. The connection between privacy, the concept of human dignity, and the need to protect it can be found as early as in the Old Testament of the Bible: Adam and Eve, realizing they were naked, made aprons out of fig leaves with which to cover their private parts (Philippa Strum, *Privacy: The Debate in the United States Since 1945* [Fort Worth, Tex.: Harcourt Brace College Publishers, 1998], 5).
70. Flaherty, *Privacy in Colonial New England,* 3–4.
71. Edward J. Bloustein, "Privacy as an Aspect of Human Dignity: An Answer to Dean Prosser," in *Philosophical Dimensions of Privacy: An Anthology,* ed. Ferdinand David Schoeman (Cambridge: Cambridge University Press, 1984), 188.
72. Stanley I. Benn, "Privacy, Freedom, and Respect for Persons," in *Privacy,* ed. J. Roland Pennock and John W. Chapman (New York: Atherton, 1971), 229.
73. Benn, "Privacy, Freedom, and Respect," 229.
74. Bazelon, "Probing Privacy," 590.

75. Fred H. Cate, *Privacy in the Information Age* (Washington, D. C.: Brookings Institute Press, 1997).

76. Cate, *Privacy in the Information Age*, 25.

77. Westin, *Privacy and Freedom*, 43.

78. Dag Elgesem, "Privacy, Respect for Persons, and Risk," in *Philosophical Perspectives on Computer-Mediated Communication*, ed. Charles Ess (Albany: State University of New York Press, 1996), 55.

79. James Rachels, "Why Privacy is Important," in *Philosophical Dimensions of Privacy: An Anthology*, ed. Ferdinand David Schoeman (Cambridge: Cambridge University Press, 1984), 292.

80. Avrum Geurin Weiss, "Privacy and Intimacy: Apart and a Part," *Journal of Humanistic Psychology* 27 (1987): 121.

81. Janna Malamud Smith observes that at first glance, we might think of the wish for privacy as only a desire for aloneness when, in fact, one of its most important attributes is that it enables a deeper, more chosen openness. Privacy encourages self-expression and elaborates aspects of intimacy. She believes that the current flowering of memoirs is a perfect illustration of this seeming paradox: as people feel more separated, it may heighten their wish to recount very personal experiences (*Private Matters*, 8–9).

82. Fried, *Anatomy of Values*, 142.

83. Bazelon, "Probing Privacy," 591.

84. Barry Schwartz, "The Social Psychology of Privacy," *American Journal of Sociology* 73 (1968): 741.

85. Rotenberg, "Data Protection Board," 80. In Rotenberg's opinion, it is not a coincidence that a primary attribute of totalitarian societies and the dystopias that are often found in science fiction is that individuals lack personal privacy.

86. Bazelon, "Probing Privacy," 591–92.

87. Bazelon, "Probing Privacy," 592.

88. Gerard Salton, "A Progress Report on Information Privacy and Data Security," *Journal of the American Society for Information Science* 31 (1980): 76.

89. Alderman and Kennedy, *Right to Privacy*.

90. Amitai Etzioni, *The Limits of Privacy* (New York: Basic, 1999).

91. Robert Gellman, "Privacy," in *Federal Information Policies in the 1990s: Views and Perspectives*, ed. Peter Hernon, Charles McClure, and Harold C. Relyea (Norwood, N.J.: Ablex, 1996).

92. Martha Montague Smith, "Information Ethics," *Annual Review of Information Science and Technology* 32 (1997): 339–36.

93. Strum, *Privacy: The Debate in the United States*.

3

Ownership of Personal Data

YOUR NAME AND ADDRESS[1]

If asked who has the right to control access to your name and address, most would assert that your name and address are a peculiar personal asset and, therefore, should be under your strict control. This is the simple, idealistic view: in reality, your name and address are public knowledge. In most cases, such data are available to anyone who takes the effort to collect them.

The average consumer is on approximately 100 mailing lists and in at least 50 databases. Many of these lists are comprised of public information in the public domain, required for public purposes and from which our names cannot be removed. As David Linowes points out, your name gets on mailing lists by:[2]

1. Merely being—e.g., living at a particular address, subscribing to utility services, voting in an election, or registering for almost anything whether legally required or not.
2. Functioning like a human being—e.g., getting married or divorced, having a baby, attending school, procuring a job, relocating, or purchasing a car.

3. Responding to mail solicitation, which merchants take as a
   sign that you are likely to purchase what they have to offer.

A fine example of a source for mailing list compilers is the United
States Postal Service (USPS). Every night, all the change-of-address
postcards are consolidated at the USPS's 200 regional data processing centers. The cards are then forwarded to a computer in Mem-
phis, TN, where the data are inputted into a national address system
at the National Change of Address (NCOA) database and a Delivery
Sequence File (DSF) that contains almost all the deliverable postal
addresses in the country.[3] After that, the NCOA list is made available to some twenty-odd licensed address list managers serving
mass mailers, who, in turn, jam our mailboxes with direct mail
solicitations.[4]

Even though the change-of-address cards warn that the addresses
may be given to others, the truth is that they inevitably *will* be. The
USPS does not offer any alternatives; if you want your mail forwarded, you must accept that very soon, unsolicited mail will catch
up with you at your new address. According to the USPS, providing
individuals with the opt-out option would be financially and tem-
porally inefficient: these inefficiencies far outweigh the inconvenience to customers of disposing unwanted mail. Besides, the postal
service claims its role is not "to monitor the preferences of individuals or to tell mailers to whom they can or should address the mail."[5]

The USPS claims that the NCOA and DSF save the agency some
$30 million a year for every 1 percent of the more than 160 billion
pieces of mail automatically processed by computers. It also claims
that dissemination of computer-coded mailing addresses greatly en-
hances its ability to deliver mail promptly on top of quashing the
enormous costs associated with forwarding mail to relocated customers. The agency claims to give the changed addresses only to
mailers whose computers already have those customers and only to
companies acting as its agents. Mail managers who have an address
that can be "matched" in the NCOA will receive the new address
promptly. Those who do not will not be able to use change-of-address cards to build up their lists unless they already have at least 90
percent of the addresses within a given ZIP code. Even though the
name of the new occupant may not be known, the old address is still
known to the computer. This explains the large amount of mail addressed to "the occupant."

Thus, we have a conflict between the interest of those who wish to maintain some control over the mail they receive and the economic interests of the USPS and the direct mail marketing industry. Current practice comes down on the side of the USPS which does have a legitimate interest in streamlining its operation and continuing to provide employment for its three-quarter million workers. The real winners are the direct mail marketers who have their mailing lists automatically updated through the efforts of the USPS and its customers. The ultimate loser is probably the ecosystem since forests are pillaged to produce the paper on which junk mail is printed. Only 1 percent to 2 percent of the public actually respond to direct mail solicitations which means that a great deal ends up as rubbish. According to the Stop Junk Mail Association, an area the size of Los Angeles County is consumed by approximately 41 pounds of direct mail sent to each adult in a year. There is also the cost of disposing such items, leading to the inevitable tax hikes. Recycling costs escalate, much of the increase going toward the recycling of paper that has not yet had a useful first life.

YOUR TELEPHONE NUMBER[6]

Historically, telephone companies have viewed the telephone number as their property. The Supreme Court, in essence, supports this by refusing to recognize that a telephone customer has either a privacy or a property interest "in information he voluntarily turns over to third parties."[7] It may have been the case of *Smith vs. Maryland* in 1979 that telephone users realized that their numbers were public knowledge. In March 1976, Patricia McDonough of Baltimore, MD, began receiving threatening and obscene calls from a man who claimed to be the person who had robbed her. To track down the culprit, a "pen register"—a device that reveals telephone numbers directed to her number—was installed on McDonough's telephone. The caller turned out to be Smith who claimed a constitutional right of privacy to the telephone numbers he had dialed. At the trial, he moved under the "search and seizure" clause of the Fourth Amendment, to suppress the pen record claiming that they constituted an unwarranted search. The case went all the way to the Supreme Court. The majority of justices held that Smith could expect this evidence to be withheld only if he had a legitimate expectation of privacy in the telephone numbers he used and called:

> We doubt that people in general entertain any actual expectation of privacy in the numbers they dial. . . . Telephony users, in sum, typically know that they must convey numerical information to the phone company; that the phone company has facilities for recording this information; and that the phone company does in fact record this information for a variety of legitimate business purposes. Although subjective expectation cannot be scientifically gauged, it is too much to believe that telephone subscribers, under these circumstances, harbor any general expectation that the number they dial will remain secret.[8]

Recognition that the telephone number is a valuable commodity rather than an inconsequential fact is the first step in protecting telephone numbers. Determining the locus/loci of control constitutes the second. Some issues to grapple with are: Should the issuer or the user of the numbers, or the government, have the ultimate authority over its deployment? To what entities must it be disclosed and for what purposes? Most important, who is to pay for the imposition of technological "fixes" for serving diverse needs—the user, the provider, or the public officers? These are not questions that can be solely decided by the marketplace or even by judges and juries in a case-by-case litigation. Moreover, there are obviously trade-offs that must be considered in this complex matter.

YOUR E-MAIL[9]

The notion of the privacy and sanctity of mail comes from the moral traditional and relatively recent legal sanction prohibiting opening another person's letters transmitted through the USPS. However, this practice has not been applied to large corporate electronic mail systems. A case in point: in January 1990, Alana Shoars, then administrator for the e-mail system at Epson American, Inc., noticed printouts on her boss's desk that looked like the contents of password-protected e-mails she supervised.[10] When she criticized her manager for reading what she considered private messages, she was told to ignore the matter. The day after the altercation, Shoars was fired. Epson America denied that the dismissal was related to her questioning the e-mail procedures. Instead, the company claimed that she was terminated for allegedly obtaining her own personal MCI Mail account against company policy, which constituted a gross insubordination.

Consequently, Shoars filed a million-dollar wrongful discharge and slander suit and was joined by several former Epson America employees in a class action suit questioning the invasion of privacy. The company maintains that it reserves the right to inspect its e-mail systems, but claimed it did not abuse this privilege. The lower court agreed with Epson's lawyer that neither state privacy statutes nor federal statutes address confidentiality of e-mail in the workplace and dismissed the case. The court found that Shoar's attorney, Neil Shipman, failed to provide sufficient proof that Shoars and the other Epson workers had an expectation of privacy in their e-mail. The court also found that the submitted e-mail messages were, with few exceptions, business-related, and that the California state constitutional right of privacy covered only *personal* information. Therefore, the court found insufficient legal or factual basis for extending the right to privacy to cover business-oriented communications.[11] As for Shoars' personal suits, her slander suit was settled in 1994 for an undisclosed sum, but she lost her wrongful discharge suit.

Since the Shoars case, there have been a number of proposals to regulate the new realm of e-mails, including a full-fledged constitutional amendment guaranteeing First Amendment rights to all electronic systems. Before this can occur, several legal issues need to be resolved as First Amendment rights can include both the right of a "publisher" to publish without government censorship and the right of privacy of the individual to control access to personal information. Moreover, it is unclear as to what extent the right of anonymity will be preserved, a right that has firm legal roots.

Another obstacle lies in the fact that it is becoming more and more difficult to identify the nature of the various messages because they are embedded in a digital electronic stream in which the signals are in binary form without spelling out whether they purport to be news, mail, book, conference call, or private conversation. Thus, what legal rubric would be appropriate to cover them is not easily determined.

Finally, how to reconcile the jurisdictional authority over a global entity such as the World Wide Web remains a challenge, if not a legal nightmare.

Thus, when using e-mail under the current situation, one should assume that "if the corporation owns the equipment and pays for the network, that asset belongs to the company, and it has a right to look and see if people are using it for purposes other than running the business."[12]

The following chapter will examine the various ways privacy can be protected. These methods range from what an individual can do to what the government has done and can do further.

NOTES

1. Most of the information in this section comes from Anne Wells Branscomb, *Who Owns Information? From Privacy to Public Access* (New York: Basic Books, 1994), 9–29.
2. David F. Linowes, *Privacy in America: Is Your Private Life in the Public Eye?* (Urbana: University of Illinois Press, 1989), 140–41.
3. The master NCOA file, the only USPS file containing actual names, records some 90 million moves per year.
4. For more information about mailing lists, see Linowes, *Privacy in America*, 140–55.
5. Testimony of Robert G. Krause (Director, Office of Address Information Systems, United States Postal Service) Before the U.S. House of Representatives, Government Information, Justice, and Agriculture Subcommittee Hearing on U.S. Postal Service Address Correction Activities, 14 May 1992, quoted in Branscomb, *Who Owns Information*, 10.
6. Most of the information in this section comes from Branscomb, *Who Owns Information*, 30–53.
7. *Smith vs. Maryland*, 442 U.S. 735 (1975), quoted in Branscomb, *Who Owns Information*, 36.
8. *Smith vs. Maryland*, 442, quoted in Branscomb, *Who Owns Information*, 37
9. Most of the information in this section comes from Branscomb, *Who Owns Information*, 92–105.
10. For further details, see Ellen Alderman and Caroline Kennedy, *The Right to Privacy* (New York: Vintage Books, 1997), 310–17.
11. Alderman and Kennedy, *Right to Privacy*, 315.
12. Michael Simmons, Chief Information Officer, Bank of Boston, quoted in Wayne Eckerson, "Privacy Suit Forces Users to Examine E-mail Policies: Case Against Epson Raises Troubling Questions," *Network World* 17 (17 September 1990): 1.

4

Means of Protecting Privacy

LEGISLATION

In the United States, concern for privacy protection began in the late 1960s when a multitude of technological (e.g., computerized record systems, telephone wiretaps, parabolic microphones, lie detectors, personality tests, and miniaturized cameras) and social changes (e.g., media coverage and scholarly studies that have increased public concern about surveillance) precipitated challenges to individual privacy. By the mid-1960s, public and congressional concern spurred inquiries into the capabilities and uses of these techniques and the development of legislative actions to prevent or alleviate privacy invasions.

Since the 1970s, the United States Congress has passed more than a dozen laws protecting individual privacy.[1] Most appeared on the congressional agenda in response to technological changes that were perceived as threats to individual privacy. Information privacy laws (i.e., those involving questions about the use of personal information collected by financial institutions, the federal government, educational institutions, the retail sector, etc.) account for three-quarters of these. Communication privacy laws (i.e., those involving questions about who can legitimately intercept verbal, printed, or electronic discussions between two parties) account for two-thirds. Psy-

Title III of the Omnibus Crime Control and Safe Streets Act of 1968 protects the privacy of wire and oral communications by prohibiting electronic surveillance of aural communications except for law enforcement surveillance under a court order, specified telephone company monitoring for service purposes, and cases where one participant consents to the surveillance.

Fair Credit Reporting Act (FCRA) of 1970 requires credit investigations and reporting agencies to make their records available to the subjects of the records, provides procedures for correcting information, and permits disclosures only to authorized customers.

Family Education Rights and Privacy Act of 1974, a.k.a. the "Buckley Amendment," requires educational institutions to grant students or parents access to student records, establishes procedures to challenge and correct information, and limits disclosure of third parties.

Privacy Act of 1974 provides individuals rights of access to and correction of information held by federal agencies and places restrictions on federal agencies' collection, use, and disclosure of personally identifiable information.

Foreign Intelligence Surveillance Act of 1978 establishes legal standards and procedures for the use of electronic surveillance to collect foreign intelligence and counter intelligence within the United States.

Right to Financial Privacy Act of 1978 provides bank customers some privacy regarding their records held by banks and other financial institutions and stipulates procedures whereby federal agencies can gain access to such records.

Privacy Protection Act (PPA) of 1980 prohibits government agencies from conducting unannounced searches of press offices and files if no one in the office is suspected of having committed a crime.

Cable Communications Policy Act of 1984, a.k.a. "1984 Cable Act" or "Cable Act," requires cable services to inform subscribers of the nature of personally identifiable information collected and the nature of the use of such information; the disclosures that may be made of such information; the period during which such information will be maintained; and the times during which subscribers may access such information about themselves. It also places restrictions on the cable services' collection and disclosure of such information.

Electronic Communications Privacy Act (ECPA) of 1986 extends Title III protection and requirements to new forms of voice, data, and video communications, including cellular phones, electronic mail, computer transmissions, and voice and display pagers.

Figure 4.1 Major Privacy Legislations[2]

Computer Matching and Privacy Protection Act of 1988 requires agencies to formulate procedural agreements before exchanging computerized record systems for purposes of searching or comparing those records and establish Data Integrity Boards within each agency.

Employee Polygraph Protection Act of 1988 prohibits the private sector's use of lie detector tests for employment purposes, except under certain circumstances.

Video Privacy Protection Act of 1988 prohibits video stores from disclosing their customers' names and addresses and the specific videotapes rented or bought by customers except under certain circumstances.

Telephone Consumer Protection Act (TCPA) of 1991 restricts telemarketing calls, especially those made by autodialers.

Driver's Privacy Protection Act of 1994 restricts the public disclosure of personal information contained in state Department of Motor Vehicle (DMV) records.

Communications Assistance for Law Enforcement Act (CALEA) of 1994, a.k.a. Digital Telephony Act, requires telephone companies to modify their networks to ensure government access to all wire and electronic communications, as well as call-identifying information. The law also includes several provisions enhancing privacy such as a section that increased the standard for government access to transactional data.

Telecommunications Act of 1996 requires telephone companies to obtain customers' approval before using information about users' calling patterns to market new services.

Health Insurance Portability and Accountability Act of 1996 contains a section known as "Administrative Simplification" which mandates the development and adoption of standards for electronic exchanges of health information. It also requires that Congress and the Secretary of Health and Human Services develop privacy rules to govern such electronic exchanges; however, these rules may not be in place before the electronic system is implemented.

Children's Online Privacy Protection Act (COPPA) of 1998 requires commercial websites and other online services directed at children 12 years and under, or which collect information regarding users' age, to provide parents with notice of their information practices and obtain parental consent prior to the collection of personal information from children. The Act further requires such sites to provide parents with the ability to review and correct information about their children collected by such services.

(Figure 4.1 continued)

chological privacy laws (i.e., those involving questions about the degree and type of probing to determine individuals' thoughts and attitudes) account for the smallest portion of privacy legislation. Figure 4.1 describes privacy laws that have been enacted in the United States so far.

SELF-REGULATING VOLUNTARY CODES

Many sectors, from banking and insurance to direct marketing and telecommunications, have created their own privacy codes in an effort to fend off legislation and to raise low consumer confidence. These industry codes are primarily based on the Organization for Economic Cooperation and Development's (OECD) Code of Fair Information Practices (FIPs) which offer protections regarding limited collection, notification of intended uses, consent for secondary uses, and the right to access one's file and amend errors.[3] Industry associations such as the Direct Marketing Association and the Information Industry Association of America, too, have introduced their own privacy codes. Several businesses such as American Express, Equifax, IBM, and Dun & Bradstreet have written their own company privacy codes. In addition, a number of companies such as AT&T and Verizon have attempted to address the question of privacy in the services they offer.

Self-regulating voluntary codes have the advantage of being tailor-made to the particular circumstances of one sector, allowing for greater flexibility in applying information practices. It is also more likely that sector-specific protections will suit the needs of the customers as well as the particular regulatory environment in which the industry operates. However, voluntary privacy codes are also believed to be less effective than privacy legislation mainly due to an inadequate enforcement mechanism. Moreover, consumer advocates claim that such codes have little, if any, consumer input. They tend to be poorly monitored and poorly communicated, and leave consumers with little recourse if their complaints are not resolved.[4] However, this view may be changing with the introduction of privacy seal programs.

Online privacy seal programs require their licensees to implement certain FIPs and to submit to various types of compliance monitoring in order to display a privacy seal on their websites. These programs are still in their infancy, but if widely adopted, they promise an efficient way to alert consumers to licensees' information practices and to demonstrate licensees' compliance with program requirements. Below is a description of the three major online privacy seal programs available at present:

- *TRUSTe* (www.truste.com), the first online privacy seal program, was founded by Lori Fena, Executive Director of the Electronic Frontier Foundation, and Charles Jennings, founder and CEO of Portland Software. TRUSTe is a nonprofit, global initiative operating independently from both industry and government. Its core tenets to which licensees must abide include: (1) Notice, whereby licensees must post clear notice of what personally identifiable information is gathered and with whom it is shared. This disclosure must be easy to read and accessible by one click of a mouse from the home page; (2) Choice, where users must have the ability—through opt-in or opt-out functions—to choose whether to allow secondary uses of that personal information; (3) Access, where users must have reasonable access to information maintained about them by the website to correct any inaccuracies in the data collected; and (4) Security, where the website must provide reasonable security to protect the data collected.[5]
- *BBBOnline Privacy Seal* (www.bbbonline.org) was launched in March 2000. The Better Business Bureau has licensed over 450 sites representing 244 companies to post its seal. In order to be licensed, online merchants must meet BBBOnline Privacy Program's requirements regarding notice, choice, accountability, and security in terms of identifiable information collected online. These companies must post privacy notices telling consumers what personal information is being collected, how it will be used, choices consumers have in its usage, and licensees must verify security measures taken to protect this information. Qualifying websites must abide by their posted privacy policies, agree to a comprehensive independent verification by BBBOnline, and participate in the program's dispute resolution service.[6]
- *CPA WebTrust* (www.cpawebtrust.org) is the third major privacy seal program available. The WebTrust Program requires

independent verification through a licensed CPA firm, or its international counterpart, to ensure that an online business complies with its set of e-business "best practices."[7,8] The CPA firm tests the website at least every six months to verify that it continues to comply with the Program requirements. A site that complies with all Program requirements for the module(s) it has chosen, earns the right to display a WebTrust Seal of Assurance on its website.[9] Visitors can click on the seal to view the independent CPA's report, the site management's assertions, and disclosures related to the particular WebTrust module(s). The Program requires the use of third party arbitration to resolve customer complains; in the U.S., the National Arbitration Forum has established an effective, low-cost arbitration and mediation process. Although it is not mandatory for WebTrust clients to select the Forum as its third party arbitrator, it is required that the organization selected for the role follow the guidelines of the WebTrust Program.[10]

YOURSELF

Probably, the best weapon in protecting your privacy is yourself. As consumers, you must seriously consider your privacy and what it means to you when engaging in everyday transactions in the marketplace. In view of this, the following is a primer on how to become your own privacy watchdog. Points in Figure 4.2 deal with privacy in general, regardless of medium; points in Figure 4.3 deal specifically with Internet privacy.

SUMMARY

The ability to retain control over your personal information and to choose if, when, and how it is used, ultimately lies with you. While privacy is not an absolute, it is a fundamental human right that must be recognized and protected. Therefore, become your own privacy watchdog: be proactive, not reactive.

1. Every time you are asked for your personal information, question why it is needed and what will be done with the information.

2. Having satisfied yourself that the information is being collected for a legitimate purpose, give only the *minimum* amount required.

3. Ask who has access to your personal information (e.g., third parties).

4. Challenge the sale, rental, or exchange of your personal information to third parties for secondary uses beyond the immediate transaction.

5. Check off the opt-out box on any form seeking your personal information. If there is none, create your own by adding a sentence stating that you do not want your information sold, rented, or exchanged with other organizations for purposes beyond the immediate transaction.

6. Periodically, ask for access to your personal information gathered by companies to ensure that the information is correct and up-to-date. If not, have the company correct it.

7. Whenever possible, pay with cash as this will minimize the amount of information on your preferences and habits as a consumer.

8. Demand that your name, address, and telephone number be removed from mailing and telephone lists by contacting the Direct Marketing Association (DMA Mail Preference Service, P. O. Box 9008, Farmingdale, NY 11735-9008. Telephone 212-768-7277). Call back in a few months to double-check that your name has been added to the "Do Not Mail/Do Not Call" lists.

9. Ask your physician who may have access to your medical records outside of the office and for what reason; ask if your records have ever been reviewed during an audit and indicate your wish to be notified when such a situation arises; ask to see your records before your doctor sends them to a third party; and ask your healthcare providers (including pharmacists) how they keep your records confidential.

10. Write to the Medical Insurance Bureau (P. O. Box 105, Essex Station, Boston, MA 02112) to obtain a copy of your medical record file.

11. Use the Call Blocking feature (*67) on your telephone if you do not want your number to be traceable.

12. Complain to the heads of organizations that do not respect their clients' privacy, and tell government representatives that privacy issues are important to you and ask what they are doing to protect your privacy.

Figure 4.2 General Ways to Protect Your Privacy[11]

1. Look for privacy policies on the web. An increasing number of websites has begun to provide privacy policies that detail the sites' information practices. Study these carefully. If there is no policy, write and tell the company that you are a user of their site, your privacy is important to you, and you would like to see them post a policy.

2. Obtain a separate account for personal e-mail. As seen in Chapter 3, your employer has a legal right to read any and all correspondence in your workplace account or on your work computer at any time. Getting a separate account for home allows you to check your personal messages without using your workplace e-mail server.

3. Clear memory cache after browsing the web. After you have surfed the web, copies of all accessed pages and images are saved on your computer's memory. While these make subsequent visits to the same sites faster, your web activities may be traced, particularly if you share a computer or browse at work. To delete most of your online trail, go into the "Preferences" folder in your browser and click on the "Empty Cache" button. Sometimes, this option is in the "Advanced" menu of the browser preferences.

4. Use online forms while in secure mode. New browsers are designed to indicate whether the accessed page allows encrypted transfers. The most common icons used to indicate security is a key or a padlock. If a page is secure, the key is intact or the padlock is locked. Conversely, if the page is insecure, the key is broken or the padlock is unlocked. The icon appears in the corner of the browser screen. Clicking on the icon will inform you of additional security information about the page.

5. Reject unnecessary cookies. Cookies enable websites to store information about your visit on your computer's hard drive. These are also used to create a profile of you, and thus, to target advertisements to you. You can search your hard drive for a file with the word "cookie" in it to view any that have been attached to your computer. Newer browsers allow you to recognize sites that send you cookies and reject them outright by accessing the "Advanced" screen of the "Preferences" menu.

6. Use anonymous remailers (See following section, "Technologies," for an explanation of anonymous remailers).

7. Encrypt your e-mail (See following section, "Technologies," for an explanation of encryption).

8. Use anonymizers while browsing (See following section, "Technologies," for an explanation of anonymizers).

Figure 4.3 Ways to Protect Your Internet Privacy[12]

TECHNOLOGIES

On the one hand, technologies designed to meet the information needs of government and businesses have deprived individuals of the power to control their personal information. Moreover, communication technologies have enabled collectors to share data amongst themselves for a variety of purposes, and most egregiously, without the knowledge or consent of data subjects. On the other hand, technology can be designed to empower users to make decisions about the collection, use, and disclosure of personal information every time they go online. Some tools protect privacy by cloaking information likely to reveal identity, or decoupling this identity information from the individual's activities. Other tools make it possible to browse the web without revealing one's identity and purchase goods with the anonymity of cash. Below is a sample of the technological tools available at this time that protect online privacy.[13]

Ad Blocker

Advertising banners can be downloaded by your browser from any Internet server. Besides requiring extra time to download and taking up disk space, some advertising companies track the web movements of people seeing the ads (see Chapter 4, "Doubleclick" section for an illustration of this procedure). Ad blockers disable advertisements from many web pages. Examples of Ad blockers are AdDelete, AdSubtract, Guidescope, Internet Junkbuster Proxy, and Proxomitron.

Anonymizer

An anonymizer is a computer that sits between you and the Internet, filtering out your private information such as IP (Internet Protocol) Address, computer type, or browser information. Examples of anonymizers are Aixs, Anonymity 4, Anonymouse, Cloak, I-Safetynet, No Proxy, Secure Anticensorship Proxy, Anonymizer, CGIProxy, Crowds, Cyberpress, Easy Access, IDecide Privacy Companion, IDZap, Interfree Anonymizer, Naviscope, net HUSH, Ponoi, Privacy Proxy, PrivacyX, Private Idaho, Rewebber, Sami, Siege Surfer, Silent Browser, Simple Anonymity, Space Proxy, and ZixCharge.

Cookie Management

A cookie is a piece of information unique to you that your browser saves and sends back to a web server when you revisit a website. Cookie management programs help computer users know what is going on in and out of the browser. Examples of cookie management software are Buzof, Cookie Central, Cookie Cop, Cookie Cop Plus, Cookie Crusher, Cookie Cutter 1.0 for Macintosh, Cookie Jar, Cookie Pal, Cookie Sweeper, Cookie Terminator, Crumbler97, Luckman's Anonymous Cookie for Internet Privacy, Magic Cookie Monster for Macintosh, PGPcookie.cutter, and ZDNet Cookie Master.

Encryption

Encryption (a.k.a. encoding) is a mathematical process that disguises the content of messages transmitted. There are two main types of encryption: symmetric cryptosystems and public key systems. In symmetric systems, one common key is shared by both parties for encrypting and decrypting messages. One problem with such a system is that for the recipient to decrypt the message, the sender must tell the recipient what the key is. When that information is transmitted via a public network it may be intercepted, thus, defeating the whole point of encryption.

Conversely, a public key system is asymmetric because two different keys are involved: one public (widely distributed for encryption), the other, private (only known to the recipient and sender for decryption). What is encoded with one key may be decoded only with the corresponding key in the pair. Under a public key system, the public key is published in a directory of public keys for subscribers to the system. A secure message could be sent to you by anyone encrypting it with your public key. However, only you, the holder of your private key, could decode the message. The process of using someone's public key to encode a confidential message is known as the encryption mode. A public key may also be used as the decoding key with the private key serving as the encoder. Since your private key is known only to you when it is used to encode a message, it is uniquely associated with you, much like your handwritten signature. Thus, when a message is encoded with your private key, it, in effect, serves as your "digital signature" to verify the identity of the sender and to ensure the integrity of the message. This form of encryption is referred to as the authentication mode.

One of the disadvantages of public key systems is that they tend to be slower than symmetric systems. However, it is possible to combine the advantages of both systems in a "hybrid" cryptosystem to yield the best encryption system.

Examples of encryption software are AACrypt, BestCrypt, Cypherus, F-Secure SSH, Fortify, Mailcrypt, PGP, Scramdisk, Secure File System, SecureDrive, SecuriPhone, seNTry 2020, and TMC-SL-200 Universal Secure System.

File Management

Your computer keeps track of your activities on your hard drive as you surf the Internet. These tools help you manage what information is stored about your surfing habits. Examples of file management software are Burn 2.5, Complete Cleanup, DiskVac, Eraser, File Wiper for DOS, Mutilate, NSClean & IEClean, Window Washer, and X-Ray Vision.

Profile Management

These tools allow you to create multiple profiles as you surf. For example, Digitalme enables you to choose to give different "business cards" to different people depending on your relationship with them; Privaseek helps consumers control the use and distribution of their personal information on the Internet; and Freedom is a software that allows you to create untraceable online identities called "pseudonyms" ("nyms").

PRIVACY ADVOCATES

The privacy advocacy community is critical in mobilizing support and keeping the issue alive on the public and congressional agenda. The following section recounts the genesis of this community and briefly describes selected privacy advocacy groups based in the United States.

Privacy Advocates: Individuals[14]

In the mid-1960s, the Social Science Research Council proposed to establish a National Data Center. This event presented Congress with the first opportunity to discuss and debate issues of privacy. The meetings of the Senate Subcommittee on Administrative Practice and Procedure in March and June 1966 (chaired by Senator Edward Long), the Special Subcommittee on Invasion of Privacy in July 1966 (chaired by Representative Cornelius Gallagher), and the Subcommittee on Constitutional Rights in 1971 (chaired by Senator Sam Ervin) invited a number of people to participate who eventually became members of the privacy community: Arthur R. Miller, then law professor at the University of Michigan and author of *The Assault on Privacy;* Alan Westin, the author of *Privacy and Freedom;* and Hope Eastman, acting director of the ACLU's Washington, D.C., office.

Toward the end of the 1960s, computer specialists became active in the privacy community, particularly in the area of information privacy. Willis Ware of the RAND Corporation chaired the Health, Education, and Welfare's (HEW) Secretary's Advisory Committee on Automated Data Systems which developed the Code of Fair Information Practices. Lewis Branscomb, an IBM vice president and chief scientist, testified on privacy and data security issues. Michael Baker, along with Alan Westin, received funding from the Russell Sage Foundation in 1968 to study computers, record keeping, and privacy for the National Academy of Sciences.

The Westin and Baker study brought several individuals into the privacy community, many of whom are still active. Lance Hoffman, then assistant professor of electrical engineering and computer sciences at the University of California at Berkeley, was a staff associate of the project. He later became a professor at George Washington University and chair of the Second Annual Conference on Computers, Freedom, and Privacy (Washington, D.C., March 1992). Robert Belair, then a student at Columbia University Law School, was a research assistant for the study. He continued his privacy interests as an attorney. Kenneth Laudon, then a graduate student of Westin at Columbia, participated in site visits and later worked on the Office of Technology Assessment (OTA) study on criminal history records and penned *Dossier Society.*

Many of the above testified at congressional hearings before the passage of the 1974 Privacy Act. These sessions also provided an opportunity for new individuals to be involved in the privacy community. Christopher Pyle, a former captain in army intelligence and a doctoral student of Westin at Columbia, testified at the 1971 and

1974 hearings of Senator Ervin's Subcommittee on Constitutional Rights. G. Russell Pipe, formerly an aide to Representative Barry M. Goldwater, Jr., submitted a statement for the record in support of Senate bill S. 3418. He went on to found and edit *Transnational Data Reports*, which report on information policies and practices worldwide.

Discussion and passage of the Privacy Act of 1974 aroused the media's interest. Several journalists such as David Burnham of *The New York Times* and author of *The Rise of the Computer State,* Robert Ellis Smith of *Privacy Journal,* and Evan Hendricks of *Privacy Times* developed a lifelong interest in privacy issues and followed congressional activity in this area.

With the establishment of the Privacy Protection Study Commission (PPSC) in 1976, old and new people flocked to the privacy community. The veterans included Willis Ware who was vice chair of PPSC; Carole Parsons, who had a key role in writing the report of the HEW advisory committee, was executive director; Representative Barry Goldwater who headed the Republican Task Force on Privacy, and Representative Edward Koch, who was active in polygraph issues as well as information privacy issues, were also on the PPSC. Alan Westin served as a specialist consultant, as did James Rule, author of *Private Lives Public Surveillance,* and Russell Pipe. New individuals included Ronald Plesser, Fred Weingarten, Arthur Bushkin, and Lois Alexander. Plesser served as general counsel for the commission and later organized the American Bar Association's (ABA) efforts in the early 1980s on behalf of privacy. Fred Weingarten was a professional staff member of the PPSC on detail from the National Science Foundation (NSF). He became program director of the Communications and Information Technology Program at the OTA during the period when the agency was conducting a number of studies on a range of privacy and technology issues. Arthur Bushkin was a PPSC project manager responsible for assessing the Privacy Act and later participated in the privacy initiative in the Carter administration. Lois Alexander was on detail from the Social Security Administration and was a project manager for research and statistics.

In the late 1970s, the OTA began a study of the societal aspects of national information systems at the request of the Senate and House Judiciary committees and the House Post Office and Civil Service Committee. As part of this assessment, the OTA formed an advisory panel for its reports on national information systems and electronic message systems. Members of the panel included a number of people who had been actively involved in information privacy issues before (i.e., Arthur Miller, Russell Pipe, James Rule, Willis Ware, and Alan Westin). Lance Hoffman served as a member of a special advisory panel on information technology. As part of the assessment, the OTA also established an advisory panel for its report on computerized criminal history systems. This panel was chaired by Arthur Miller and composed of other recognized members of the information privacy community: Jerry Berman, then legislative counsel for the ABA; Lance Hoffman; Christopher Pyle; and James Rule. Marcia Naughton served as director of the criminal history systems study from October 1978 to July 1980, and Kenneth Laudon was a contractor for the study.

In 1984, the ABA, ACLU, and the Public Interest Computer Association (PICA) sponsored a series of meetings which were primarily funded by the Benton Foundation. Ronald Plesser and George Trubow represented the ACLU; John Shattuck and Jerry Berman represented the ACLU. Marc Rotenberg, then an intern with the ACLU's Privacy and Technology Project and later head of the Washington, D.C., office of the Computer Professionals for Social Responsibility (CPSR), represented PICA which was largely his creation. These conferences not only provided a forum where members of the privacy community could meet and discuss legislative proposals and strategies, but also broadened the focus of the privacy community from mainly information privacy to communications privacy.

An international dimension crept into the privacy community in the 1980s. International issues had entered policy discussions in the 1970s when private sector firms lobbied against their inclusion in the Privacy Act partly due to concerns about the free flow of information and transborder data flows. Besides Russell Pipe, who monitored privacy developments in other countries as head of the Transnational Data Reporting Service, no individual was concerned with international privacy issues. In the 1980s, as criticisms of the Privacy Act and its implementation mounted, interest in the European model of data protection, with oversight by an advisory or regulatory body, grew in the U.S. David Flaherty, a former student of Alan Westin and author of *Privacy in Colonial New England*, testified at House hearings in 1984 about the need for such a body in the U.S.

Flaherty became an active member of the privacy community in this country, as well as abroad, and served as the information and privacy commissioner in British Columbia, Canada.

In the mid-1980s, the OTA began a study on the civil liberties and congressional oversight implications of federal agency use of new information technologies. Members of the advisory panel included several privacy veterans: Jerry Berman, David Flaherty, George Trubow, and Alan Westin. In addition, two workshops on privacy issues took place, one on electronic record systems and the other on electronic surveillance. Participants in the workshop on electronic record systems included two longtime members of the privacy community: Robert Belair and James Rule. Two federal agency representatives at the workshop—William Cavaney of the Defense Privacy Board and Robert Veeder of the Office of Information and Regulatory Affairs at the OMB—had also been actively involved in the privacy community following the passage of the Privacy Act of 1974. The workshop on electronic surveillance included luminaries such as Gary Marx, Ronald Plesser, Christopher Pyle, and James Rule.

Since the 1980s, the privacy community has been relatively stable in its perspective and strategy, reflecting shared values, shared concerns, and shared problem definition. It has been nonhierarchical and open in its membership. Within the privacy community, individuals assume a variety of roles such as advocate, expert, and facilitator. The following section discusses the four organizations that are prominent privacy advocates in the United States.

Privacy Advocates: Groups

American Civil Liberties Union (ACLU)[15]

Founded in 1920 by Roger Baldwin, Crystal Eastman, Albert DeSilver, and colleagues, the American Civil Liberties Union is the largest nonprofit, nonpartisan public interest law firm in the nation.[16] The organization is comprised of a 50-state network of staffed, autonomous affiliate offices. A national board of directors sets policy, while a national office in New York coordinates work with the help of a legislative office in Washington, D.C., and a legal department in New York.

The ACLU's mission is to preserve all of the protections and guarantees laid out in the U.S. Constitution's Bill of Rights. In other words, freedom of speech, association, and assembly; freedom of press and religion; the right to equal protection under the law regardless of race, sex, age, and religion; the right to due process; and the right to privacy. A number of national projects address specific civil liberties issues: AIDS, capital punishment, lesbian and gay rights, immigrants' rights, prisoners' rights, reproductive freedom, voting rights, women's rights, and workplace rights. Some of ACLU's more notable cases are "The Scopes Case" (1925) where biology teacher John T. Scopes was charged with violating a Tennessee ban on teaching evolution; "The *Ulysses* Case" (1933) where a New York federal court lifted a U.S. Customs Service ban on the sale of James Joyce's novel in the United States; School Desegregation (1954) where the May 17 decision by the Supreme Court declared racially segregated schools to be in violation of the Fourteenth Amendment; Flag Burning (1989) where the House of Representatives passed an amendment to the Constitution requiring punishment to desecrators of the flag, but the Senate rejected it on the ACLU's warnings.

The ACLU is supported by annual dues and contributions from its members as well as grants from private foundations and individuals: the organization does not receive any government funding. Most of the Union's clients are ordinary people who have experienced an injustice and have decided to fight back.

Center for Democracy and Technology (CDT)[17]

The Center for Democracy and Technology, a Washington, D.C.-based group founded in December 1994, is a nonprofit public policy organization dedicated to promoting democracy on the Internet. The organization's mission is to develop and implement public policies to protect and advance civil liberties and democratic values in new interactive media. Its mission is, in turn, guided by six principles of (1) the unique nature of the Internet, (2) freedom of expression, (3) privacy, (4) surveillance, (5) access, and (6) democratic participation. Examples of the CDT's work include analysis of the constitutional, legal, and enforcement problems posed by the Exon bill (a.k.a. Communications Decency Act of 1995) with which the Department of Justice concurred; expert testimony for the Senate Judiciary Subcommittee on Terrorism and Technology on free speech issues posed by the availability of bomb manuals on the Internet; monitoring the implementation of the Digital Telephony Bill; and studying the alternatives to the "Clipper Chip."[18]

The CDT pursues its mission through research and public policy development in a consensus-building process based on working groups comprising of public interest and commercial representatives of divergent views. These working groups lie in the areas of online privacy, digital security, and free expression (e.g., The Interactive Working Group, and The Digital Privacy and Security Working Group). Since working groups are educational in nature, they do not take formal positions on legislation.

The CDT promotes its own policy positions in the United States as well as abroad through public policy advocacy, online grassroots organizing with the Internet user community, public education campaigns, litigation, and the development of technology standards and online information resources.[19]

In terms of financial support, the CDT is funded by contributions from industry and foundations.[20] Most supporters join and fund one or more working groups, activities, and projects. Working group and special project participants attend CDT-coordinated forums on policy issues, and are kept informed through the Center's e-mail, fax, online policy posts, issue briefs, and reports.[21]

In the next chapter, the genesis of the CDT will be described.

Electronic Frontier Foundation (EFF)[22]

The Electronic Frontier Foundation is a San Francisco-based, donor-supported membership organization that works to protect American's fundamental rights regardless of technology. The Foundation aims to educate the media, policymakers, and the public in general about civil liberties issues related to technology, and acts as a defender of those liberties. Among its various activities, the EFF opposes misguided legislation, initiates and defends court cases preserving individuals' rights, launches global public campaigns, introduces leading edge proposals and papers, hosts frequent educational events, engages the press regularly, and publishes a comprehensive archive of digital civil liberties information.

In the following chapter, the EFF will be described in more detail.

Electronic Privacy Information Center (EPIC)[23]

Founded in 1994 by Marc Rotenberg (former intern at the ACLU and head of the Washington, D.C., office of the CPSR), the Electronic Privacy Information Center is a public interest research center based in Washington, D.C. Its purpose is to focus public attention on emerging civil liberties issues and to protect privacy, the First Amendment, and constitutional values. EPIC works in association with Privacy International—an international human rights group based in London—and is a member of the Global Internet Liberty Campaign, the Internet Free Expression Alliance, the Internet Privacy Coalition, the Internet Democracy Project, and the Trans Atlantic Consumer Dialogue (TACD).

Like the ACLU, CDT, and EFF, EPIC depends on public donations and funding from foundations.

Privacy Rights Clearinghouse (PRC)[24]

Established in 1992 with funding from the Telecommunications Education Trust (a part of the California Public Utilities Commission), the Privacy Rights Clearinghouse is a nonprofit consumer information and advocacy program and is a project of the Utility Consumers' Action Network (UCAN) (a San Diego-based nonprofit membership organization advocating consumers' interests vis à vis telecommunications and the Internet). In the beginning (1992 through October 1996), the PRC was administered by the Center for Public Interest Law of the University of San Diego School of Law.

The purposes of the PRC are: (1) to raise consumers' awareness of how technology affects personal privacy; (2) to empower consumers to take action to control their own personal information by providing practices on privacy protection; (3) to respond to specific privacy-related complaints from consumers, and when necessary, refer them to appropriate organizations for further assistance; (4) to document the nature of consumers' concerns about privacy in reports and make them available to policymakers, industry representatives, and consumer advocates; and (5) to advocate consumers' privacy rights in local, state, and federal public policy proceedings such as legislative testimony, regulatory agency hearings, task forces, study commissions, conferences, and workshops.

The PRC was originally funded by the Telecommunications Education Trust (TET), a program of the California Public Utilities Commission, from 1992 until mid-1996. Other past funders include the James and Frederica Rosenfield Foundation; legal settlement from attorneys Neville Johnson & Brian Rishwain; a cy pres class action settlement; Consumer Federation of America; Office Depot; Fellowes Manufacturing; Bank of America Consumer Education Fund; Pacific Bell/GTE Community Education Program for Caller ID Blocking; Fieldstone Foundation; American Express; and the Luella Morey Murphy Foundation. Present funders include the Metromail Cy Pres Settlement Fund; Deer Creek Foundation; Consumer Federation of America; Electronic Privacy Information Center Trust Fund; Greenville Foundation; California Consumer Protection Foundation; and Utility Consumers' Action Network.

CONCLUSION

Prior to the passage of legislation and the accumulation of records of the uses of new technologies and their effects on privacy, no privacy "experts" had existed: advocates were the lead actors. However, over time, several of these actors became recognized experts on legal issues, implementation strategies, and likely effects of new technologies. A number of academics who wrote about privacy in the 1960s and were instrumental in getting privacy and technology issues on the public agenda have become privacy experts. Most notable in this category are Alan Westin, Arthur Miller, and James Rule. Several lawyers are recognized as privacy experts, especially Ronald Plesser and Robert Belair. A number of computer scientists, namely Willis Ware and Lance Hoffman, are regarded as privacy and security experts. Knowledge of the international privacy scene fell upon David Flaherty and Russell Pipe. Several members of the press have played important roles in facilitating the development of a privacy community and in keeping privacy initiatives on the public agenda. For example, Evan Hendricks and Robert Ellis Smith with their newsletters; David Burnham and John Markoff of the *New York Times*; and Michael Miller of the *Wall Street Journal*.

Several organizations have been in the forefront of privacy issues. The American Civil Liberties Union, Center for Democracy and Technology, Electronic Frontier Foundation, Electronic Privacy Information Clearinghouse, and Privacy Rights Clearinghouse have been instrumental in developing and monitoring the implementation of policies, creating tools to protect our online privacy, defending ordinary citizens from violations in their private lives, and raising public awareness on the topic.

Without the establishment of a group of privacy experts and privacy organizations, stability and continuity of the issue of privacy, as well as a certain amount of legitimacy and credibility to the cause, would not be possible.

NOTES

1. It should be noted that the number of laws does not reflect the enormous policy success by privacy advocates. Above all, the actual number of laws passed is inversely proportionate to the amount of congressional activity devoted to the subject plus the number of laws not passed (e.g., pertaining to medical privacy, personality tests, the sale of personal information, and the use of social security numbers). From 1965 through 1974, nearly 50 congressional hearings and reports investigated a range of privacy issues. From 1965 through 1972, over 260 bills related to privacy were introduced; only the Omnibus Crime Control and Safe Streets Act of 1968 and the Fair Credit Reporting Act of 1970 were passed.

2. Sources for Figure 4.1 are Center for Democracy and Technology, *Chapter Three: Existing Federal Privacy Laws,* 2000b, http://www.cdt.org/privacy /guide/protect/laws.html (17 Aug. 2001); and Priscilla M. Regan, *Legislating Privacy: Technology, Social Values, and Public Policy* (Chapel Hill: University of North Carolina Press, 1995), 6–7.

3. Developed in 1980, the essence of Fair Information Practices is that (1) only the information that is absolutely needed should be collected; (2) where possible, it should be gathered directly from the individual to whom the data pertains (i.e., data subject); (3) the data subject should be informed as to why the data are needed; (4) the information should be used only for the intended purpose; (5) the information should not be used for other (i.e., secondary) purposes without the data subject's consent; and (6) data subjects should be given the opportunity to see their personal information and amend it if needed. FIPs apply to anyone wishing to obtain your personal information (e.g., government agencies, banks, insurance companies, etc.). The code imposes certain responsibilities on data users. In exchange for your information, users must follow a series of rules when using it. For instance, restrictions are placed on how data users are permitted to obtain the information; either they must have the legal authority to do so or they must "need" the information in order to perform their duties.

4. Ann Cavoukian and Don Tapscott, *Who Knows: Safeguarding Your Privacy in a Networked World* (New York: MacGraw-Hill, 1996), 182.

5. TRUSTe, *Building Trust Online: TRUSTe, Privacy and Self Governance,* n. d., http://www.truste.org/about/truste/index/html (19 Aug. 2001).

6. BBBOnline, *How the BBBOnline Privacy Program Works,* 2001, http://www. bbboline.org/privacy/how.asp (19 Aug. 2001).

7. Codeveloped by the American Institute of Certified Public Accountants (AICPA) and the Canadian Institute of Chartered Accountants (CICA), WebTrust is currently offered by specially trained and licensed CPA firms in Argentina, Australia, Canada, Denmark, France, Germany, Hong Kong, Ireland, Italy, the Netherlands, New Zealand, Spain, the United Kingdom, and the United States.

8. WebTrust Program "best practices" include nonrepudiation, confidentiality, availability, business practices and transaction integrity, security, online privacy, and certification authorities.

9. The WebTrust Program consists of six sets of "modules" or "standards" from which websites can choose any combination that best meets the assurance needs of their customers and business partners. These six standards/modules are:

Online Privacy standards assure that the site properly discloses its privacy practices for e-commerce transactions, maintains effective controls to provide reasonable assurance that information is protected, and the private information is restricted to authorized individuals.

Business Practices & Transaction Integrity standards assure that the site can deliver on its sales promises by fulfilling what was ordered at the agreed-upon price in the requested time-frame and as disclosed on the site.

Security standards assure that the site maintains effective controls and practices to address security matters such as encryption of private and confidential customer information; protection of information once it reaches the site; protection against virus transmission; and customer approval before the site stores, alters, or copies information on the customer's computer.

Nonrepudiation standards assure that the site discloses its practices for nonrepudiation, complies with such controls and appropriate records to provide reasonable assurance that the authentication and integrity of transactions and messages received electronically are provable to third parties in conformity with its disclosed nonrepudiation practices.

Confidentiality standards assure that the site discloses its confidentiality practices for e-commerce transactions, complies with such confidential practices, and maintains effective controls to provide reasonable assurances that customer information obtained as a result of e-commerce is protected according to its disclosed confidentiality practices and restricted to authorized individuals.

Availability standards assure that the site discloses its availability practices, complies with such practices, and maintains effective controls to provide reasonable assurance that its e-commerce systems and data are available as disclosed.

10. CPA WebTrust, *About WebTrust*, 2001, http://www.cpawebtrust.org/factsheet.htm (1 Sept. 2001).

11. Sources for Figure 4.2 are Cavoukian and Tapscott, *Who Knows;* Center for Democracy and Technology, *Getting Started: Top Ten Ways to Protect Privacy Online*, 2000e, http://www.cdt.org/privacy/guide/basic/topten/html (17 Aug. 2001); Stanton McCandish, *EFF's Top 12 Ways to Protect Your Online Privacy*, 2001, http://www.eff.org/Privacy/eff_privacy_top_12.html (17 Aug. 2001); and Privacy Rights Clearinghouse, *Privacy in Cyberspace: Rule of the*

Road for the Information Superhighway, 2001, http://privacyrights.org /fs/fs18-cyb.htm (17 Aug. 2001).

12. Sources for Figure 4.3 are Cavoukian and Tapscott, *Who Owns;* Center for Democracy and Technology, *Getting Started;* McCandish, *EFF's Top 12 Ways;* and Privacy Rights Clearinghouse, *Privacy in Cyberspace.*

13. Most of the information in this section comes from the Center for Democracy and Technology, *CDT.org Resource Library: Privacy Tools: Categories,* 2001, http://www.cdt.org/resourcelibrary/Privacy/Tools (17 Aug. 2001).

14. Most of the information in this section comes from Regan, *Legislating Privacy,* 191–202.

15. American Civil Liberties Union, *The American Civil Liberties Union: Freedom is Why We're Here* (New York: American Civil Liberties Union, 1999).

16. More than 60 ACLU staff attorneys on the national and affiliate levels collaborate with at least 2,000 volunteer attorneys in handling close to 6,000 cases per year. The ACLU appears before the U.S. Supreme Court more than any other organization besides the U.S. Department of Justice (American Civil Liberties Union, *Freedom is Why We're Here*).

17. Center for Democracy and Technology, *CDT Principles,* 2000a, http://www.cdt. org/mission/principles.shtml (24 Jan. 2000).

18. See the CDT's annual reports for further information.

19. For example, working through the Global Internet Liberty Campaign, CDT cosponsored a conference on human rights organizations in Budapest, Hungary, and produced the report *Regardless of Frontiers: Protecting Human Rights to Freedom of Expression on the Global Internet* (http://www.cdt.org /gilc/report/html).

20. For the names of CDT funders, see "Population Studied" in appendix A.

21. Center for Democracy and Technology, *Supporting CDT,* 2000g, http://www.cdt.org/mission/supporters.shtml (24 Jan. 2000).

22. Electronic Frontier Foundation, *About the Electronic Frontier Foundation,* 1996, http://www.eff.org/pub/Misc/EFF/about.eff (21 Sept. 2000).

23. Electronic Privacy Information Center, *About EPIC,* n. d., http://www. epic.org (15 Aug. 2001).

24. Privacy Rights Clearinghouse, *More About the Privacy Rights Clearinghouse,* n. d., http://www.privacyrights.org/about_us.htm (15 Aug. 2001).

5

Major Results of the Center for Democracy and Technology

This chapter details the major results of the Center for Democracy and Technology (CDT) in terms of its work on Internet privacy. The first section contains a brief background on the Electronic Frontier Foundation (EFF) which is the organization from which the CDT developed. In the prologue, the events leading up to the creation of the CDT will be reviewed, followed by an examination of the Center's role in the implementation of the Communications Assistance for Law Enforcement Act (CALEA). Next will be a narrative on the organization's work toward the defeat of the Communications Decency Act (CDA). Even though the CDA is considered primarily a freedom of speech and expression issue, it is included here as it also relates to privacy, albeit to a lesser extent. A history of the CDT's involvement with Doubleclick and Intel's Pentium III chips will conclude the chapter.

BACKGROUND ON THE ELECTRONIC
FRONTIER FOUNDATION

In 1990, the Federal Bureau of Investigation (FBI) was in pursuit of the NuPrometheus League whose crime was stealing and distributing source code used in Macintosh ROMs. Two of the people to whom the agency paid a visit were Mitch Kapor, the founder of Lotus Corporation, and John Perry Barlow, a Wyoming rancher and lyricist for the Grateful Dead. Both men were alarmed by the Feds' lack of knowledge about emerging information technology, and as anti-establishmentarians, they were greatly disturbed by the Secret Service sorties against young hackers and questionable searches and seizures at computer bulletin board services (BBS's).[1] Convinced defensive action was urgently needed, Kapor and Barlow created the Electronic Frontier Foundation in 1990. The EFF is a nonprofit, nonpartisan, public interest group whose purpose is to "civilize cyberspace" (i.e., to protect civil rights in cyberspace, to educate the public and policymakers in the opportunities and challenges posed by computer technology and telecommunications, and to encourage the spread of new information and communications technology to everyone, not just the information rich).[2]

Within a year of the EFF's debut in Cambridge, MA, the Internet boomed. The National Science Foundation (NSF) lifted its ban on commercial use of the Internet backbone and Tim Berners-Lee posted his code for the web, thus paving the way for mass exodus to the online world. Also, the incoming Clinton Administration was highly interested in the potential of the Internet which made the time seem ripe for the EFF to promote its policy views.[3] Thus, in 1992, the organization opened an office in the capital with Jerry Berman, formerly of the American Civil Liberties Union (ACLU), as its director.[4] The following year, the EFF moved all of its operations from Cambridge to Washington, and appointed Berman as the organization's first executive director. The reasons for relocating were that maintaining an office in two cities had been "expensive, logistically difficult, and politically painful. Many functions were duplicated. The two offices began to diverge philosophically and culturally." The EFF "had more good ideas than efficient means for carrying them out."[5]

In 1995, the EFF moved to San Francisco. According to *The Industry Standard*, the organization portrayed the relocation as forward momentum: with other cyber-libertarian organizations in place to watch over the Beltway, the EFF would influence the development of technology in Silicon Valley, and mine the region's wealth for much needed funding.[6] Perhaps a more accurate reason for the move was that the group had reached a low point in its existence. As Lori Fena, Berman's successor at the EFF, said, "I spent some time looking at where things were at and it was pretty bleak. The organization had gone through quite a bit of strife. Board members had gotten to be fairly contentious. The organization was seriously in debt, and it had such a big agenda."[7] Also, the Washington experience had left the group burned out and disillusioned. As Kapor explained, "I went to Washington not a government-hating libertarian but a kind of genetic liberal. But after that experience, I'd rather deal with the worst of the business world. I think I was—and the organization was—naive about the whole process of influencing public policy. It was very educational, but that was not the place to have an influence, given the roots of the EFF in taking a strong moral stand about protecting people's rights. I think we thought we could game the system, and we ended up being gamed."[8] With its move to the west coast, the EFF has shifted its focus to advocacy for open architecture to technology companies. The EFF now persuades the technology industry to consider policy implications of new products and engineer them in ways that give individuals maximum freedom to exercise their rights.

PROLOGUE: THE DIGITAL TELEPHONY BILL AND THE BIRTH OF THE CENTER FOR DEMOCRACY AND TECHNOLOGY

As the United States' telephone system gradually changed from analog to digital, the wiretapping capabilities of law enforcement agencies (LEAs) diminished. In the analog age, any agent with a warrant could attach alligator clips to a copper wire to eavesdrop on a drug deal, an assassination plot, or a bookmaker's bets. In the digital age, it became more difficult to make sense of interceptions because voice and data transmissions on fiber-optic networks are broken into electronic bits that travel at warp speeds, on various routings, and are reassembled immediately before they reach their destination. On such networks, conventional wiretaps would produce only cacophony.

Ever since the Bush Sr. Administration, law enforcement has been in search of a solution to this problem. As far as the FBI is concerned, telecommunications carriers should be mandated to somehow adapt their new equipment so that LEAs could continue wiretapping as in the analog days. Several influential politicians supported this view, most notably Joseph Biden (D-DE) who chaired the Senate Judiciary Committee during the Bush Sr. era. In 1991, Biden introduced Senate resolution S. 266 that proposed to rectify the FBI's problem.[9] However, the measure never proceeded to a vote. Nonetheless, the issue was now on the political table. Consequently, the emboldened FBI drafted a full-fledged wiretap bill, but it lacked support on Capitol Hill, in part due to opposition from civil liberties groups such as the EFF.

The situation changed in 1992 when Bill Clinton came into office. The new administration recognized the wiretap problem and framed the debate under the rubric of technology rather than privacy. Not surprisingly, the president's view was shared by the director of the FBI, Louis Freeh, a Clinton appointee. Freeh was a tireless pro-wiretapping lobbyist whose prophecies about the adverse effects of no wiretapping became more and more ominous over time. In 1994, he cautioned the American Law Institute to "just wait and see what happens if the FBI one day soon is no longer able to conduct court-approved electronic surveillance."[10] In March of the following year, he told the House of Representatives that wiretaps were "crucial to the fight against drugs, terrorism, kidnapping, and sophisticated white-collar crime." Losing the ability to tap people's telephone lines would result in an "effect so profound that law enforcement will be unable to recover."[11]

The legislation Freeh proposed during the Bush Administration was originally called the "Digital Telephony Bill," or "DigiTel," which was later renamed the "Communications Assistance for Law Enforcement Act" (CALEA), but is more commonly known as the "wiretap bill." Senator Biden attempted to introduce such legislation in early 1994. This time, with a sympathetic administration and director at the FBI, various policymakers paid heed. As pro-surveillance sentiments were gaining ground on Capitol Hill, the EFF-initiated umbrella organization, the Digital Privacy Working Group (DPWG), contacted Senator Patrick Leahy (D-VT) and Representative Don Edwards (D-CA), both highly regarded by privacy proponents.[12] At the group's behest, Leahy and Edwards asked Biden to delay introducing his bill so that the group could have time to rewrite some of the more ominous passages in the bill. Biden consented, but on the condition that a version of the bill would be on the table soon.

The resulting draft was partly based on recommendations made by Jerry Berman, then executive director of the EFF.[13] According to Stanton McCandish, EFF's online services manager, the final version of the Leahy-Edwards draft erased "as much FBI language from the bill as possible" and inserted "as much pro-privacy legislation as possible."[14,15] Berman told the EFF board that an updated wiretap law seemed inevitable. Therefore, the options were either to work within the system to defend and salvage privacy principles or to avoid any involvement with the bill.[16] After much contemplation, the EFF chose the former for the following four reasons:[17]

1. Louis Freeh was gradually convincing lawmakers that he needed updated wiretapping authorities. In view of the recent World Trade Center bombing and Congress's overall toughness on crime, it was obvious to the EFF that a new wiretap bill was imminent.
2. The EFF was worried that the FBI had already abused its powers without due regulation or oversight. The EFF believed that a new wiretap law with some compromises would terminate such practice.
3. Representative Edwards, the EFF's chief ally in the House, was about to retire.
4. Since the 1994 elections, the political climate had become increasingly conservative. If the 103rd Congress did not deal with the wiretap issue, and the 104th Congress turned out to have a Republican majority in the House and the Senate (which it did), law enforcement interests would likely supercede privacy concerns. Therefore, it was imperative to bring the wiretap bill to the floor before the Republicans took over.

The final legislation, and its smooth passage in October 1994, caused a fracas amongst the cyber-cognoscenti.[18] Many of the EFF's grassroots supporters were appalled by what they considered to have been spineless pandering, a missed opportunity to oppose, and, perhaps, to prevent a law that was unconstitutional. According to them, the EFF had lost its credibility in the eyes of the online community, and this incident confirmed their worst fears about Washington's corrupting influence.[19,20] As far as they were concerned, the deterioration began with the EFF's move from Cambridge, MA, to the capital in 1992. It was taken as a sign that the foundation had chosen to abandon the quasi-bohemian counterculture of Harvard Square for the power-obsessed and insincere atmosphere of Capitol Hill.[21] The EFF's involvement in a new law that ran counter to the group's principles was the final straw. However, John Perry Barlow defended the organization's actions:

> Politics is simply the art of the possible. If you're a purist, you go down to defeat almost every time, and the things you care about ultimately suffer. Maybe your honor and dignity will remain intact, but the environment or civil liberties or whatever your cause is won't. Sometimes you have to do a bit of nasty dealing. We got right down to the floor of the sausage factory, getting ourselves smeared with blood and pig fat, and it wasn't all that pleasant. But we did what we felt we had to do, and I'm proud of that.[22]

On record, the EFF has not revealed what had occurred during the July 1994 board meeting when the group decided not to oppose the Leahy-Edwards legislation on principle, but to work to improve it. Off record, participants conceded that the gathering was highly charged. *Wired* quoted former board member, Denise Caruso, as describing the meeting as "monumental, dramatic.[23] I was sick in my stomach." She declined to reveal the vote, but confessed that she had abstained.[24] Another anonymous source confirmed to the magazine that Caruso was one of three abstainers; six members of the board voted for collaboration; only one person—John Gilmore—voted against it.[25] Time proved a factor in some members' decisions; they felt they had no choice but to work with the FBI and the policymakers on Capitol Hill. As Caruso explained to Rogier van Bakel, "If we had known two or three months earlier how rapidly the legislation was advancing, we could have done something about it. We could have had a campaign, we could have taken it to the people, and they would have gone batshit."[26]

There was yet another reason why the EFF ultimately did not "take it to the people." David Johnson, a board member, recounted to Bakel a negotiation session inside a hearing room on the Hill.[27] When the talk turned to transactional records (data showing which online areas a computer user frequents, and which telephone numbers he or she calls), the EFF delegation argued that transactional records deserved extra protection from government snoops as they revealed much more about a person's interests, opinions, and affiliations than do lists of phone numbers called by the same individual. Johnson, with the aid of a glass jar filled with sand and a couple of stones, explained that the stones were telephone calls, and the grains of sand were the online transactional records. "[I]f law enforcement can isolate and examine every grain of sand, not just the stones, it's obviously a grave threat to a person's privacy."[28] The analogy seemed to have had an effect on the Congressional aides, for when the EFF team was invited back into the room after the government's "private deliberation," the government offered increased protection for transactional records if the EFF agreed not to further oppose the DigiTel bill. A deal was struck.

With the passage of the wiretap bill, Jerry Berman was accused by some outside the EFF of being the main culprit, both in terms of the EFF's alleged moral corruption and the passage of the bill.[29,30] Officially, Berman's departure was not related to the row over DigiTel.[31,32] Brock Meeks reported in *Wired* that according to several EFF board members who had asked not to be identified, the executive director's limited accounting and administrative experience was the reason the EFF asked him to leave.[33] The organization's newfound mission as a legal and education force, as opposed to a policy group, was another reason.[34] All that happened to have occurred in the aftermath of DigiTel. The split seemed amicable, but one unnamed source close to the process said that Berman "got so wrapped up in the game that he lost sight of the goal. Jerry's a loose cannon: he would go off and say things that he hadn't consensus on. On the other hand, it's really hard to get consensus within the EFF board. Especially with Digital Telephony, there was an incredible amount of soul-searching. It was the most divisive issue the EFF ever confronted."[35] Berman countered that he had never negotiated anything without a solid mandate from his colleagues. "I have all the papers and electronic records to back that up."[36]

Thus, the political process led to a philosophical split within the ranks of the EFF which, in turn, resulted in Berman's new civil liberties group—the Center for Democracy and Technology—an organization that would confront policymakers on their own turf.[37]

COMMUNICATIONS ASSISTANCE FOR LAW
ENFORCEMENT ACT (CALEA)

From the outset, the implementation of CALEA has been mired in controversy.[38] Ever since the law was enacted in 1994, it seems that the FBI has been trying to rewrite the statute in ways that would nullify the balance Congress intended. The agency has sought to use CALEA to require new surveillance features in the nation's telecommunications systems: (1) location tracking capability for all wireless phones to be controlled by the government; (2) carriers using packet switching protocols to provide the government the full content of customer communications when the government is only authorized to intercept the less sensitive addressing data that indicates who is communicating with whom; (3) the ability to continue monitoring parties on a conference call after the subject of the wiretap order has dropped off the call; (4) the collection of more detailed information identifying each party on a call, including those not subject to the investigation; (5) the collection of all numbers dialed by a customer on a touchtone pad after a call is connected, such as credit card and bank account numbers that the government is not authorized to intercept; and (6) instant notification when a customer has a voice mail waiting or makes any changes in service.[39] Such a wish list would, in turn, have driven the initial cost of compliance to somewhere between $3 billion and $5 billion. The FBI had tried to shift the financial burden onto carriers, thereby evading the budgetary constraints that Congress thought would force the FBI to moderate its surveillance demands.[40]

Under the Act, disputes can be taken to the Federal Communications Commission (FCC) whose job is to balance the competing interests of privacy, law enforcement, and industry. Thus, the CDT had been submitting comments to the agency in response to every proposal issued by the FBI.[41] In August 1999, the FCC neglected its duty as the overseer to a fair implementation of CALEA and ruled that wireless companies must provide location information on callers, that companies were allowed to deliver packet communications to the government even though the latter was not authorized to intercept them, and that carriers had to build six additional surveillance capabilities sought by the FBI.[42]

The following month, the telecommunications industry and privacy groups challenged the FCC decision by filing judicial appeals which were later consolidated in the U.S. Court of Appeals in the

District of Columbia. The CDT filed its petition jointly with the Cellular Telecommunications Industry Association (CTIA). Their petition challenged the FCC's requirement that companies locate and track wireless phone users. The two organizations also asked the court to overturn the Commission's ruling that allowed the government to intercept the content of packet communications without a judicial warrant.[43]

A little less than a year later, the Federal Court of Appeals for the District of Columbia rejected the FBI's demands for added surveillance features, but affirmed the FCC's ruling that wireless phones be able to provide general location information about users. In a unanimous opinion, the three-judge panel found that the FCC's decision requiring carriers to build additional surveillance features into their networks was "an entirely unsatisfactory response" to the privacy provisions of CALEA and failed to take into account the financial burden on industry. The Court held that the Commission was correct in requiring carriers to build into their systems a location capability for wireless phones. However, the judges noted that the requirement was limited only to the location of the antenna handling a call. The court also stressed that location information could not be obtained by the government under the weaker pen register standard, even if that legal standard is unclear.[44,45] It is up to Congress to decide what should be the legal standard for government access to cell phone tracking information. In a separate portion of the opinion dealing with newer packet technologies, the court signaled that interception of newer packet technologies must meet the highest legal standards.[46] The court upheld the FCC's interim conclusion that carriers should not be required to separate the addressing information from contents, but it rejected the agency's assumption that the government would be able to intercept both routing information and call content under the less demanding standard of approval required for pen register and trap and trace orders. The court held that the FCC's assumption "was simply mistaken." According to the judges, the government would need to meet the higher standard required for interception of communications content, even if it claimed it was only interested in the addressing information.[47]

As of writing, CALEA issues will return to the FCC on September 20, 2000, when the telephone industry must file a report detailing how it intends to carry out surveillance of packet communications. Thus, the debate on CALEA continues.

COMMUNICATIONS DECENCY ACT (CDA)

When the first automobiles started showing up on the roads, a whole series of incredibly stupid laws were enacted to control them. One law required drivers to exit the car at every intersection, walk to the center of the intersection and make several loud noises before proceeding across. In Pennsylvania, drivers were even asked to fire a rocket into the air every mile and wait 10 minutes for the road to clear. The Communications Decency Act was the modern equivalent of such laws: reactionary legislation for a feared new technology.[48]

On 1 February 1995, Senators James Exon (D-NE) and Slade Gorton (R-WA) introduced the Communications Decency Act (S. 314) in order to expand the FCC regulations on obscene and indecent audiotext to cover all content carried over all forms of electronic communications networks.[49] The bill's purpose was to protect minors from accessing controversial material and material of a sexually inappropriate nature in interactive media including the Internet, commercial online services, and electronic BBSs.[50] The bill, essentially, compelled service providers to choose between severely restricting the activities of the subscribers (i.e., closely monitoring every private communication, electronic mail message, public forum, mailing list, and file archive carried by or available on their network) or completely shutting down their services under the threat of criminal liability.

Nine days after the bill was introduced, the Interactive Working Group (IWG), an ad hoc coalition chaired by the CDT consisting of public interest organizations, members of the computer and communications industry, and associations representing librarians and the press, sent a letter to Senator Larry Pressler (R-SD, Chair of the Senate Commerce Committee), Senator Exon, and other members of the Senate Commerce Committee to express their grave concerns about S. 314 in terms of the First Amendment and the viability of the entire communications industry.[51,52] In view of their apprehensions, the coalition urged Senators Pressler and Exon to not incorporate S. 314 into Senate telecommunications reform legislation which was to be introduced later on in February.

Not only did the CDT chair the IWG, but it also joined forces with other organizations to create "a single Congressional net campaign to stop the Communications Decency Act."[53,54] CDT and colleagues used as a conduit for legislative feedback and activism, the Voters

Telecommunications Watch (VTW), a New York-based Internet civil liberties group that organizes citizens in individual Congressional districts, lobbies on state and Federal legislation, and occasionally raises money for worthy causes.[55] The VTW's posting of 17 March 1995, warned members that sometime during the following week, the CDA bill would be marked up in the Commerce committee. "Win this battle, and we've won the fight for this year and stopped the bill. Lose it and we'll be on the ropes in the Senate for the rest of the session. Only you can make the difference, and it will only take two minutes," read the alert.[56] What the VTW urged was that the public contact Senators Pressler, Exon, and Bob Packwood (R-OR, Chairman of the Communications Subcommittee) by telephone, fax, or e-mail (in that order of preference due to time constraints) and encourage the Senators to prevent S. 314 from being incorporated into telecommunications reform legislation. They should, instead, support Senator Leahy's efforts to explore alternatives to the Exon bill.[57]

On 24 March 1995, as the CDA was reported out of the Senate Commerce Committee, a revision was added to the Senate telecommunications reform legislation. Senator Exon offered an amendment that would make it a felony to send certain kinds of communications over computer networks even though some of these are otherwise constitutionally protected speech under the First Amendment. As Senator Leahy said in his Floor Statement opposing the CDA:

> Under this Exon Amendment, those of us who are users of computer e-mail and other network systems would have to speak as if we were in Sunday School every time we went online. . . . The Exon Amendment makes it a felony punishable by two years imprisonment to send a personal e-mail message to a friend with "obscene, lewd, lascivious, filthy, or indecent" words in it. This penalty adds new meaning to the adage, "Think twice before you speak." All users of Internet and other information services would have to clean up their language when they go online, whether or not they are communicating with children.
>
> Meanwhile, the amendment is crafted to protect the companies who provide us with service. They are given special defenses to avoid criminal liability. Such defenses may unintentionally encourage conduct that is wrong and borders on the illegal.[58,59]
>
> On the other hand, another defense rewards with complete immunity any service provider who goes snooping for smut through private messages. According to the language of the amendment, online providers who take steps "to restrict or prevent the transmission of, or access to" obscene, lewd, filthy, lascivious, or indecent communica-

tions are not only protected from criminal liability, but also from any civil suit for invasion of privacy by a subscriber. We will thereby deputize and immunize others to eavesdrop on private communications. Overzealous service providers, in the guise of the smut police, could censor with impunity private e-mail messages or prevent a user from downloading material deemed "indecent" by the service provider.

The Exon Amendment would totally undermine the legal authority for law enforcement to use court-authorized wiretaps. . . [It] would impose blanket prohibition on wiretapping digital communications. No exceptions allowed. This means that parents of a kidnapping victim could not agree to have the FBI listen in on calls with the kidnapper, if these calls were carried in a digital mode. Or, that the FBI could not get a court order to wiretap the future John Gotti, if his communications were digital.

The CDT, too, proclaimed the amended bill "an unconstitutional intrusion of the free speech and privacy rights of Internet users and all content providers in interactive media."[60,61] The Center, with the help of Senator Leahy and other civil liberties advocates in Congress, vowed to keep the CDA

> from being enacted and continue to search for alternatives to this dangerous legislation. The CDT believes that federal legislation is needed to solidify free speech rights and clarify online service provider liability. Without such legislation, a series of state legislative proposals as bad or worse than the Exon/Gorton bill will proliferate. . . . We will work with concerned legislators and the Interactive Working Group. . . to develop alternatives.[62]

A little more than a week after Senator Leahy condemned the CDA, he introduced the "Child Protection, User Empowerment, and Free Expression in Interactive Media Study Bill" (S. 714) as an alternative to the Exon-Gorton bill.[63] Leahy's bill would have directed the DoJ, in consultation with the Commerce Department, to conduct a study to address technical means for empowering users to control information they receive over interactive communications systems. The agencies would have examined:[64]

- Whether then current laws prohibiting the distribution of obscenity and child pornography by means of computers were sufficient.

- Whether then current law enforcement resources were sufficient to enforce then existing laws.
- The availability of technical means to enable parents and other users to control access to "commercial, noncommercial, violent, sexually explicit, harassing, offensive, or otherwise unwanted" content.
- Recommendations to encourage the development and deployment of such technologies.
- The availability of technical means to promote the free flow of information consistent with Constitutional values.

In an effort to seek a compromise among the disparate critics of the then current language in the CDA, Senator Exon's staff, in consultation with industry, social issues groups, and the DoJ, drafted an alternative legislative proposal on 26 May 1995, in the Senate Telecommunications Reform bill.[65] Based on the CDT's initial analysis of the draft, the Center believed that although it contained several significant improvements over the original language, it still contained unconstitutional prohibitions against First Amendment-protected speech and failed to fully account for the unique characteristics of interactive media.[66] The CDT, in partnership with People for the American Way (PFAW), offered the following commentary on the new language of the draft proposal:[67]

1. Unconstitutional restrictions on indecent speech online: banning the "seven dirty words" on the net

The newly added Section (e) effectively illegalized the use of the "seven dirty words" in Internet public forums. Such items would have included rap music lyrics (both the text and the sound files), *Lady Chatterley's Lover*, public declarations that one is "pissed off" or that someone is a "shit," and Calvin Klein ads with naked models. The constitutional flaw in this section laid in the critical distinction between "obscenity" (i.e., that which is truly hardcore pornography), and "indecency" (sexually explicit material that may be offensive to some or considered by some to be inappropriate for minors, but which is protected by the First Amendment). Under the First Amendment, Congress has broad power to regulate obscenity, but can only regulate indecency under very narrow circumstances (e.g., in broadcast media where there is a captive audience). Even under such circumstances, such regulation must be the "least intrusive means" for accomplishing the government's goal of protecting children. Given the availability of filtering/blocking software, the CDA did not constitute the "least restrictive means" established by the Supreme Court. Moreover, the government may not regulate indecent material in a way that would deny adults access to such material which would be precisely the outcome of this new draft.

2. Unfair treatment of individual users, educational institutions, and other noncommercial services: preemption against restrictive state laws only for commercial services

The new draft proposed to protect commercial service providers from additional censorship by state legislatures, but left all noncommercial users such as libraries, schools, community groups, and individuals to additional regulation and censorship under state law. The CDT and PFAW found no valid public policy argument to support greater protection to commercial speech than to noncommercial users of the Net.

3. Failure to take full advantage of user and parental control features inherent in interactive media

As drafted, the proposal suggested possible FCC rule making on the issue of determining what is and is not indecent, but it did not guarantee that the Commission would take this course of action. The authors suggested that Congress identify both legal and voluntary means to encourage the development of increasingly flexible and accessible user control techniques instead of simply transferring this critical question to a regulatory body.

Coming on the heels of his recent attack on "sex and violence" in the entertainment industry, Senator Bob Dole (R-KS) cosponsored a bill with Senator Charles Grassley (R-IA) on 7 June 1995 that would have been more sweeping than the CDA.[68] "The Protection of Children from Computer Pornography Act" was offered as a freestanding bill and not as an amendment to the pending Senate Telecommunications Reform bill (S. 652) of which the CDA is part. The Dole/Grassley bill would have created new penalties in Title 18 for all operators of electronic communications services who knowingly transmit indecent material to anyone under 18 years of age. It would also have created criminal liability for system operators who willfully permit minors to use an electronic communications service to obtain indecent material from another service. Criminal liability would have been applied to online service providers, Electronic Bulletin Board (EBB) operators, as well as any other entity that used computer storage to deliver information to users such as video dial tone services, cable television video on demand services, etc. The degree of knowledge required to impose liability was unclear, but an entity could be said to have had the requisite knowledge if it was merely informed by a third party that some material on its system are indecent.[69] According to opponents of the CDA, the introduction of the Dole/Grassley bill meant an even greater need for support of Senator Leahy's alternative (S. 714): if the Senate rejected the Leahy bill, it would pass either the Exon bill or the even more draconian Dole/Grassley S. 892.[70]

On 14 June 1995, the Senate passed the CDA by a vote of 84 to 16.[71] Senator Leahy, in an effort to defeat the Exon Amendment, cited the 35,000-plus signatures on the Internet petition, as well as the serious First Amendment and privacy concerns raised by the Exon proposal.[72,73] The CDT stated in its policy post of the same day that it "remains adamantly opposed to this legislation," and that they "will continue to fight it as the bill moves to the House of Representatives."[74] The Center's main objections to the Senate-passed version were that (1) it was an unconstitutional ban on "indecent" material in most parts of the Internet; (2) it offered second-class free speech rights for all interactive media; (3) it criminalized "annoying" messages; (4) it bestowed the FCC jurisdiction over content and technical standards on the Internet; (5) its provisions were ineffective in that they were designed to protect online service providers from liability; (6) "good faith defense" for service providers may encourage violations of user privacy; and (7) it placed undue burden on individual users, content providers, and small system operators.[75]

On 21 June 1995, Representatives Chris Cox (R-CA) and Ron Wyden (D-OR) announced that they were developing a different approach to the problem of children's access to controversial material on the Internet (H. R. 1978). They declared that they would seek to encourage the development of blocking and filtering technologies that empower parents to screen the material to which their children have access. Simultaneously, they hoped to keep the growing Internet free from intrusive and ineffective regulation by the FCC.[76] Daniel Weitzner, then CDT Deputy Director, praised Representatives Cox and Wyden for knowing that "federal content censorship such as has existed in radio and television mass media will not be effective in protecting children."[77] Jerry Berman lauded Newt Gingrich for also condemning the Exon/Coats Act the previous evening as a "clear violation of free speech and . . . a violation of the right of adults to communicate with each other."[78] The Speaker of the House made his comments on the program "Progress Report" on National Empowerment Television as part of a discussion with Representative Bob Walker (R-PA) and Jay Keyworth, Chairman of the Progress and Freedom Foundation. Gingrich remarked:

> I think that the Amendment you referred to by Senator Exon in the Senate will have no real meaning and have no real impact and in fact I don't think will survive. . . . I don't agree with it and I don't think it is a serious way to discuss a serious issue, which is, how do you maintain the right of free speech for adults while also protecting children in a medium which is available to both? That's also frankly a problem with television and radio, and it's something we have to wrestle with in a calm and mature way as a society. I think by offering a very badly thought out and not very productive amendment, if anything, that put the debate back a step.[79,80]

In August 1995, the House passed the Cox/Wyden/White "Internet Freedom and Family Empowerment Act" (H. R. 1978) which would have prohibited the FCC from imposing content or other regulations on all interactive media, removed disincentives which prohibit online service providers from deploying blocking and filtering applications, and created a uniform national policy of user control, rather than government censorship, for addressing objectionable material online.[81] However, the House also passed the so-called "Managers Amendment" at the same meeting which would have criminalized the transmission of indecent material to minors.[82]

In November 1995, as the telecommunications conferees were reconciling the various versions of the CDA passed by the Senate and the House, the IWG sent a letter to Senator Pressler (Chairman, Senate Commerce Committee), Senator Ernest Hollings (D-SC, Ranking Democrat, Senate Commerce Committee), Representative Thomas Bliley (R-VA, Chairman, House Commerce Committee), Representative John Dingell (D-MI, Ranking Democrat, House Commerce Committee), Representative Henry Hyde (R-IL, Chairman, House Judiciary Committee), and members of the Conference Committee on telecommunications reform legislation urging "a consensus policy that empowers families, places liability on creators of illegal content instead of passive service providers, and avoids constitutionally suspect new laws that will only delay enforcement."[83,84] According to the coalition, a comprehensive and effective policy approach to this issue should be based on the following principles:[85]

- *Parental empowerment:* Maximum reliance on, and encouragement of, private sector innovation to produce technologies that enable parents, not government regulators, to choose what is best for their own children.
- *No vicarious liability:* Because of the tremendous flow of information through public as well as private networks, holding service providers, systems, access software providers, or any other third parties liable for the content of illegal messages created by persons not under their authority or control would be ineffective at protecting children as well as a threat to the privacy of users.
- *Enforceable, narrowly tailored, and constitutionally sound criminal laws:* Any new criminal laws should focus on bad actors and based on constitutionally sound standards. Existing proposals, which rely on the vague and untested indecency standard, do not fall into such a category.
- *Uniform national policy:* Given the national, and even global, nature of online services, uniform national rules governing liability are essential. Allowing state regulation of content in interactive media would force service providers and systems to conform to inconsistent and contradictory regulations and undermine the national interest.

The coalition also expressed that it would welcome the opportunity to demonstrate interactive technologies for protecting children and to brief the conferees on additional cooperative efforts currently underway in the private sector. In addition, the IWG would be pleased to brief the conferees on ongoing efforts to assist law enforcement in cases where criminal activity has occurred.[86]

In the run-up to the House conference committee vote on which of the two proposals to pass (i.e., the Hyde/Christian Coalition bill or the Cox/Wyden/White bill), Representative Rick White (R-WA) sent an open letter to the Internet community outlining his proposal on the controversial "cyberporn" issue as a last-minute pitch.[87] To the best of the CDT's knowledge, that was the first time a member of Congress had posted a public message to a usenet group.[88] In it, the Congressman explained the highlights of his proposal:

- Substitutes the narrow, "harmful to minors" standard instead of the broad, vague, and constitutionally suspect "indecency" standard. The "harmful to minors" standard refers to material that is sexually explicit and, taken as a whole, lacks serious literary, artistic, political or scientific value for minors.
- Prohibits the Federal government from regulating online content or from having oversight over the underlying technologies of the Net.
- Would prohibit displaying material that is "harmful to minors," but create immunity for those who make good faith and reasonable efforts to implement parental empowerment technologies that enable screening of unwanted content.
- Would impose liability on online service providers merely for transmitting the messages of their users.

Representative White's lobbying efforts seemed successful, for the House conferees voted 20–13 to accept his proposal on 6 December 1995.[89] However, it also approved by a vote of 17–16 Representative Bob Goodlatte's (R-VA) amendment to substitute "indecency" for the "harmful to minors" standard in White's proposal.[90] Thus, the approved provision mirrored the Exon/Coats CDA in that it relied on the "indecency" standard and contained defenses for online service providers.

12 December 1995 was designated as the Internet's Day of Protest. A variety of Net-activists and telecommunications-related services exhorted the online community to call a selected group of Senators and Representatives to protest against the CDA. As the Senate members of the Telecommunications Reform conference committee contemplated portions of legislation concerning "indecent" material online, their staffers were being overwhelmed by telephone calls.

Senator Daniel Inouye's (D-HI) office reported that they were "getting lots and lots of calls and faxes."[91] Senator Trent Lott's (R-MS) office also reported that they were being "flooded with calls."[92] Senator Ted Stevens' (R-AK) office received so many calls that they could not keep a complete tally.[93] The fax machine was "backed up" at Senator Exon's office, and at one point, activists could not get through to Senator Gorton. The VTW estimated that "there were well over 50,000 phone calls and faxes made on the one day."[94] Steven Cherry of the VTW arrived at this rough figure from the VTW's Alerts which asked people to send them an e-mail after they had called Congress. The message count peaked in the late afternoon at over 70 per minute. By 7:30 P.M. (EST), the organization had received 14,000 messages. By Wednesday morning, the count was well above 18,000. Of course, an approximate figure was also factored in for those who had called, but never sent the VTW an e-mail.[95] In addition to the Day of Protest, a protest was held the same day at the Cybercafé at 273A Lafayette Street in New York City at 2 P.M. Rallies were previously held on 4 December 1995 in San Francisco and Seattle.

Despite the fact that the Republican leadership had instructed the conferees to have the final CDA bill ready for the full House and Senate vote during the week of 1 December 1995 Congress broke for the year without voting on the Telecommunications Deregulation bill.[96,97] In a New Year alert, the VTW urged activists to "begin face-to-face meeting with the staff of your local legislator."[98] Concerned citizens should schedule a meeting which, ideally, should include an Internet user, an Internet business person, and a librarian, where one person acts as the emcee. In preparing for the appointment, the VTW advised that citizens become familiar with the CDA FAQ (http://www.vtw.org/pubs/cdafaq) for a sense of the myths they may have to dispel during the meeting. The VTW also recommended that activists review and bring a copy of the organization's Internet Parental Control FAQ (http://www.vtw.org/pubs/ipcfaq) to support claims that there are many such devices available. While at the meeting, activists may need to bring staffers up to date on the Internet, as well as why it needs no new laws. The VTW suggested being polite, dressing appropriately, making sure that everyone has a chance to speak, answer any questions staffers might have, and leaving one's name and telephone number in case staffers have any questions to ask later. After the meeting, cyber-activists should send a thank you letter to the local legislator, and let the VTW know via e-mail that they had had the meeting.[99]

On 4 January 1996, the House/Senate Telecommunications conferees released a preliminary draft of the final Telecommunications Deregulation bill. According to the CDT, although the conferees had made several important changes to the legislation, none of them were particularly favorable to cyberspace-rights advocates. Among other things, the preliminary draft:[100]

- Relied on the vague and blatantly unconstitutional "indecency" standard.
- Prohibited transmission of "indecent" material directly to a minor or making indecent material available for display in a manner available to a minor (including WWW pages, ftp sites, or usenet groups).
- No longer contained the provision of Cox/Wyden/White bill prohibiting the FCC from imposing content or other regulations on interactive media.
- Contained weaker protections for content providers who label content and enable others to block it.
- Allowed states to impose additional restrictions on noncommercial activities such as free-nets, BBS's, and nonprofit content providers.
- Created a new crime for the solicitation of minors using a computer, the US mail, or any other means of interstate or foreign commerce.

On 31 January 1996, the VTW sent out a somewhat despondent bulletin alerting that Congress was poised to vote on the Telecommunications Deregulation bill on 1 February, and that even a massive public outcry would not be enough to defeat the bill.[101] However, the VTW still felt that activists should continue to be vocal, and remind Congress that they are concerned about the callousness with which they treated the First Amendment in a medium in which they often have little experience. The VTW pointed out that no matter how bad it got that year, someone would probably introduce a similar bill the following year, and they would need to continue to educate these people all over again.[102]

As the VTW predicted, Congress approved the Telecommunications Deregulation bill on 1 February 1996. The House passed the measure on a vote of 414 to 16, while the Senate concurred a few hours later on a vote of 91 to 5. Coincidentally, the vote occurred exactly one year to the day after Senator Exon originally introduced the proposal.[103] The CDT in its *Policy Post* of the same date announced:

> Although we did not accomplish all our most important objectives, we have become a powerful force. This is not the last time Congress will consider issues vital to the interests of Internet users across the United States. We must never lose sight of the fact that, despite the apparent defeat today, there is still a tremendous amount of work to be done.[104]

A week later, President Clinton signed the bill into law, as expected.[105] In response, people all over the world made their web pages blank (with white text) for 48 hours to illustrate the far-reaching effect of the CDA.[106] Over 1,500 sites participated including Senator Leahy, Representative Jerrold Nadler (D-NY), Yahoo!, Soft-Watch Software, and Netcom.[107]

On 26 February 1996, the Citizens Internet Empowerment Coalition (CIEC), a group coordinated by the CDT, America Online, American Library Association and colleagues filed a lawsuit in a Federal Court in Philadelphia, PA, seeking to overturn the recently enacted CDA.[108] In a 55-page complaint, the CIEC aimed to educate the court on how the Internet functions and why the broad content regulations imposed by the CDA threatened the very existence of the Internet as a viable medium for free expression, education, and commerce.[109] Among other things, the CIEC challenge argued that:

- The Internet is a unique communications medium which deserves First Amendment protections at least as broad as those afforded to print media.
- Individual users and parents, not the Federal Government, should determine for themselves and their children what material enters their homes based on their own tastes and values.
- The CDA will be ineffective at protecting children from "indecent" or "patently" offensive material online.

On 1 March 1996, the CIEC filed a motion for preliminary injunction of the CDA. In the motion, the coalition argued that:

In sum, this Court should accord to the interactive computer medium the most vigilant protection from government censorship and over-reaching. The unparalleled potential of cyberspace to effectuate the core policies of the First Amendment calls for a reaffirmance of our "profound national commitment" to public discourse that is "uninhibited, robust, and wide-open."

The challenged provisions of the Act, however, represent an indiscriminate and damaging retreat from that commitment, one that reflects an as yet poor legislative understanding even of the basic operating methods of cyberspace. Those provisions are facially invalid because they abridge far too much protected speech while affording little incremental protection for minors, and threaten to disrupt the rapidly unfolding development of a salutary communications revolution that, until now, has flourished with a minimum of governmental interference.[110]

Included in the CIEC filing were declarations from individuals, libraries, online service providers, content providers, publishers, nonprofit groups, civil liberties advocates, and even a U.S. Senator.[111] The declarations detailed the potential impact the CDA would have on their rights to free speech on the Internet, and were considered by the court as evidence in the case.[112]

The court began to hear the case on 21 March 1996. The CDT, with cooperation from the DoJ, the clerk of the Philadelphia Federal Court, and Bell Atlantic, wired the courtroom for Internet access. A T1 line and a small Local Area Network (LAN) with at least three computers were installed to enable the court to see the Internet and view demonstrations of parental control technologies. That represented the first time a Federal Court had been wired to the Internet for the purposes of a trial.[113]

At 9 A.M. on 12 June 1996, the panel of three federal judges for the U.S. District Court for the Eastern District of Pennsylvania granted the CIEC request for a preliminary injunction against the CDA. In a unanimous decision, the judges ruled that the CDA would have violated free speech, and therefore, the CDA was unconstitutional. U.S. District Judge Stewart Dazell wrote in his opinion:

If the goal of our First Amendment jurisprudence is the "individual dignity and choice" that arises from "putting the decision as to what views shall be voiced largely into the hands of each of us," then we should be especially vigilant in preventing content-based regulation of a medium that every minute allows individual citizens actually to make those decisions. Any content-based regulation of the Internet, no matter how benign the purpose, would burn the global village to roast the pig.

Our findings of fact—many of them undisputed—express our understanding of the Internet. These findings lead to the conclusion that Congress may not regulate indecency on the Internet at all.

The Judges concluded that the "plaintiffs ha[d] shown irreparable injury, no party ha[d] any interest in the enforcement of an unconstitutional law, and therefore the public interest [would] be served by granting a preliminary injunction."[114]

Having previously announced its plans in a letter to Senator Exon on 26 June 1996, the DoJ formally filed an appeal of the Philadelphia Federal Court ruling on 1 July 1996.[115,116] In an unusual move for an appeal, not only did the DoJ ask the Supreme Court to overturn the Philadelphia decision, but it also requested the Justices to consider new arguments not made during the lower court hearings such as a contention that the CDA should be construed to cover only those who provide so-called "commercial pornography." As the CIEC remarked in its *Trial Bulletin*, "[i]n essence, the government [was] asking the Supreme Court to rewrite the law—something that the Court ha[d] been reluctant to do in previous cases."[117] In turn, the CIEC asked the Court to hear the appeal and to carefully consider the detailed factual record created in the Philadelphia case including:

- The Internet is a unique communications medium which deserves First Amendment protections *at least* as broad as those enjoyed by the print medium.
- When it comes to otherwise constitutionally protected speech, individual users—not the federal government—are the best and most appropriate judges of what material is and is not appropriate for themselves and for their children.
- User control technologies such as SurfWatch, CyberPatrol, and PICS are the only effective and constitutional method of limiting minors access to objectionable material on the Internet.

On 6 December 1996, the Supreme Court agreed to hear the government's appeal of the CDA. The DoJ and a coalition of "pro-family" groups who supported the CDA filed briefs the following month in support of the statute, thus beginning the formal process of Supreme Court review.[118,119]

On 26 June 1997, the Supreme Court ruled unanimously that the CDA violated the First Amendment. Writing for the court, Justice John Paul Stevens stated that

> As a matter of constitutional tradition, in the absence of evidence to the contrary, we presume that governmental regulation of the content of speech is more likely to interfere with the free exchange of ideas than to encourage it. The interest in encouraging freedom of expression in a democratic society outweighs any theoretical, but unproven benefit of censorship.[120]

Thus, the Justices held that "the CDA place[d] an unacceptably heavy burden on protected speech" and found that all provisions of the CDA were unconstitutional as they applied to "indecent" or "patently offensive" speech.[121]

At a news conference held shortly after the ruling, plaintiffs and the attorneys in the case made statements on the outcome of the case.[122] Their sentiments echoed that offered by Jerry Berman:

> By rejecting the CDA, the Supreme Court has guaranteed that the First Amendment and the free flow of ideas will thrive in the Information Age. Today's decision is not only a victory for free speech, but also for the right of users to surf the net in a manner consistent with family and individual values.[123]

Other reactions were offered including those of Congress people who had opposed the CDA. Senator Leahy said that "this ruling comes as a vindication for the 15 Members of the Senate who joined with me to vote against the CDA."[124] Senator Russ Feingold (D-WI) expressed gratitude "that the Supreme Court, and the lower court before it, correctly recognized what I have long contended—that Congress failed in its efforts to protect children on the Internet while simultaneously trampling on the rights of all Americans to free speech."[125] Likewise, Representative Ed Markey (D-MA) was "gratified that the Supreme Court . . . held a lower court's ruling that the CDA was unconstitutional. . . ." Representative White said, "This case will have a lasting impact on how the government treats the Internet."[126,127] Representative Nadler was pleased that "a majority of the Supreme Court has recognized that this law was the cyberspace equivalent of book burning. The Court's decision will ensure that Americans will not have to sacrifice their fundamental rights when they log on to the Internet. . . . I hope that Congress and the President will read the Court's decision and learn from it. . . . I am thankful that the Supreme Court has joined the choir of voices that have declared the bill an indecent assault on American liberty."[128]

COMMUNICATIONS DECENCY ACT: AFTERMATH

In reaction to the landmark Supreme Court ruling on the CDA, Cathy Cleaver, Director of the Family Research Council Legal Policy, said:

> Today's ruling means that pornographers can open their doors to children on the Internet. But pornographers beware: this will not be the last work on protecting children from your corrupting influence. . . . With no legal liability for those who pursue children with graphic images and language on the Internet, we need to act fast and firmly to ensure that our country does not give pornographers special rights.[130]

And "fast and firmly" did Congress act. Congresswoman Zoe Lofgren (D-CA) introduced the "Internet Freedom and Child Protection Act" (H. R. 774) as soon as the CDA was struck down. Lofgren's bill required all Internet providers to offer some version of screening software (e.g., Net Nanny, SurfWatch, or Cybersitter) so that parents could limit access to material they deem inappropriate for their children.[131] Senator Patty Murray (D-WA) in her CDA press release previewed her "Childsafe Internet Act of 1997" which was a seven-point plan to: (1) ensure that every parent with a computer had access to filtering software; (2) create a parental warning alongside copyright protections on each homepage; (3) create incentives for web page creators to rate their own pages for content; (4) make it a criminal offense to misrate websites; (5) make it a criminal offense to steal sites previously rated as childsafe; (6) make it a felony for anyone to solicit childsafe chat rooms; and (7) create a toll-free telephone number to provide concerned parents with a mechanism to report harmful material on the Internet.[132]

However, Congress latched onto none of the proposals above. Instead, they approved, on 21 October 1998, H. R. 3683 "Child Online

Table 5.1 Chronology of the Communications Decency Act (CDA)[129]

2/1/95	S. 314 introduced by Senators James Exon (D-NE) and Slade Gorton (R-WA). S. 314 referred to the Senate Commerce Committee.
2/21/95	H. R. 1004 introduced by Representative Tim Johnson (D-SD). H. R. 1004 referred to the House Commerce and Judiciary Committees.
3/23/95	S. 314 amended and attached to the Telecommunications Reform Bill by Senator Gorton. Language provides some provider protection, but continues to infringe on e-mail privacy and free speech.
4/7/95	Senator Patrick Leahy (D-VT) introduces S. 714, an alternative to the Exon/Gorton bill, which commissions the Department of Justice to study the problem to see if additional legislation (such as the CDA) is necessary.
5/24/95	The House Telecommunications Reform Bill (H. R. 1555) leaves committee in the House with the Leahy alternative attached to it, thanks to Representative Ron Klink (D-PA). The CDA is not attached to it.
6/14/95	The Senate passes the CDA as attached to the Telecommunications Reform Bill (S. 652) by a vote of 84-16. The Leahy bill (S. 714) is not passed.
6/21/95	Several prominent House members publicly denounced the CDA, including Speaker of the House Newt Gingrich (R-GA), Representatives Chris Cox (R-CA) and Ron Wyden (D-OR).
6/30/95	Cox and Wyden introduce the "Internet Freedom and Family Empowerment Act" (H. R. 1978) as an alternative to the CDA.
8/4/95	House votes 421-4 to attach H. R. 1978 to Telecommunications Reform bill (H. R. 1555). House votes to attach Managers Amendment to Telecommunications Reform bill (H. R. 1555). House passes H. R. 1555 which goes into conference with S. 652.
9/26/95	Senator Russ Feingold (D-WI) urges committee members to drop Managers Amendment and the CDA from the Telecommunications Deregulation bill.

(Table 5.1 continued)

12/7/95	The House half of the Telecommunications conference committee votes the "indecency" standard for online speech into the Telecommunications Deregulation bill.
1/4/96	The House/Senate Telecommunications conference committee releases a preliminary draft of the final Telecommunications Reform bill.
1/31/96	The House and Senate prepare to signoff on the conference report for the Telecommunications bill and rush the vote to the floor.
2/1/96	The House and Senate pass the Telecommunications Bill (S. 652/H. R. 1555) 414-16 and 91-5, respectively.
2/8/96	President Bill Clinton signs S. 652/H. R. 1555 into law.
2/26/96	Citizens Internet Empowerment Coalition (CIEC) files suit against CDA in Federal Court.
3/21/96	U.S. District Court for the Eastern District of Pennsylvania begins hearings on the CDA case.
6/12/96	Court grants CIEC request for preliminary injunction against CDA.
7/1/96	Department of Justice (DoJ) files appeal of CDA ruling.
12/6/96	Supreme Court agrees to hear DoJ's appeal.
6/26/97	Supreme Court rules CDA unconstitutional.

Protection Act" (COPA), the more narrowly crafted "Son of CDA" or "CDA II" bill sponsored by Representative Michael Oxley (R-OH), which was attached to an omnibus appropriations bill.[133] COPA would have required entities that knowingly make, for commercial purposes over the World Wide Web, communications that are "harmful to minors" to place such information behind an age-verification barrier intended to exclude children age 17 and under. Unlike the CDA which sought to regulate "indecency," COPA applied to a legally recognized category of speech, that which is "harmful to minors." But like its predecessor, COPA federalized enforcement of what had previously been left to the states.[134]

The bill provided for criminal and civil fines. Site operators could face up to $100,000 in fines and six months imprisonment for violation.[135] Like the CDA, the bill offered an affirmative defense against conviction to those who use a credit card or adult verification system to limit access to the site. Also, those who transmit content created by others are exempted. It also limited the use and disclosure of personal information collected by those who provide credit card or adult verification systems. The one provision that seemed more encouraging than in the CDA was that a commission be established for the study of methods for protecting children from harmful content.[136,137]

COPA was immediately challenged by the ACLU and others. This time, the CDT was not one of the plaintiffs. Instead, it formed part of a coalition of 17 public interest groups and hi-tech trade associations who filed an amicus brief on behalf of the ACLU.[138,139,140] In its brief, the coalition argued that COPA was too broad and stifled adult speech by potentially cutting off access to an array of content:

> The effect of the Act, like the Communications Decency Act, is to restrict adults from communicating and receiving expression that is clearly protected by the Constitution.[141]

Filtering technologies are more effective than laws when it comes to protecting children on the Internet, according to the coalition.

On 3 February 1999, Federal Judge Lowell Reed granted a preliminary injunction prohibiting the enforcement of COPA. Judge Reed concluded that the law was likely unconstitutional and that enforcement, unless blocked, would cause irreparable harm to website users. He also found that the law's provision requiring websites with harmful materials to minors to place adult verification in front of that material was an undue burden on speech.[142]

Following Judge Reed's injunction, the DoJ filed an appeal in the U.S. Court of Appeals for the Third Circuit.[143] At the time of writing, the Court of Appeals found that "the proof of age requirement places an undue economic burden on publishers, who would have to pay for a screening system and could lose users who did not want to register." It also said that the act's definition of harmful material as that which offends "contemporary community standards" is impossible to enforce because community standards vary, and Internet publishers do not know where their users live. Moreover, the law is not the least restrictive way to protect children from harmful material, noting that parents can install blocking software on their own computers.[144] Therefore, the court would most likely uphold Judge Reed's injunction against the measure. A DoJ spokeswoman said it was too early to say whether they would be appealing the decision.[145]

DOUBLECLICK

The profiling activities of advertisement networks, such as Doubleclick, which currently commands approximately 60 percent of the market share, are the leading edge of a growing industry built upon the widespread tracking and monitoring of an individual's online behavior. . . . The increasingly pervasive use of surreptitious monitoring systems breed consumer distrust and undermines consumers' efforts to protect their privacy by depriving them of control over their personal information.—Deirdre Mulligan, Staff Counsel, CDT[146]

"Doubleclick is the industry leader at leveraging technology and media expertise to create solutions that help advertisers and publishers unleash the power of the web for branding, selling products, and building relationships with customers."[147] The company came into prominence using two business strategies.[148] First, it licenses to 11,000 clients software that places advertisements on web pages.[149] Second, and far more controversial, is a service it provides to its advertising network of 1,500 companies that receive their advertisements direct from Doubleclick: the monitoring of individual consumers as they move around Internet sites which are affiliated with Doubleclick.[150,151] When Doubleclick first serves the visitor an advertisement, "the company assigns you a unique number and records that number in a cookie file of your computer. Then, when you visit a website on which Doubleclick serves ads, Doubleclick reads this number to help target ads to you." If you refuse cookies in your web browser's preferences, the company claims that you can get a "blank" or "opt out" cookie that prevents data from being associated with your browser.[152]

Even though Doubleclick's privacy statement reports that the company does not link its profiles with personal identification such

Table 5.2 Timeline of the Center for Democracy and Technology

12/94	CDT founded.
2/1/95	Communications Decency Act (S. 652) introduced in Senate.
6/14/95	S. 652 passed in Senate.
6/30/95	Internet Freedom and Family Empowerment Act (H. R. 1555) introduced in House.
2/1/96	House and Senate pass S. 652 and H. R. 1555.
2/8/96	President Clinton signs S. 652/H. R. 1555 into law.
2/26/96	CDT and colleagues file suit against CDA in Federal Court.
6/12/96	U.S. District Court grants CDT and colleaues request for preliminary injunction against CDA.
7/1/96	Department of Justice appeals CDA ruling.
6/26/97	U.S. Supreme Court rules CDA unconstitutional.
1/20/99	Intel announces Pentium III (P3) processors will include Processor Serial Numbers.
2/26/99	Intel releases P3 on the market. CDT and colleagues file complaint against Intel to Federal Trade Commission (FTC).
4/8/99	CDT and colleagues file supplemental complaint against Intel with FTC.
2/3/00	CDT launches website to expose Doubleclick and enable Internet users to "opt out."
2/29/00	CDT files report to FTC alleging Doubleclick's invasion of privacy.
3/2/00	Doubleclick announces delay in plans to combine online and offline consumer data.
4/27/00	Intel announces PSNs will no longer be a feature in new chips.

as a visitor's name, e-mail address, home address, telephone number, and so forth, concerns over privacy arose in 1999 because the company's Abacus Alliance service (created after Doubleclick bought the database company, Abacus Direct, in 1991) began combining its online data with information gleaned from consumer's offline purchases from major retailers, catalog companies, and publishers.[153] Thus, an alliance member who sells printer toners could receive a list of 1,000 people who have bought computer printers from retail stores in the last six months. When these same people are surfing other alliance sites for information on replacement toners, Doubleclick could show them an ad for one that matches their printer.[154]

In self-defense, Doubleclick stressed that only members of the Abacus alliance received the extra data. The company assured that Internet users would be notified of the tracking and afforded the opportunity to opt out of the program. Moreover, it pledged that the alliance would not gather data on medical, financial, or sexual behavior of adults, or on children's surfing habits.[155] Even though such behavioral monitoring is beneficial to both consumers as well as businesses, Doubleclick, in actual fact, considers the company was playing fair. As Kevin Ryan, President of Doubleclick, pointed out, "Catalog and retail data have been combined for years. Right now online and offline seem very different, but look at a bookstore, which can have a site, a store, and a catalog. Our clients won't be thinking of people as online or offline pretty soon." This privacy scare is like the "overblown fear over credit card fraud, which set back e-commerce two years."[156]

Still, such declarations did little to mollify privacy groups because, to begin with, the company is under no legal obligation to live by those restrictions and it is free to change its policy unilaterally. Thus, on 29 February 2000, the CDT filed a report to the FTC alleging that Doubleclick may be collecting sensitive information about user purchases, including video titles, salaries, and search terms, through its ad-serving technology.[157] The filing also asserted that Doubleclick may be linking information collected about user surfing habits to individual identities in its Abacus Online database.[158] As Ari Schwartz, a policy analyst at the CDT, said, "Companies could be transporting information that could be possibly used by Doubleclick in a personally identifiable way without the company's knowledge. . . . [Companies] could be violating their own privacy policy without knowing it."[159]

As a result of the CDT's filing, several companies have reexamined their relationship with Doubleclick. For example, home-delivery service Kozmo.com has distanced itself from the advertising powerhouse due to these potential lapses.[160] AltaVista, an Internet search service, has limited the amount of user information it makes available to Doubleclick.[161]

Not only did the CDT battle Doubleclick through the federal government, but they also fought the company using grassroots efforts. The Center created the "Operation Opt-Out" website (http://opt-out.cdt.org) to help consumers protect their privacy from "online profiling" and limit the sale of their personal information. As Oldenburg wrote, the "Opt-Out Program" is a "must-do for any consumer troubled by increasingly invasive telemarketers and direct mailers."[162] The website provides links to major companies that allow "opting-out" online; for other companies that do not have such service, the CDT also provides a section that generates ready-to-mail opt-out forms complete with addresses to the ten largest national banks, credit card solicitors, the Direct Marketing Association's mail preference and telephone preference lists, state vehicle registration and driver's license lists, etc.[163,164]

Bowing to pressure from hundreds of consumers who had objected to Doubleclick's plans via the CDT's website, Doubleclick announced on 2 March 2000, that it would delay plans to combine online and offline data that it collects on consumers. "It is clear . . . I made a mistake by planning to merge names with anonymous user activity across websites in the absence of government and industry privacy standards," the company's CEO, Kevin O'Connor, admitted in a statement on Doubleclick's website.[165] However, this retraction does not necessarily signify the end of the plan; rather, Doubleclick has pledged only to postpone moving forward until new guidelines on privacy have been negotiated between the government and industry.[166] "The absence of standards has led to confusion and uncertainty. We need clarity to get rid of the uncertainty," said O'Connor.[167]

Another result of pressures from privacy groups and the public is that Doubleclick hired two prominent New York consumer advocates to spearhead its online privacy efforts. Jules Polonetsky, consumer affairs commissioner to Mayor Rudolph Giuliani, was appointed as the company's chief privacy officer. He will work with the company's clients and consumers to publicize and enforce Doubleclick's privacy policies. Bob Abrams, former New York state attorney general, was appointed as chair of the company's Privacy Advisory Board. He will oversee a board comprised of outside privacy and security experts whose function will be to advise Doubleclick in developing and revising its policies.[168] To further combat negative publicity, Doubleclick promised to educate the industry and demonstrate to consumers the benefits of sharing personal information. The company took out full-page ads in several newspapers in February 2000, to announce a privacy-education campaign, and to notify the public that they could opt-out of Doubleclick's monitoring by visiting Privacychoices.org, a site it had developed. Ryan is convinced that, once the company explains what it is doing and how it is doing it, people will feel more comfortable with online monitoring.[169]

PENTIUM III

> The gains that it [Pentium III Processor Serial Number] could give us for the proposed line of security features were not sufficient to overcome the bad rep it would give us.—Unidentified Intel engineer[170]

In January 1999, Intel announced that all new Pentium III (P3) processors would include a unique identifier called the Processor Serial Number (PSN).[171, 172] The PSN was embedded in the microchip during the manufacturing process, and served as an identifier for the processor, and by association, its system.[173] The PSN control utility was a Windows program that enabled or disabled the reading of the P3 PSN by software. This allowed users control of which software programs or websites could have permission to read the PSN. When installed, the utility ran automatically each time the system was booted. An icon was placed in the Windows system tray to give the user a visual indication of the state of the PSN feature, and it could be hidden if the user so wished. The PSN could be disabled any time, but enabling the serial number required the processor to be reset (typically a restart or power off/on button, depending on the computer manufacturer).[174,175] According to the manufacturer, the benefits of such a device were that "corporate I. T. departments [could] use it to track assets and manage systems in a more efficient manner to help reduce total cost ownership. For consumers, the potential of the Internet promises new ways to shop online, manage

Table 5.3 Chronology of Doubleclick

1999	Doubleclick's Abacus Alliance service begins to combine its online data with information gleaned from consumer's offline purchases.
2/3/00	CDT launches website to expose Doubleclick and to enable users to opt-out of personal information collection.
2/29/00	CDT files report to the Federal Trade Commission (FTC) alleging that Doubleclick may be collecting sensitive information about user purchases and that the company may be linking information collected about user surfing habits to individual identities in its Abacus Online database. As a result companies have distanced themselves from Doubleclick. CDT launches Operation Opt-Out (http://opt-out.cdt.org).
3/2/00	Doubleclick announces it will delay plans to combine online and offline data it collects on consumers.
3/8/00	Doubleclick announces the hiring of Jules Polonetsky and Bob Abrams to spearhead its online privacy efforts.

their lives, and access and disseminate information. Used in combination with other identifiers such as passwords and user names, the PSN [could] provide added levels of confidence."[176,177] In other words, the PSN would, essentially, eliminate theft on the Internet. For cyber-merchants, having proof-positive of their customers would end consumer fraud and decrease the cost of conducting business with customers they cannot see.[178] Not only would the device benefit consumers, but the manufacturing company as well. The ID scheme would solve the problem of illegal clocking, which is the act of running the processor at higher speeds such as by a hardware hacker. Such a hardware hacker could be an employee of a computer maker that would purchase 300 MHz Celeron processors, overclock them to 400 MHz, and then sell the ware as a 400 MHz processor. Of course, this results in revenue lost as well as liability for Intel, for if the overclocked processor has problems functioning at the higher speed, Intel would be the one to be blamed, not the PC maker. Thus, with the PSN, consumers could conceivably check their processor against Intel's database of products to see at which speed the processor was sold.[179]

Despite the fact that the PSN control utility reportedly could be enabled or disabled by the consumer, it was shown that rogue web-sites and software manufacturers were able to access the PSN even if it were disabled in the first place. For example, Andreas Stiller, the processor expert of *C't magazine,* a German technology publication, announced that he had discovered a theoretical method of retrieving the identification information.[180,181] Mario Contestabile, a programmer at the Montreal-based security firm, Zero-Knowledge, developed an ActiveX application that skirted Intel's PSN Control Utility and placed a cookie file inside the user's system. Once the cookie was in place, the number could be broadcast, even if the user had turned off the PSN.[182,183,184]

On 28 January 1999, the ACLU, CDT, Consumer Action, Private Citizen, and Privacy Rights Clearinghouse sent a letter to Craig R. Barrett, President and CEO of Intel, to express their deep concern about the privacy implications of the PSN in P3s. The advocates believed that

> technical and policy solutions must be developed that provide strong security, offer robust and varied authentication tools to support electronic commerce, and protect individual privacy and anonymity. Based on what we know so far, the Pentium III unique identifier does not meet this standard. In our view, the privacy risks inherent in this unique ID feature outweigh the security it potentially provides.[185,186]

Therefore, the five organizations urged Intel to revise its plan to issue unique IDs and to develop products that support individual privacy as well as commerce.

Hoping to appease the CDT and other privacy groups, Intel announced earlier that week that it had fine-tuned the ID feature in the P3 chip.[187,188,189] The company said it would provide a software patch that will leave the serial number disabled unless the individual user activated it (the original plan was that the PSN would have been automatically enabled each time a computer was booted, and the user would have had to disable it him-/herself). However, there were three snags with the software: first, the patch would not be available until several months after the P3 ships. Second, the user or computer manufacturer would have to install it themselves. Last, it could be tampered with or disabled by hackers or another software program.[190]

About three weeks after urging Intel to reconsider its plans, the CDT sent a questionnaire to nine leading PC manufacturers asking how they planned to implement Pentium III's ID feature.[191] The CDT believed that these computer distributors could assist in limiting the privacy risks P3 chips posed by disabling the PSN in the BIOS of their computers and publicizing whether they are shipping Pentium III products with the ID disabled in the interest of informed consumer choice. CompUSA, Gateway 2000, Packard-Bell/NEC, and Toshiba never replied.[192] The PSN had been disabled in the BIOS for Compaq, Dell, and IBM computers. In addition, Dell users could request the utility to be enabled, and IBM pledged to provide information on its PSN settings via online help and literature shipped with its products.[193,194,195] Sony replied that their PSN default was ON, but consumers may go to Intel's or Sony's website to download software utility to control the PSN setting. Also, each PC box will contain a notice saying that the PSN is on. Eventually, the PSN in all future shipments will be disabled by a preinstalled software utility.[196] As for Hewlett-Packard, it was unclear what its default setting was, but the company said that users would be given a choice on the matter. The company would also make "very clear" whether PSN is enabled or disabled in its products.[197]

On 26 February 1999, the CDT, Privacy Rights Clearinghouse, Consumer Action, and Private Citizen formally asked the FTC to investigate and halt distribution of the P3 as a violation of individual privacy, and therefore, an unfair and deceptive trade practice under Section 5 of the FTC Act.[198,199] The complaint stated that as the largest chip manufacturer in the consumer marketplace, Intel's product design decisions have extensive impact on consumers' online privacy.[200] The combination of the company's dominance, coupled with the lack of accurate information about the privacy implications of the PSN, and the inability of individuals to control the use of the device, placed consumer privacy at risk. Therefore, the coalition asked the FTC to immediately enjoin Intel from shipping Pentium III processors with PSN and to begin an investigation into the privacy issues posed by the technology. In addition, due to the large number of chips already in the hands of computer makers, the FTC was asked to enjoin manufacturers from shipping P3 PSN-equipped computers unless the PSN had been securely switched off.[201,202] On 5

March 1999, the ACLU, Center for Media Education, Consumer Federation of America, National Consumers League, and *Privacy Times* sent a letter to Donald Clark, Secretary of the FTC, in support of the complaint filed by CDT and colleagues.[203] Nevertheless, CDT and colleagues' action did not deter Intel, for the chipmaker introduced P3s with PSN capability a few days after the document was filed. On 8 April 1999, the CDT, Consumer Action, Gay & Lesbian Alliance against Defamation (GLAAD), and Privacy Rights Clearinghouse filed a supplemental complaint against Intel.[204,205] The document detailed the potential harm to consumers—particularly children and teenagers—posed by the PSN. The brief argued that

> The PSN . . . has the potential to transform the World Wide Web from a largely anonymous environment into one where individuals are expected, or even required, to identify themselves in order to participate in online activities, communicate, and make purchases. . . This is a far cry from the world we live in today—either offline or online—and would represent a grave erosion of consumers' online privacy.[206]

The complaint also discussed key differences between PSN and existing identifiers on the Internet such as "cookies."[207]

On 27 April 2000, after feedback from marketing, privacy, and engineering representatives who were opposed to the device, an Intel management committee decided not to include the PSN feature in the "Willamette" chip scheduled for release in Fall 2000.[208,209, 210, 211] According to George Alfs, the company had "made the decision earlier [that] year," and he also cited the rise of digital signature technology as making chip identification obsolete.[212] Thus, he implied that public opinion on the PSN had little influence on Intel's decision to withdraw the PSN since the company had already made the decision before the height of the crisis, and that newer, more sophisticated technology also became a factor in the decision.

CONCLUSION

The Communications Assistance for Law Enforcement Act, the Communications Decency Act, Doubleclick, and Intel Pentium III chips form the answer to Research Question (RQ) 1, "What have been the major results of the Center for Democracy and Technology

Table 5.4 Chronology of Intel Pentium III

1/20/99	Intel announces Pentium III (P3) processors will include Processor Serial Numbers (PSNs).
Week of 1/24/99	Intel announces it has fine-tuned identification feature in P3 chip.
1/28/99	CDT, American Civil Liberties Union (ACLU), Consumer Action, Private Citizen, and Privacy Rights Clearinghouse send letter to Craig R. Barrett, President and CEO of Intel, to express their concern about privacy implications of the PSN.
2/16/99	CDT sends questionnaire to leading PC manufacturers inquiring how they plan to implement P3's identification feature.
2/17/99	Intel previews P3 chip at San Jose Convention Center.
2/26/99	Intel officially releases P3 on the market.
	CDT, Privacy Rights Clearinghouse, Consumer Action, and Private Citizen file a complaint against Intel with the Federal Trade Commission (FTC).
3/5/99	ACLU, Center for Media Education, Consumer Federation of America, National Consumers League, and Privacy Times send letter to Donald Clark, Secretary of the FTC, in support of CDT and colleagues' complaint.
4/8/99	CDT, Consumer Action, Gay and Lesbian Alliance Against Defamation, and Privacy Rights Clearinghouse file supplemental complaint against Intel with the FTC.
4/27/00	Intel announces PSN feature will not be included in the "Willamette" chip scheduled for release in Fall 2000.

in terms of its work on Internet privacy?" These events are considered as major due to (1) the amount of materials that could be found pertaining to them; (2) the leading role the CDT took in these events; (3) the victories the CDT gained at the outcome of these episodes; and (4) the varied means for obtaining these results (e.g., litigation as in the CDA; activism in the form of online petitions, electronic newsletters, online campaigns such as Operation Opt-Out; expressions of CDT's concerns to lawmakers, federal agencies, and the technology industry in the form of letters, reports, policy analyses, and formal complaints; and the formation of coalitions so that in greater number, civil libertarians' may be heard rather than ignored if each were fighting the system on its own).

Having determined what have been the major results of the CDT, the following chapter will deal with RQ 2, "How has the CDT been perceived by the American public as reflected in the mass media?"

NOTES

1. For details, see John Perry Barlow, *A Note; Terribly Brief History of the Electronic Frontier Foundation,* 8 November 1990, http://www.eff.org/pub/Misc /EFF/history.eff (21 Sept. 2000); and David Gans and Ken Goffman, *Mitch Kapor and John Barlow Interview,* 5 August 1990, http://www.eff.org/pub /Misc/Publications/John_Perry.../barlow_and_kapor_in_wired.interview (21 Sept. 2000).

2. Electronic Frontier Foundation, *New Foundation Established to Encourage Computer-Based Communications Policy,* 10 July 1990, http://www.eff.org /pub/EFF/Historical/eff_founded.announce (21 September 2000); Mitchell Kapor and John Perry Barlow, *Across the Electronic Frontier,* 10 July 1990, http://www.eff.org/pub/Misc/EFF/electronic_frontier.eff (20 September 2000); and Sandra Stewart, "Whatever Happened to the EFF?" Industry Standard (20 March 2000): 156–172.

3. Stewart, "Whatever Happened."

4. Electronic Frontier Foundation, *Berman to Head New EFF Washington Office,* 15 January 1992, http://www.eff.org/pub/Misc/EFF/Historical/eff_dc_office.announce (21 Sept. 2000).

5. Mitch Kapor et al., *Major Changes at the Electronic Frontier Foundation,* 13 January 1993, http://www.eff.org/pub/Misc/EFF/Historical/major_changes. announce (21 Sept. 2000).

6. Stewart, "Whatever Happened."

7. Stewart, "Whatever Happened."

8. Stewart, "Whatever Happened."

9. Joseph Biden, *Comprehensive Counter Terrorism Act of 1991,* 24 January 1991, http://thomas.loc.gov/cgi-bin/bdquery/D?d102:1:./temp/~bdtnWx: @@@L/bss/d102query.html (23 Sept. 2000).

10. Rogier van Bakel, "How Good People Helped to Make a Bad Law," *Wired* (Archive 4.02 1996), http://www.wired.com/wired/archive/4.02 /digi-tel_pr.html (18 July 2000).

11. Louis Freeh, *Prepared Statement of Louis J. Freeh, Director, Federal Bureau of Investigation, Before the House Committee on the Judiciary Subcommittee on Crime*, 30 March 1995, available from Congressional Universe (23 Sept. 2000).

12. The Digital Privacy Working Group comprised of such civil liberties groups as the EFF and ACLU, as well as representatives from the technology industry such as IBM, MCI, Microsoft, and AT&T.

13. Some of the pro-privacy features that the EFF helped to implement in the final version of the DigiTel bill were:

> • In order to obtain transactional records (a log of when, where, and for how long a party visited an information service, and when and with whom he or she exchanged e-mail) of online or regular telephone traffic, a law enforcement officer would need a court order as opposed to a mere subpoena.
>
> • Internet service providers (ISPs), online information services, and private bulletin boards would not have to implement new technology to facilitate wiretaps.
>
> • When presented with a court order, telephone companies have to give law enforcement encrypted messages sent over the companies' wires and decrypt them, even if they do not possess the key.
>
> • The "radio part" of cordless telephone calls (i.e., the transmission between handset and base), which the government could listen in on with impunity, receives the same protection as any other telephone call (a court order is needed to wiretap).
>
> • The Department of Justice (DoJ) can no longer set standards for new digital networks. The industry is free to develop its own standards, albeit "in consultation with the Attorney General."
>
> • The telephone industry will be reimbursed for software and equipment modifications required by the bill. The federal government promised to set aside $0.5 billion for this purpose, subject to appropriation, so that implementation costs will not lead to higher telephone rates.

14. For Stanton McCandish's biography, see http://www.eff.org/pub/Misc /EFF/bios.eff.

15. Bakel, "How Good People."

16. Stewart, "Whatever Happened."

17. Bakel, "How Good People."

18. The vote was a unanimous "yes" in the Senate, and only one "no" in the House.

19. Brock N. Meeks, "Berman's Bailout," *Wired*, Archive 3.03 1995, http://www.wired.com/wired/archive/3.03/eword.html?pg=8 (6 Aug. 2000).

20. Stewart, "Whatever Happened."

21. In its announcement of major changes at the EFF (Kapor et al., *Major Changes*), the board members wrote:

> We expect that the foregoing [i.e., changes] may not sit well with many on the Net. We may be accused of having "sold out" our bohemian birthright for a mess of Washington pottage. It may be widely, and perhaps hotly, asserted

that the "suits" have won and that EFF is about to become another hand-maiden to the large corporate interests which support our work on telecommunications policy.

However plausible, these conclusions are wrong. We made these choices with many of the same misgivings our members will feel. . . . We believe that our decisions will go far to focus EFF's work and make it more effective. The decision to locate our one office in Washington was unavoidable; our policy work can only be done effectively there. . . .

We recognize that inside the Beltway there lies a very powerful reality distortion field, but we have a great deal of faith in the ability of the online world to keep us honest. We know that we can't succeed in insightful policy work without a deep and current understanding of the networks as they evolve—technically, culturally, and personally. . . .

We are deeply concerned that, in moving to Washington, EFF is in peril for its soul. But we are also convinced that we have made the best decisions possible under the circumstances, and that EFF will be stronger as a result. . . .

22. Joshua Quittner, "The Merry Pranksters Go to Washington," *Wired*, Archive 2.06 1994, http://www.wired.com/wired/archive/2.06/eff_pr.html (26 July 2000).
23. For Denise Caruso's biography, see http://www.eff.org/pub/Misc/EFF /bios.eff.
24. Bakel, "How Good People."
25. For John Gilmore's biography, see http://www.eff.org/pub/Misc /EFF/bios.eff.
26. Bakel, "How Good People."
27. For David Johnson's biography, see http://www.eff.org/pub/Misc/EFF/bios. eff.
28. Bakel, "How Good People."
29. Bakel, "How Good People."
30. According to Meek's article ("Berman's Bailout"), board members were upset because they believed Berman had cost the EFF street credibility in the eyes of the online community, and they were wary of the political insider role he was crafting for the group. However, they praised his efforts in the arduous negotiations to get DigiTel passed.
31. Bakel, "How Good People."
32. Dinah Zeiger, "Internet Watchers Split Over Policies," *Denver Post*, 22 January 1995, H.05.
33. Meeks, "Berman's Bailout."
34. The EFF's mission statement (*About the Electronic Frontier Foundation*, 1996, http://www.eff.org/pub/Misc/EFF/about.eff [21 Sept. 2000]), which was last updated in December 1996, states that the EFF will

• engage in and support educational activities which increase popular understanding of the opportunities and challenges posed by developments in computing and telecommunications
• develop among policymakers a better understanding of the issues underlying free and open telecommunications, and support the creation of legal and structural approaches which will ease the assimilation of these new technologies by society

• raise public awareness about civil liberties issues arising from the rapid advancement in the area of new computer-based communications media
• support litigation in the public interest to preserve, protect, and extend First Amendment rights within the realm of computing and telecommunications technology
• encourage and support the development of new tools which will endow nontechnical users with full and easy access to computer-based telecommunications.

35. Meeks, "Berman's Bailout."
36. Meeks, "Berman's Bailout."
37. Zeiger, "Internet Watchers."
38. Center for Democracy and Technology, *FCC Wiretap Decision Challenged,* 2000d, http://www.cdt.org/digi_tel/appeal (15 Aug. 2000).
39. In packet switching system, communications are broken up into individual packets, each of which contains addressing information that gets the packets to their intended destination where they are then reassembled.
40. James X. Dempsey, *Status Report on the Communications Assistance for Law Enforcement Act (CALEA): FBI Seeks to Impose Surveillance Mandates on Telephone System; Balanced Objectives of 1994 Law Frustrated,* 1999, http://www.cdt.org /digi_tel/status.html (22 Aug. 2000).
41. See Cellular Telecommunications Industry Association et al., *Communications Assistance for Law Enforcement Act (CALEA): Industry and Privacy Advocates Response to FBI Implementation Plan,* 29 April 1997, http://www.cdt.org /digi_tel/970429_resp_over.html (22 Aug. 2000); Center for Democracy and Technology, *Comments on the FBI's Second CALEA Capacity Notice,* 18 February 1997, http://www.cdt.org/digi_tel/970218_comments.html (22 Aug. 2000); Center for Democracy and Technology, *Comments of the Center for Democracy and Technology in the Matter of Communications Assistance for Law Enforcement Act,* 20 April 1998, http://www.cdt.org/digi_tel/ calea052098.html (15 Aug. 2000); Center for Democracy and Technology, *Comments of the Center for Democracy and Technology in the Matter of Communications Assistance for Law Enforcement Act: Extension of October 1998 Compliance Date,* 2 April 1998, http://www.cdt.org/digi_tel/cdtcomments.html (22 Aug. 2000); Center for Democracy and Technology, *Petition for Rulemaking Under Sections 107 and 109 of the Communications Assistance for Law Enforcement Act,* 26 March 1998, http://www.cdt.org/digi_tel/980426_ fcc_calea.html (22 Aug. 2000); Center for Democracy and Technology, *Reply Comments of the Center for Democracy and Technology in the Matter of Communications Assistance for Law Enforcement Act,* 12 June 1998, http://www.cdt.org/digi_tel/cdtreplycom.html (15 Aug. 2000); Center for Democracy and Technology, *Reply Comments of the Center for Democracy and Technology,* 27 January 1999, http://www.cdt.org/digi_tel /cdtreply012799. shtml (24 Jan. 2000); Center for Democracy and Technology, Electronic Frontier Foundation, and Computer Professionals for Social Responsibility, *Comments of the Center for Democracy and Technology, The Electronic Frontier Foundation, and Computer Professionals for Social Responsibility,* 12 December 1997, http://www.cdt.org /digi_tel/971212_nprm_comments. htm (22 Aug. 2000); Center for Democracy and Technology and Computer

Professionals for Social Responsibility, *Reply Comments of the Center for Democracy and Technology and Computer Professionals for Social Responsibility Regarding Implementation of the Communications Assistance for Law Enforcement Act (CALEA)*, 11 February 1998, http://www.cdt.org/digi_tel/980211_fcc.html (22 Aug. 2000); United States Federal Bureau of Investigation, *Communications Assistance for Law Enforcement Act (CALEA) Implementation Plan*, 3 March 1997, http://www.cdt.org/digi_tel /CALEA_plan.html (22 Aug. 2000); United States Federal Bureau of Investigation, *Electronic Surveillance—Report on the FBI's Publication of the Second Notice of Capacity*, 14 January 1997, http://www.cdt.org/digi_tel/970114fbi1.html (22 Aug. 2000); United States Federal Bureau of Investigation, *Reply Comments of the FBI Regarding Implementation of the Communications Assistance for Law Enforcement Act (CALEA)*, 11 February 1998, http://www.cdt.org/digi_tel/CALEA_FBI_Reply_980211. html (22 Aug. 2000).

42. Center for Democracy and Technology, *FCC Wiretap Decision Challenged.*

43. Cellular Telecommunications Industry Association et al., *Communications Assistance for Law Enforcement Act (CALEA)*; United States Telephone Association, Cellular Telecommunications Industry Association, and Center for Democracy and Technology, *CTIA/CDT/USTA vs. FCC Reply Brief*, 4 April 2000, http://www.cdt.org/digi_tel/appeal/000404cdt-ctia-ustareply.shtml (15 Aug. 2000); United States Telephone Association, Cellular Telecommunications Industry Association, and Center for Democracy and Technology, *USTA/CTIA/CDT vs. FCC Brief*, 20 January 2000, http://www.cdt.org /digit_tel/appeal/000120cdt-ctia-ustabrief.shtml (15 Aug. 2000).

44. Pen registers are electronic surveillance devices that capture every number dialed from a particular telephone; trap and trace devices record the originating phone numbers of all incoming calls on a particular telephone line. Both pen registers and trap and traces are not supposed to reveal the content of communications; they should not even identify the parties to a communication or whether a call was connected. To obtain a pen register or trap and trace order, the government need merely certify that the information likely to be obtained is relevant to an ongoing criminal investigation.

45. David S. Tatel, *USTA, et al. vs. FCC: Court Opinion*, 15 August 2000, http://pcaer.cadc.uscourts.gov/common/opinions/200008/99-1442a.txt (23 Aug. 2000).

46. Tatel, *USTA, et al. vs. FCC: Court Opinion.*

47. Tatel, *USTA, et al. vs. FCC: Court Opinion.*

48. Eamonn Sullivan, "Web Laws: Less is Definitely More," *PC Week* (8 July 1996): 57.

49. This legislation was identical to another proposed by Senator Exon in 1994, which failed along with the Senate Telecommunications reform bill (S. 1822, 103rd Congress, Sections 801–804).

50. In discussing the CDA on the MacNeil/Lehrer News Hour, Senator Exon explained the catalyst for his bill (MacNeil/Lehrer News Hour, *Focus—Sex in Cyberspace?*, 22 June 1995, http://www.cdt.org/speech/cda/950622macneill_ lehrer.html [16 Aug. 2000]):

I had a book that was downloaded with pictures that I showed to many of my colleagues in the United States Senate, they did not know it was available. It's pornography at its worst. It's obscenity at its worst. And to say it's indecent is an understatement. . . . I simply say the Exon-Coats Bill. . . is a step in the right direction. It's not a cure-all, but it will provide a deterrent to stop the profiteering that's going on today that are polluting the minds of our youth. We can't just sit idly by and say, oh, this is so complicated we can't do anything about it. . . . We've got to do something to protect kids.

51. The IWG consisted of America Online, American Advertising Federation, American Association of Advertising Agencies, American Association of Law Libraries, American Library Association, American Society of Newspaper Editors, Apple Computer, Association of National Advertisers, Association of Research Libraries, AT&T, Bell Atlantic, Business Software Alliance, Cavanagh Associates, Center for Democracy and Technology, Coalition for Networked Information, Commercial Internet eXchange, Compuserve, Computer & Communications Industry Association, Consumer Electronics Manufacturers Association, Consumer Federation of America, Cox Enterprises, Discovery Channel, Electronic Frontier Foundation, Electronic Messaging Association, Institute of Electrical and Electronic Engineers—United States Activities, Information Technology Association of America, Information Technology Industry Council, Interactive Services Association, MCI, Media Access Project, Microsoft, Microsystems Software, National Cable Television Association, National Newspaper Association, National Retail Federation, Netscape, Newspaper Association of America, Pacific Telesis, People for the American Way, Recreational Software Advisory Council, SmithKline Beecham, Software Industry Coalition, Software Publishers Association, SurfWatch Software, Targetbase Marketing, TCI, The Internet Company, The Media Institute, and Time Warner.

52. Internet Working Group, *Letter to Senators Pressler, Exon, and the Senate Commerce Committee,* 9 February 1995, http://www.cdt.org/publications/pp30302.html (18 Aug. 2000).

53. Other VTW members were the American Civil Liberties Union, American Communication Association, Center for Public Representation, Computer Communicators Association, Computing Professionals for Social Responsibility, CyberQueer Lounge, Electronic Frontier Foundation, Electronic Frontier Foundation-Austin, Electronic Frontiers Australia, Electronic Frontiers Houston, Electronic Privacy Information Center, Florida Coalition Against Censorship, Hands Off! the Net petition drive, National Coalition Against Censorship, National Libertarian Party, National Public Telecomputing Network, National Writers Union, People for the American Way, and Society for Electronic Access.

54. Voters Telecommunications Watch, *Campaign to Stop the US Communications Decency Act* (S. 314/H. R. 1004), 17 March 1995, http://www.cdt.org/speech/cda/950317s314campaign.html (16 Aug. 2000).

55. For more information, see VTW's homepage http://www.vtw.org.

56. Voters Telecommunications Watch, *Campaign to Stop the U.S. Communications Decency Act.*

57. A sample communiqué offered by the VTW was:

> I'm a resident of _____. Please support Senator Leahy's efforts to ex-
> plore alternatives to S. 314. Please keep S. 314 out of the telecommunications
> reform bill, and remove S. 314 from the fast track. Thanks.

58. Patrick Leahy, *Senate Floor Statement of Senator Leahy on Censoring Cyberspace*, 30
    March 1995, http://www.cdt.org/publications/pp070330.html (16 Aug.
    2000).

59. On 3 May 1995, the DoJ sent a letter to Senator Leahy detailing its objections to
    the CDA. In reference to hindrances to LEAs resulting from the bill, Acting
    Assistant Attorney General, Kent Marcus, wrote (Kent Marcus, *Department of
    Justice's Letter to Senator Patrick Leahy Regarding the Communications Decency
    Act*, 3 May 1995, http://www.cdt.org/speech/cda/950503doj_ltr.html [18
    Aug. 2000]):

> With respect to the Communications Decency Act, while we understand that
> section 402 is intended to provide users of online services the same protection
> against obscene and harassing communications afforded to telephone sub-
> scribers, this provision would not accomplish that goal. Instead, it would sig-
> nificantly thwart enforcement of existing laws regarding obscenity and child
> pornography, create several ways for distributors and packages of obscenity
> and child pornography to avoid criminal liability, and threaten important
> First Amendment and privacy rights. . . .
>
> Nearly ten years of litigation, along with modifications of the regulations,
> were necessary before the current statute as applied to audiotext services, or
> "dial-a-porn" calling numbers, was upheld as constitutional. . . . The pro-
> posed amendment in Section 40-2 of the bill would jeopardize the enforce-
> ment of the existing dial-a-porn statute by inviting additional constitutional
> challenges, with the concomitant diversion of law enforcement resources. . . .

60. Center for Democracy and Technology, *CDT Policy Post 3/30/95, Number 7*, 30
    March 1995, http://www.cdt.org/publications/pp070330.html (16 Aug.
    2000).

61. For details, see Center for Democracy and Technology, *CDT Policy Post 3/24/95,
    Number 6*, 24 March 1995, http://www.cdt.org/publications/pp060323. html
    (16 Aug. 2000),"Section II: Analysis of Current Proposal." Senator Exon, on
    the other hand, did not consider his bill to be a violation of free speech, for
    he said on the MacNeil/Lehrer Newshour (*Focus—Sex in Cyberspace?*):

> It's not a violation of free speech, and I called on a lot of well-known lawyers
> to make sure that this bill could test—to be properly tested on the constitu-
> tional rights provision. We never know what the courts are going to do. We
> based this on the law that has been in effect and been approved out in no-
> man's land. We're running on the record of courts' decisions that have said
> you can use community standards to protect especially kids on telephones
> and in the mails. We're trying to expand that as best we can to the Internet.

62. Center for Democracy and Technology, *CDT Policy Post 3/30/95*.

63. Patrick Leahy, *Child Protection, User Empowerment, and Free Expression in Interac-
    tive Media Study Bill* (S. 714), 7 April 1995, http://thomas.loc.gov/cgi-
    bin/query/C?c104:./temp/~c104JwzSa3 (18 Aug. 2000).

64. Center for Democracy and Technology, *CDT Policy Post 4/7/95, Number 8,* 7 April 1995, http://www.cdt.org/publications/pp080407.html (16 Aug. 2000).

65. "Draft Bill Would Give FCC Role in Regulating On-Line Speech," *Communications Daily,* 1 June 1995, http://www.cdt.org/speech/cda/950601ed.html (16 Aug. 2000).

66. Center for Democracy and Technology, *CDT Policy Post 5/26/95, Number 14,* 26 May 1995, http://www.cdt.org/publications/pp140526.html (16 Aug. 2000).

67. Jerry Berman et al., *Analysis of Proposed Revision of Exon CDA,* 1995, http://www.cdt.org/publications/pp140526.html (16 Aug. 2000).

68. Charles Grassley, *Protection of Children from Computer Pornography Act of 1995,* 1995, http://thomas.loc.gov/cgi-bin/query/C?c104:./temp/~104p7KJCK (18 Aug. 2000).

69. Center for Democracy and Technology, *CDT Policy Post 6/6/95, Number 16,* 6 June 1995, http://www.cdt.org/publications/pp160606.html (16 Aug. 2000).

70. Center for Democracy and Technology, *CDT Policy Post 6/6/95, Number 16.*

71. Center for Democracy and Technology, *CDT Policy Post 6/14/95, Number 18,* 14 June 1995, http://www.cdt.org/publications/pp180614.html (16 Aug. 2000).

72. The following are some of the organizations that signed the petition: Art on the Net, Californians Against Censorship Together, Center for Democracy and Technology, Cyber-Rights Campaign, Electronic Frontier Foundation, Electronic Frontier Canada, Electronic Frontiers Houston, Feminists for Free Expression, Florida Coalition Against Censorship, Hands Off! The Net, Inner Circle Technologies (a.k.a. Novalink), National Libertarian Party, Marijuana Policy Project, MindVox, National Public Telecomputing Network, National Writers Union, Panix Public Access Internet, People for the American Way, Society for Electronic Access, The Well, and Voters Telecommunications Watch.

73. For the text of the petition, see *Voters Telecommunications Watch, Petition to Help Senator Leahy Fight the Communications Decency Act and to Prevent the Federal Government from Regulating Online Speech,* 15 October 1995, http://www.cdt.org/speech/cda/951005petition.html (16 Aug. 2000). According to *CDT Policy Post 5/26/95, Number 14,* the petition generated 10,000 signatures in its first week of existence. By the end of the second week, the number of signatures had doubled *(CDT Policy Post 6/6/95, Number 16).* When the petition finally closed just under 5 months from its inception, more than 115,000 signatures were collected (Voters Telecommunications Watch, *The Petition is CLOSED,* 5 October 1995, http://www.cdt.org/speech/cda/951005petition.html [5 Oct. 2000]).

74. Center for Democracy and Technology, *CDT Policy Post 6/14/95, Number 18.*

75. For details, see Jerry Berman and Daniel Weitzner, *CDT Analysis of Senate Passed Exon/Coats Communications Decency Act,* 1995, http://www.cdt.org/publications/pp190620.html (16 Aug. 2000).

76. Center for Democracy and Technology, *CDT Policy Post 6/21/95, Number 20,* 21 June 1995, http://www.cdt.org/publications/pp200621.html (16 Aug. 2000).

77. Center for Democracy and Technology, *CDT Policy Post 6/21/95, Number 20.*

78. Center for Democracy and Technology, *CDT Policy Post 6/21/95, Number 20.*

79. Center for Democracy and Technology, *CDT Policy Post 6/21/95, Number 20.*

80. Previously, in an interview with Sir David Frost on PBS, Gingrich said (Newt

Gingrich, *Interview with David Frost*, PBS 5/31/95, 1995, http://www.cdt.org /speech/cda/950531gingrich_exon.html [16 Aug. 2000]):

It's [i.e., Exon bill] probably illegal under our Constitution is my guess. We have a very strong freedom of speech provision. On the other hand, I've been advocating quite openly that major advertisers ought to announce that they will not advertise on radio stations that broadcast songs encouraging the rap- ing and the torture and the physical violence again women. I mean, freedom of speech doesn't mean subsidized speech. And we have every right as a cul- ture, not as a government, but as a culture; we have every right for wise lead- ership to say we won't support that. We won't tolerate that. . . .

Now, first of all. . . computers. There is a problem, nowadays. . . . I was quite surprised when I was told this by an expert. There is a problem nowadays, pedophiles—using computer networking to try to pursue children. It's truly amazing. I think there you have a perfect right on noncensorship basis to in- tervene decisively against somebody who would prey upon children. And that I would support very intensely. It's very different than trying to censor willing adults.

81. Center for Democracy and Technology, *CDT Policy Post 12/1/95, Number 30*, 1 December 1995, http://www.cdt.org/publications/pp301201.html (16 Aug. 2000).

82. Center for Democracy and Technology, *House Approves New Unconstitutional In- decency Statute*, 1995, http://www.cdt.org/speech/cda/950804hsecrim.html (19 Aug. 2000).

83. Legislators on the conference committee were Representatives Bob Barr (R-GA), Joe Barton (R-TX), Howard Berman (D-CA), Thomas Bliley (R-VA), Rick Boucher (D-VA), Sherrod Brown (D-OH), Ed Bryant (D-TN), Steve Buyer (R- IN), John Conyers (D-MI), John Dingell (D-MI), Anna G. Eshoo (D-CA), Jack Fields (R-TX), Michael Flanagan (R-IL), Dan Frisa (R-NY), Elton Gallegly (R- CA), Bob Goodlatte (R-VA), Bart Gordon (D-TN), Dennis Hastert (R-IL), Mar- tin Hoke (R-OH), Henry Hyde (R-IL), Sheila Jackson-Lee (D-TX), Scott Klug (R-WI), Blanche Lincoln (D-AR), Edward Markey (D-MA), Carlos Moorhead (R-CA), Michael Oxley (R-OH), L. William Paxon (R-NY), Bobby Rush (D-IL), Daniel Schaefer (R-CO), Patricia Schroeder (D-CO), Robert Scott (D-VA), Cliff Stearns (R-FL), and Rick White (R-WA); and Senators Conrad Burns (R-MT), James Exon (D-NE), Wendell Ford (D-KY), Slade Gorton (R-WA), Ernest Hollings (D-SC), Daniel Inouye (D-HI), Trent Lott (R-MS), John McCain (R- AZ), Larry Pressler (R-SD), John Rockefeller (D-WV), and Ted Stevens (R-AK).

84. Internet Working Group, *Child Protection and Parental Empowerment in Interactive Media*, 9 November 1995, http://www.cdt.org/speech/cda/951109_ iwg_ltr.html (18 Aug. 2000).

85. Internet Working Group, *Child Protection and Parental Empowerment*.

86. Internet Working Group, *Child Protection and Parental Empowerment*.

87. Representative Hyde endorsed a proposal offered by conservative religious groups in October (a.k.a. the Reed/Schafly/Meese Proposal), which was more restrictive than the Exon proposal *(CDT Policy Post 12/1/95, Number 30)*. The proposal would have made Internet providers, online services, and li- braries criminally liable for expression online. It would have created a stan-

dard for criminalizing "indecency" online, dumbed down every web page, newsgroups, discussion forum, and chat system. Last, the bill would have given the FCC jurisdiction over speech in cyberspace and software that might be used to filter children's access to the Net.

88. Rick White, *An Open Letter to the Internet Community*, 4 December 1995, http://www.cdt.org/speech/cda/951204white_ltr.html (18 Aug. 2000).

89. Center for Democracy and Technology, *CDT Policy Post 12/6/95, Number 32*, 6 December 1995, http://www.cdt.org/publications/pp321206.html (16 Aug. 2000).

90. Representative White did NOT vote for the Goodlatte Amendment *(CDT Policy Post 12/6/95, Number 32)*.

91. Voters Telecommunications Watch, *Press Release on National Day of Protest from the Net*, 13 December 1995, http://www.cdt.org/speech/cda/951213protest_pr.html (16 Aug. 2000).

92. Voters Telecommunications Watch, *Press Release on National Day of Protest from the Net*.

93. Voters Telecommunications Watch, *Press Release on National Day of Protest from the Net*.

94. Voters Telecommunications Watch, *Press Release on National Day of Protest from the Net*.

95. Voters Telecommunications Watch, *Press Release on National Day of Protest from the Net*.

96. Center for Democracy and Technology, *CDT Policy Post 12/4/95, Number 31*, 4 December 1995, http://www.cdt.org/publications/pp311204.html (16 Aug. 2000).

97. Voters Telecommunications Watch, *Campaign to Stop the Unconstitutional Communications Decency Act*, 1 January 1996, http://www.cdt.org/speech/cda/06-1-1protest_alert.html (16 Aug. 2000).

98. Voters Telecommunications Watch, *Campaign to Stop the Unconstitutional Communications Decency Act*, 1 January 1996.

99. Voters Telecommunications Watch, *Campaign to Stop the Unconstitutional Communications Decency Act*, 1 January 1996.

100. Center for Democracy and Technology, *CDT Policy Post 1/4/96, Number 33*, 4 January 1996, http://www.cdt.org/publications/pp33010496.html (16 Aug. 2000).

101. Voters Telecommunications Watch, *Campaign to Stop the Unconstitutional Communications Decency Act: January 31, 1996* (Expires February 29, 1996), 31 January 1996, http://www.cdt.org/speech/cda/960131alert.html (16 Aug. 2000).

102. Voters Telecommunications Watch, *Campaign to Stop the Unconstitutional Communications Decency Act: January 31, 1996* (Expires February 29, 1996).

103. Center for Democracy and Technology, *CDT Policy Post 2/1/96, Volume 2, Number 5*, 1 February 1996, http://www.cdt.org/publications/pp_2.5.html (16 Aug. 2000).

104. Center for Democracy and Technology, *CDT Policy Post 2/1/96, Volume 2, Number 5*.

105. Center for Democracy and Technology, *CDT Policy Post 2/8/96, Volume 2, Number 6,* 8 February 1996, http://www.cdt.org/publications/pp_2.6.html (16 Aug. 2000).

106. Voters Telecommunications Watch, *Join Hundreds and Thousands of Other Internet Users in 48 Hours of Protest After President Clinton Signs the Bill That Will Censor the Internet,* 3 February 1996, http://www.cdt.org/speech/cda /960203_48hrs_alert.html (19 Aug. 2000).

107. Center for Democracy and Technology, *CDT Policy Post 2/8/96, Volume 2, Number 6.*

108. Members of the CIEC included the Association of American University Presses, Association of National Advertisers, Association of Research Libraries, Center for Democracy and Technology, Coalition for Networked Information, Media Access Project, Media Institute, Microsystems Software, National Association of State Universities & Land Grant Colleges, National Newspaper Association, People for the American Way, Recording Industry Association of America, Software Publishers Association, Special Libraries Association, SurfWatch Software, University of California Santa Barbara Library, and Voters Telecommunications Watch.

Named plaintiffs in the challenge included the American Library Association; America Online; American Booksellers Association; American Booksellers Foundation for Free Expression; American Society of Newspaper Editors; Apple Computer; Association of American Publishers; Association of Publishers, Editors and Writers; Citizens Internet Empowerment Coalition; Commercial Internet eXchange; Compuserve; Families Against Internet Censorship; Freedom to Read Foundation; HotWired Ventures; Interactive Digital Software Association; Interactive Services Association; Magazine Publishers of America; Microsoft Corporation; Microsoft Network; NETCOM On-Line Communications Services; Newspaper Association of America; OpNet; Prodigy; Society of Professional Journalists; and Wired Ventures.

109. Citizens Internet Empowerment Coalition, *Citizens Internet Empowerment Coalition Trial Bulletin Update No. 15,* 31 October 1996, http://www.ciec.org /trial /complaint/complaint.html (19 Aug. 2000).

110. Bruce J. Ennis et al., *ALA Plaintiffs' Memorandum of Law in Support of Their Motion for a Preliminary Injunction,* 1996, http://www.ciec.org/trial/injunction_ brief.html (19 Aug. 2000).

111. Those who filed declarations included Albert Vezza (Associate Director, Laboratory for Computer Science, MIT); America Online; American Booksellers Association; American Booksellers Foundation for Freedom Expression; American Library Association; American Society for Newspaper Editors; Association of American Universities; Association of American University Presses; Association of Publishers, Editors and Writers; Association of Research Libraries; Bantam Doubleday Dell Publishing Group; Carnegie Library of Pittsburgh; Center for Democracy and Technology; Commercial Internet eXchange; Compuserve; Families Against Internet Censorship; Fort Vancouver Regional Library; Free Library of Philadelphia; Freedom to Read

Foundation; Health Sciences Libraries Consortium; HotWired Ventures; Interactive Services Association; Media Access Project; Microsoft Corporation; Microsoft Network; Microsystems Software; NETCOM On-Line Communications Services; Newspaper Association of America; OpNet; Senator Patrick Leahy; People for the American Way; Prodigy; Recording Industry Association of America; Scott O. Brander (Office of Information Technology, Harvard University); Society of Professional Journalists; Surfwatch Software; Timothy Berners-Lee (Director, World Wide Web Consortium); University of California-Santa Barbara Library; University of Pennsylvania Libraries; Vinton Cerf (MCI Telecommunications Services); and Wired Ventures.

112. Center for Democracy and Technology, *CDT Policy Post 3/1/96, Volume 2, Number 8*, 1 March 1996, http://www.cdt.org/publicationspp_2.8.html (16 Aug. 2000).

113. Center for Democracy and Technology, *CDT Policy Post 3/14/96, Volume 2, Number 10*, 14 March 1996, http://www.cdt.org/publications/pp_2.10.html (16 Aug. 2000).

114. Dolores Sloviter, Ronald L. Buckwater, and Stewart Dalzell, *Adjudication on Motions for Preliminary Injunction*, 1996, http://www.ciec.org/decision_PA/decision_text.html (19 Aug. 2000).

115. Jamie S. Gorelick, *Text of DoJ Letter to Senator Exon*, 26 June 1996, http://www.ciec.org/SC_appeal/DOJ_Exon_ltr.html (18 Aug. 2000).

116. Michael R. Stiles, *Defendants' Notice of Appeal*, 1996, http://www.ciec.org/SC_appeal/DOJ_notice.html (9 Aug. 2000).

117. Citizens Internet Empowerment Coalition, *Citizens Internet Empowerment Coalition Trial Bulletin Update No. 15*.

118. Citizens Internet Empowerment Coalition, *Brief for the Appellants*, 1997, http://www.ciec.org/SC_appeal/970121_DOJ_brief.html (9 Aug. 2000).

119. Jepsen Ronald D. Maines, M. Kendall Brown, and Enough is Enough, *Amici Curiae Brief*, 1997, http://www.ciec.org/SC_appeal/970121_EIE_brief.html (9 Aug. 2000).

120. John Paul Stevens, *Supreme Court Opinion: Janet Reno, Attorney General of the United States, et al., Appellants vs. American Civil Liberties Union, et al., on Appeal from the United States District Court for the Eastern District of Pennsylvania*, 1997, http://www.ciec.org/SC_appeal/opinion.shtml (20 Aug. 2000).

121. In a separate concurrence, Chief Justice William Rehnquist and Justice Sandra Day O'Connor agreed that the provisions of the CDA were all unconstitutional except in their narrow application to "communications between an adult and one or more minors" (Sandra Day O'Connor and William Rehnquist, *Concurrence by Justice O'Connor and Chief Justice Rehnquist: Janet Reno, Attorney General of the United States, et al., Appellants vs. American Civil Liberties Union, et al.*, 1997, http://www.ciec/org/SC_appeal/concurrence.shtml [20 Aug. 2000]).

122. Statements were also made by Bruce J. Ennis, lead attorney from the law firm of Jenner & Block; Bill Burrington, Assistant General Counsel and Director of Law and Public Affairs at America Online; Mary R. Somerville, President of the American Library Association; Barry and Michele Fagin, founders of Families Against Internet Censorship, Colorado Springs, CO; Andrew Jay Schwartzman, President of the Media Access Project; Elliot Mincberg, Execu-

tive Director of People for the American Way; and Nigel Spicer, President of Microsystems Software (Citizens Internet Empowerment Coalition, *U.S. Supreme Court Rules on Communications Decency Act: Reactions from Plaintiffs and Attorneys,* 1997b, http://www.ciec.org/SC_appeal/970626_CIEC.shtml [20 Aug. 2000]).

123. Citizens Internet Empowerment Coalition, *U.S. Supreme Court Rules on Communications Decency Act.*

124. Patrick Leahy, *Statement on Supreme Court's Decision Declaring Unconstitutional the Communications Decency Act,* 1997, http://www.ciec.org/SC_appeal/970626_Leahy.html (20 Aug. 2000).

125. Russ Feingold, *Feingold Applauds Supreme Court Decision Striking Down Unconstitutional Internet Censorship Law,* 1997, http://www.ciec.org/SC_appeal/970626_Feingold.html (20 Aug. 2000).

126. Edward Markey, *Markey Reaction to Online Censorship Ruling,* 1997, http://www.ciec.org/SC_appeal/970626_Markey.html (20 Aug. 2000).

127. Rick White, *White Praises Supreme Court for Realizing Potential of the Internet,* 1997, http://www.ciec.org/SC_appeal/970626_White.html (20 Aug. 2000). In 1996, following the enactment of the CDA, Representative White formed the Congressional Internet Caucus (IC) to help educate Members of Congress about the Internet. He believes that through the work of the IC and with the help of the Internet community, Capitol Hill had gained a better understanding of the Internet and would be better prepared to address content-regulation issues in the future.

128. Jerrold Nadler, *Representative Nadler Hails U.S. Supreme Court Decision Striking Down the "Communications Decency Act",* 1997, http://www.ciec.org/SC_appeal/970626_Nadler.html (20 Aug. 2000).

129. Sources for Table 5.1 are Voters Telecommunications Watch, *Campaign to Stop the Unconstitutional Communications Decency Act,* 1 January 1996; and Voters Telecommunications Watch, *Campaign to Stop the Unconstitutional Communications Decency Act, January 31, 1996 (Expires February 29, 1996),* 31 January 1996.

130. Cathy Cleaver, *Court Reaffirms Government's Interest in Protecting Children from Porn, But Strikes CDA As Too Broad,* 1997, http://www.ciec.org/SC_appeal/970626_FRC.html (20 Aug. 2000).

131. Zoe Lofgren, *Congresswoman Lofgren Urges Sensible Solution Not "Knee Jerk" Posturing,* 1997, http://www.ciec.org/SC_appeal/970626_Lofgren.html (20 Aug. 2000).

132. Patricia Murray, *Murray Outlines Plan to Protect Children from Material on Internet,* 1997, http://www.ciec.org/SC_appeal/970626_Murray.html (20 Aug. 2000). A toll-free line in Great Britain has reportedly proven successful in uncovering illegal material and providing parents with a resource for action.

133. Michael Oxley, *Child Online Protection Act (H. R. 3783 IH),* 30 April 1998, http://thomas.loc.gov/cgi-bin/query/D?c105:1:./temp/~c105zg1WJj (16 Aug. 2000).

134. Center for Democracy and Technology, *Constitutional Analysis of the Oxley Bill—The Child Online Protection Act (H. R. 3783),* 1998, http://www.cdt.org/speech/copa/980924constitutional.html (16 Aug. 2000).

135. Michael Rogers and Norman Oder, "Congress Passes Coats' 'CDA II,'" *Library Journal* 123 (1998): 13.
136. Center for Democracy and Technology, *Constitutional Analysis of the Oxley Bill—The Child Online Protection Act (H. R. 3783)*.
137. The COPA Commission consists of 16 people from the high-tech industry appointed by the Speaker of the House, the Senate Majority Leader, and three Ex-officio members from the DoJ, the FTC, and the Department of Commerce. The members of the Commission are: Donald Telage (Network Solutions, Inc., and Commission Chair), Stephen Balkam (Internet Content Rating Association), John Bastian (Security Software Systems), Jerry Berman (CDT), Robert C. Cotner (Evesta.com), Arthur H. DeRosier, Jr. (Rocky Mountain College), J. Robert Flores (National Law Center for Children and Families), Albert F. Garnier III (Education Networks of America), Michael E. Horowitz (DoJ), Donna Rice Hughes (Enough is Enough/Author of *Kids Online*), C. Lee Peeler (FTC), William M. Parker (Crosswalk.com), Gregory L. Rhode (Department of Commerce/NTIA), C. James Schmidt (San Jose State University), William L. Schrader (PSINet), Larry Shapiro (Disney's Go.com), Srinija Srinivasan (Yahoo! Inc.), Karen Talbert (Amerivision Lifeline), and George Vradenburg III (AOL). The group's mission is to craft and file a report that describes and analyzes technologies and methods that could be used to achieve their goals; make conclusions and recommendations of those technologies; and recommend ways to legislatively implement those conclusions. The report should be submitted no later than one year after COPA's enactment (Center for Democracy and Technology, *COPA Commission*, 2000c, http://www.cdt.org/speech/copa/commission.html [4 Aug. 2000]).
138. Members of the coalition were American Society of Newspaper Editors, Association of American Publishers, Bibliobytes, Center for Democracy and Technology, Comic Book Legal Defense Fund, Commercial Internet eXchange Association, Computer and Communications Industry Association, Freedom to Read Foundation, Internet Alliance, Magazine Publishers of America, National Association of College Stores, National Association of Recording Merchandisers, Newspaper Association of America, People for the American Way, Periodical and Book Association of America, PSINet, Publishers Marketing Association, Recording Industry Association of America, and Society of Professional Journalists (Association of American Publishers et al., *Amici Curiae in Support of Plaintiffs*, 11 January 1999, http://www.cdt.org/speech/copa/990111amicus.html [14 Aug. 2000]). Despite the fact that many in the coalition were parties in the challenge to the CDA, they have not joined the lawsuit itself.
139. Association of American Publishers et al., *Amici Curiae in Support of Plaintiffs*.
140. The plaintiffs were American Civil Liberties Union, Androgyny Books, Different Light Bookstores, American Booksellers Foundation For Free Expression, ArtNet, Blackstripe, Addazi, Condomania, Electronic Frontier Foundation, Electronic Privacy Information Center, Free Speech Media, Internet Content Coalition, OBGYN.Net, Philadelphia Gay News, Planetout Corporation, Powell's Bookstore, Riotgrrl, Salon Internet, and West Stock (Association of American Publishers et al., *Amicus Brief: Child Online Protection Act (COPA)*, 1

September 1999, http://www.cdt.org/speech/copa/990901amicus.shtml [14 Aug. 2000]).

141. Rogers and Oder, "Congress Passes Coats' "CDA II."

142. Lowell Reed, *Text of Judge Lowell's Opinion,* 1 February 1999, http:/www. cdt.org/speech/copa/990201ACLUvsRENOdecision.shtml (14 Aug. 2000).

143. Janet Reno, *ACLU vs. RENO: Notice of Appeal,* 31 March 1999, http://www.cdt.org/speech/copa/990331appealdocument.gif (14 Aug. 2000).

144. "Cybersmut Law Injunction Upheld," *Associated Press Online,* 23 June 2000, available from Newspaper Source (6 Aug. 2000).

145. "Cybersmut Law Injunction Upheld," *Associated Press Online.*

146. "Companies Make Big Bucks Profiting Browsers," *Detroit News,* 17 February 2000, C3.

147. Doubleclick, *Doubleclick Press Kit,* 1996–2000a, http://www.doubleclick. com:8080/company_info/press_kit (10 Aug. 2000).

148. Doubleclick delivers more than 17 billion advertisements to web surfers each month. In 1999, the company grossed $316.8 million in revenue.

149. For further information on the DART software, see http://www.doubleclick.net:8080/publishers/service.

150. For a complete list of Doubleclick clients, see http://www.doubleclick.net: 8080/advertisers/network/net_sites/all_sites/default.htm.

151. Bob Tedeschi, "Critics Press Legal Assault on Tracking of Web Users," *New York Times,* 7 February 2000, C1.

152. "Companies Make Big Bucks," C3.

153. Doubleclick's Privacy Statement reads in part (Doubleclick, *Privacy Statement,* 1996–2000b, http://www.doubleclick.com:8080/privacy_policy [10 Aug. 2000]):

Internet user privacy is of paramount importance to Doubleclick, our advertisers, and our web publishers. The success of our business depends upon our ability to maintain the trust of our users. . . . In the course of delivering an ad to you, Doubleclick does not collect any personally identifiable information about you, such as your name, address, phone number, or e-mail address. Doubleclick does, however, collect nonpersonally identifiable information about you, such as the server your computer is logged onto, your browser type. . . , and whether you respond to the ad delivered.

The nonpersonally identifiable information collected by Doubleclick is used for the purpose of targeting ads and measuring ad effectiveness on behalf of Doubleclick's advertisers and web publishers who specifically request it. . . . However, as described in "Abacus Alliance" and "Information Collected by Doubleclick's Web Sites" below, nonpersonally identifiable information collected by Doubleclick in the course of an ad delivery *can be associated with a user's personally identifiable information* if that user has agreed to receive personally tailored ads.

154. Tedeschi, "Critics Press Legal Assault," C1.

155. Tedeschi, "Critics Press Legal Assault," C1.

156. Diane Anderson and Keith Perine, "Marketing the Doubleclick Way," *Industry Standard*, 25 July 2000, http://www.thestandard.com/article/display /0,1151,12400,00.html (25 July 2000).
157. Deirdre K. Mulligan et al., *In the Matter of Doubleclick: Statement of Additional Facts and Grounds for Relief* (Washington, D.C.: n. p., 2000).
158. Deirdre K. Mulligan et al., *In the Matter of Doubleclick.*
159. Jim Hu, "Consumer Group Blasts Doubleclick in Report to FTC," *CNET News.com*, 1 March 2000, http://news.cnet.com/news/0-1005-202-1561502.html (18 July 2000).
160. Hiawatha Bray, "Doubleclick Backs Off on Net Data Bows to Protests on Use of Personal Information," *Boston Globe*, 3 March 2000, C1.
161. Hiawatha Bray, "Doubleclick Backs Off."
162. Don Oldenburg, "Consummate Consumer: The Online Opt-Out Option," *Washington Post*, 15 March 2000, C04.
163. Major companies that allow online opt-out include Amazon.com, American Express (e-mail), Any Birthday, AT&T, eBay, Lexis-Nexis, About.com, AltaVista, Excite, Go.com, Lycos, MSN.com, Netscape, Wired.com, Yahoo, 24/7 Media, Adforce, AdKnowledge, Angara, AvenueA, BeFree, Cogit/Click-Safe, CoreMetrics, Doubleclick, Engage, Flycast, L90, Matchlogie, and MediaPlex.
164. These include American Express, Bank of America, Chase, Capital One, Citibank, Fleet Options, HSBC, MBNA Affiliates, MBNA Third Party, Wells Fargo, Equifax, Experian, Trans Union, Direct Marketing Association, and 1-800-US.Search.
165. Kevin O'Connor, *Statement from Kevin O'Connor, CEO of Doubleclick*, 2000, http://www.doubleclick.com. . ./company_info_press_kit?pr.00.03.02. htm (10 Aug. 2000).
166. Kevin O'Connor, *Statement from Kevin O'Connor.*
167. Evan Hansen, "Doubleclick Postpones Data-Merging Plan," *CNet News.com*, 2 March 2000, http://news.cnet.com/news/0-1005-202-1562746.html (18 July 2000).
168. Jim Hu, "Consumer Group Blasts Doubleclick."
169. Anderson and Peregrine, "Marketing the Doubleclick Way."
170. Declan McCullagh, "Intel Nixes Chip-Tracking ID," *Wired News*, 27 April 2000, http://www.wired.com/news/print/0,1294,35950,00.html (23 Aug. 2000).
171. Patrick Geisinger, RSA Data Security Conference and Expo'99: "A Billion Trusted Computers," 20 January 1999, http://www.intel.com/pressroom /archive/speeches/pg012099.htm (23 Aug. 2000).
172. It turned out that in March 1999, Intel notified its PC vendors that Pentium II and Celeron chips shipped in the Mobile Module packaging also contained the PSN technology. "In some Mobile Module products we had some prototype circuitry that we were supposed to disable as part of the process," said George Alfs, an Intel spokesperson. "On some of the processors the circuitry was not disabled" (Ephraim Schwartz and Dan Briody, "Intel's Pentium Security Woes Continue," *InfoWorld Electric*, 1999, http://www.infoworld/com /cgi_bin/displayStory.p1?990310/wepsn.htm [23 Aug. 2000]).
173. Intel, *Pentium III Processors: Processor Serial Number Questions and Answers*, 2000, http://support.intel.com/support/processors/pentiumiii/psqu.htm (23 Aug. 2000).

174. Intel, *Pentium III Processors: Processor Serial Number Control Utility*, 2000, http://support.intel.com/support/processors/pentiumiii/snum.htm (23 Aug. 2000).
175. Pentium III-powered PCs are manufactured by the following companies: Acer, AMAX, AST, AVATAR, BOLData, Calber, Ciara, Colfax, Compaq, CompUSA, Cybernetique, Cyberstar, Dell, DTK, EMPAC, Everex, Gateway, Hewitt Rand, Hewlett-Packard, IBM, ION, MediaOn, MicroCenter, MicronPC, MidwestMicro, Mitsuba, MynixTechnology, Patriot, PC Club, Polywell, Premio, Prosys, Quantex Micros, Royal Computer, Seanix, Solomon Technology, Sony, Tangent Computers, Toshiba, UMAX, Utron, and V-squared Computers (Intel, *Find Your New Intel Processor Powered PC at These Manufacturers' Web Sites*, 2000, http://www.intel.com/home/buynow/maker.htm [23 Aug. 2000]).
176. Intel, *Pentium III Processors: Processor Serial Number Control Utility.*
177. For further technical specifications, see Intel, *Pentium III Processors: Processor Serial Number Control Utility.*
178. Some experts questioned the PSN's practical value as well as general effectiveness. For example, Rebecca Duncan, an analyst at Gartner Group (Delran, NJ), predicted that the serial number could discourage users from visiting sites that required such identification for access. Moreover, users with more than one computer would presumably be required to register each machine at sites demanding such number. "Intel needs to look at what burden it is putting on the user or organization buying the PC. There is a point where people would just say no to applications that would use this number," said Duncan (Bill Roberts, "Intel Reconsiders Plans for Security Feature," *Internet World*, 1 February 1999, http://www.internetworld.c...int/1999 /02/01/news/19990201-intel.html [23 Aug. 2000]). Lance Cottrell, founder and CEO of Anonymizer, Inc., concurred. According to him, "[PSNs] are a very poor authenticator. Consider the number of people who may use a computer in an office environment. I know families where four or five people regularly use and make purchases from the same computer. In addition, many people sell or give away old computers. Using the PSN to identify the user could be a huge security breach. A computer with an upgradable processor would change its PSN each time it's upgraded. Let's not even consider Internet cafés or libraries. The opposite problem is also common. Many people use more than one computer to transact business. I have a laptop, a home PC, and several workstations in the office. I may use any of them to conduct my business and make my purchases. Any system which required me to do everything from a single CPU would not get my business for long" (Amara D. Angelica, "Identity Crisis: The Pentium III's Serial Number Feature is the Latest Flash Point in the Debate Over Privacy," *TechWeek*, 8 February 1999, http://www.techweek.com/articles/2-8-99/privacu.htm [26 Aug. 2000]). Dave Banisar, policy director for the Electronic Privacy Information Center, claimed that because the serial number would be used with a software program, the numbers would not be all that secure in the first place (Angelica, "Identity Crisis."). Bruce Schneier, President of Counterpane Systems and author of *Applied Cryptography*, wrote in his ZDNet article that "[y]es, the processor number is unique and cannot be changed, but the software that queries the processor is not trusted. If a remote website queries a

processor ID, it has no way of knowing whether the number it gets back is a real ID or a forged ID. Likewise, if a piece of software queries its processor's ID, it has no way of knowing whether the number it gets back is the real ID or whether a patch in the operating system trapped the call and responded with a fake ID. Because Intel didn't bother creating a secure way to query the ID, it will be easy to break the security" (Bruce Schneier, "Why Intel's IS Tracker Won't Work," *ZDNet News*, 26 January 1999, http://www.zdnet.com/filters/printerfriendly/0,6061,2194863-2,00.html [25 Aug. 2000]).

179. Robert Lemos, "Intel Disables ID Tracking in New Chips," *ZDNet News*, 27 April 2000, http://www.zdnet.com/intweek/stories.news/0.4164,2556671, 00.html (23 Aug. 2000).

180. Stephanie Miles, "Symantec Offers Security for Pentium III," *CNET News.com*, 1999, http://new.net.com/0-1003-202-340176.html (23 Aug. 2000).

181. Christian Perrson, "Pentium III Serial Number is Soft Switchable After All," *Heise Online*, 22 February 1999, http://www.heise.de/ct/english/99/05/news1 (23 Aug. 2000).

182. "Intel Still Wrestling Serial Number Debacle," *Reuters*, 29 April 1999, http://news.cnet.com/news/0-1003-200-341844.html?tag= (23 Aug. 2000).

183. Miles, "Symantec Offers Security."

184. Schwartz and Briody, "Intel's Pentium Security Woes Continue."

185. American Civil Liberties Union et al., *Privacy Advocates Letter to Intel on Pentium III*, 28 January 1999, http://www.cdt.org/privacy/issues/pentium3/990128intel.letter.shtml (23 Aug. 2000).

186. It must be said that not everyone agreed that the PSN posed a threat to users' privacy. For example, Computer Associates, which has developed software that will allow businesses, especially in the corporate environment, to use the PSN, said that the Intel's P3 chip will help tighten security. As Marc Sokal, Senior VP of Marketing for Computer Associates, said (Janet Kornblum, "Privacy Eclipses P3 Chip," *USA Today*, 17 February 1999, http://www. usatoday.com/life/cyber/tech/cte420.htm [23 Aug. 2000]):

    My feeling is today with the Internet, and especially with cookies, all that information [i.e., personal information] is available anyhow. A serial number is the least of your challenges. You have to trade off the benefit that the chip gives against the risks.

187. Besides the CDT et al., there were other privacy advocates that protested against the PSN such as a group led by Junkbusters and EPIC who had called for a boycott of Intel the week of 8 February 1999.

188. "Privacy Groups Want Chip Recall," *Bloomberg News*, 29 January 1999, http://news.cnet.com/news/0-1006-202-338031.html (23 Aug. 2000).

189. Compare Intel's rate of response concerning the Pentium III PSN with the lackadaisical attitude toward the mathematical glitch in 1994 that eventually forced the company into a $457 million recall of the first Pentium chips (James Lardner, "Intel Even More Inside," *U.S. News Online*, 8 February 1999, http://www.usnews.com/usnews/issue/990208/8inte.htm [26 Aug. 2000]).

190. Bill Roberts, "Intel Reconsiders Plans."

191. Center for Democracy and Technology, *CDT Asks Equipment Manufacturer How They Plan to Implement the ID Feature*, 16 February 1999,

http://www.cdt.org/privacy/issues/pentium3/990216oem.letter.shtml (23 Aug. 2000).

192. Center for Democracy and Technology, *Equipment Manufacturer's Default Setting on the Intel Pentium III PSN*, 1999, http://www.cdt.org/privacy/issues/pentium3/990414OEM.shtml (23 Aug. 2000).

193. For IBM's full response to CDT's letter, see http://www.cdt.org/privacy/issues/pentium3/990224ibmletter.shtml.

194. For more information, see http://www.dell.com/policy/Intel.htm.

195. Center for Democracy and Technology, *Equipment Manufacturer's Default Setting*.

196. Center for Democracy and Technology, *Equipment Manufacturer's Default Setting*.

197. Center for Democracy and Technology, *Equipment Manufacturer's Default Setting*.

198. Center for Democracy and Technology, *Summary of CDT Activities 1999 — Work Plan 2000*, 2000f, http://www.cdt.org/mission/activities2000.shtml (5 Oct. 2000).

199. Dan Goodin, "More Support for Pentium III Complaint," *CNet News.com*, 8 April 1999, http://news.cnet.com/news/0-1003-202-340915.html (23 Aug. 2000).

200. Intel makes 85 percent of the world's computer microprocessors (Roberts, "Intel Reconsiders Plans").

201. The Pentium III chip was previewed at the San Jose Convention Center on 17 February 1999, and officially released in systems on 26 February 1999 (Brooke Crothers and Michael Kanellos, "What Does Pentium III Bring to the Party?" *CNet News.com*, 11 February 1999, http://www.cnet.com/news/0-1006-202-338646.html [23 Aug. 2000]).

202. Center for Democracy and Technology, *CDT Asks Equipment Manufacturers*.

203. American Civil Liberties Union et al., *More Privacy and Consumer Groups Urge FTC Immediately to Prevent Harm to Consumer Privacy*, 1999, http://www.cdt.org/privacy/issues/pentium3/990305intel.moregroups.shtml (23 Aug. 2000).

204. Center for Democracy and Technology, *Summary of CDT Activities 1999*.

205. Goodin, "More Support for Pentium III Complaint."

206. Center for Democracy and Technology, *CDT Policy Post 8/31/99, Volume 5, Number 21*, 31 August 1999, http://www.cdt.org/publications/pp_5.21.html (22 Aug. 2000).

207. Center for Democracy and Technology, *CDT Policy Post 8/31/99*.

208. Center for Democracy and Technology, *Summary of CDT Activities 1999*.

209. Michael Kanellos, "Intel to Phase Out CPU Serial Number," *CNet Gamecenter.com*, 28 April 2000, http://www.gamecenter.com/News?Item?Textonly/0,78,0-4073,00.html?st.gc.gn.. pfv (23 Aug. 2000).

210. McCullagh, "Intel Nixes Chip-Tracking ID."

211. Besides the serial number, Intel also explained that support for hardware digital certificate—a feature financial institutions support—would also not be included in the new generation of Intel microchips (McCullagh, "Intel Nixes Chip-Tracking ID").

212. Lemos, "Intel Disables ID Tracking in New Chips."

6

The Public's Perceptions of the Center for Democracy and Technology as Reflected in the Mass Media

A search in the National Newspapers database produced 35 articles about the CDT that were written between 1995 and March 2000. There was one article from 1995; seven from 1996; two from 1997; eleven from 1998; nine from 1999; and five from 2000. These articles appeared most often in the *Washington Post* (nine articles) and *USA Today* (eight articles); followed by the *Denver Post* and *Wall Street Journal* (three articles each); *Houston Chronicle, San Francisco Chronicle*, and *Times-Picayune* (two each); and *Atlanta Journal, Boston Globe, Detroit News, Los Angeles Times, New York Times*, and *St. Louis Post-Dispatch* (one each). All articles mentioned the CDT and/or one of its staff.[1] However, not all of them quoted CDT personnel; 7 out of the 35 did not include CDT quotes.

The chapter will proceed with a description of the contents of these articles.

NEWSPAPERS

1995

The one article from this year appeared in the *Denver Post*, which seems rather surprising considering the subject of the story is based in Washington, D.C.[2] In her article, Dinah Zeiger, a business writer for the newspaper, debuted the CDT and explained briefly how it came to be. She also explained what would be the differences between the organization that Jerry Berman had left and this new center he had just formed: the EFF would continue to work on security and privacy issues; remain a player in the debate over universal access; and it would take on the issue of intellectual property in cyberspace. By contrast, the CDT would "focus on enforcing privacy protections in the digital wiretap law and opposing efforts to regulate content on the Net. Its involvement would build on a coalition that includes many of the industries that have helped to fund the Center."[3] Interestingly, one thing Zeiger felt certain about was that "the new order will reshape the debate on such issues as privacy and the regulation of the Internet. . . ."[4]

1996

Seven articles concerning the CDT appeared in 1996. The earliest one was published the same week as the FTC's Bureau of Consumer Protection was holding a two-day public meeting "to address consumer privacy issues posed by the emerging online marketplace."[5] In view of this, Leslie Miller, a reporter for *USA Today*, showcased the CDT's new privacy website (http://www.cdt.org/privacy) which was launched the same day as the article's publication. Miller explained that the website demonstrates the CDT's desire "to educate the public about what's going on out there and how few protections currently exist.[6] When visitors access the page, they see an eye staring back from the screen and a message displaying the information collected: e-mail address, and perhaps real name. . . , geographic location, type of computer, and web browsing software being used." The page also explains why visitors ought to care: "It is possible to construct a very detailed profile of your online activities that could be used in a variety of ways."[7] Miller cited Janlori Goldman (one of three privacy experts consulted for the background for the article. The others were Robert Ellis Smith, editor of the *Privacy*

Journal, and David Sobel, director of the Electronic Privacy Information Center) to warn of the dangers of the Internet: "People think they're invisible" but "the illusion of anonymity is completely false. . . ." The web "is not just a billboard, it's a billboard with the capacity to capture the address of every single person who looks at it. . . Used in conjunction with lists and information from other sites. . . you can imagine how easy it would be to put together a lifestyle profile" that could be used for direct marketing or even law enforcement purposes.[8]

On the same day and in the same newspaper, another piece appeared that pertains to the CDT's efforts in soliciting and posting on its website the privacy policies of online services (e.g., American Online, Compuserve, Microsoft Network, and Prodigy).[9] According to the CDT, all companies that conduct business online should warn users up front "what information they're collecting and what they're going to do with it."[10] The ultimate goal of this CDT project "is to create a demand for strong privacy policies and tools," explained Janlori Goldman.

In June, the CDT was mentioned as an example of a D.C.-based Internet public interest group in Kara Swisher's article.[11] The focus of her piece was, in fact, Internet-oriented trade groups that have increased in size and importance with the proliferation of the Net.

Two important events in early July provided the context for two articles concerning the CDT that month. First, at the conclusion of the FTC's two day hearing on individual online privacy, the Commission instructed industries engaging in e-business to find ways to better protect the privacy of online customers. Second, Representative Edward Markey (D-MA) introduced the "Communications Privacy and Consumer Empowerment Act" (H. R. 3685) that would force industry to develop and implement privacy tools for online consumers. It would require companies to notify web surfers that they are collecting data, whether they will be reused or resold, and offer consumers the right to opt-out of the collection scheme. In the articles that appeared in July, Hiawatha Bray and John Schwartz both alerted the public about the CDT's website (http://www.13x.com/cgi-bin/cdt/snoop.pl) which was created to correct the illusion that most people have of the web being anonymous.[12,13,14] This site is a more sophisticated version of the one described by Miller, for here one can obtain a report on the type of browser, the resolution settings of one's computer monitor, and the Internet access service being used, plus the general area of the country in which one is located.[15] Furthermore, the CDT website can even tell what the last Internet address one visited was, provided that the browser has such a function. Once visitors are done at the site, they may find an e-mail from the CDT awaiting them. Certain browsers such as Netscape 2.0 will reveal the user's e-mail address to any website designer who asks for it, and in turn, the site operator can share it with anyone of choice. Concluding his article on a personal note, Bray explained that since "there are very few tools right now, either to discover what information is being collected or to limit what information is being collected, the citizen's most valuable defense is prudence and common sense."[16] He tells the reader that he always assumes that whenever he is online, there will be a record of it somewhere, and that nothing done on the Internet is truly private. The reporter admits that it may seem a little paranoid, but he believes that "eternal vigilance is the price of liberty."[17]

The last article from 1996 concerning the CDT appeared on 21 August in the *San Francisco Chronicle*.[18] It was written in anticipation of the Senate vote in September on a bill intended to eliminate federal restrictions on encryption. Ramon McLeod enlists the expertise of Danny Weitzner amongst others (i.e., Laurie Fena, executive director of EFF; and Philip Zimmermann, developer of e-mail encryption software, Pretty Good Privacy) to describe and comment on the issues at stake, and explain the Clinton Administration's stance on encryption:

> Computer technology raises new issues and old conundrums. On the one hand, we want security, and on the other hand, we want privacy from government intrusions. Striking that balance won't be easy, but we'd better do it, and very soon. . . . The government is saying "Trust us and give us the keys, we won't use them without a good cause and a court order." But the temptation will be enormous. We're not talking about telephone tapping here. We are talking about a form of technology where you can quite easily set up a point-and-click [computer] system that get all kinds of information.[19]

1997

Only two articles from 1997 concerning the CDT were indexed in National Newspapers. The first piece was published the day after the House Judiciary Committee approved the "Security and Freedom through Encryption (SAFE) Act" (H. R. 695) which would loosen the government's control on encryption technology. In an overview of the debate over the pros and cons of encryption, Elizabeth Corcoran mentioned the CDT as one of the privacy advocates who contend that people will be able to protect personal information as better encryption products become available.[20]

A month after the House Judiciary Committee approved the SAFE Act, President Clinton announced that the government would work with the Internet industry to use existing laws and technology to help parents protect their children from objectionable material in cyberspace. While the government was increasing the number of investigators and lawyers at the DoJ who specialize in prosecuting people who transmit indecent material over the Net, industry was also doing its part. Corcoran listed the CDT's website (http://www.netparents.org)—a tool to help parents navigate a safe course for their children online—as one of the examples of what the industry had come up with. Other organizations mentioned were America Online, National Parent Teachers Association, and search engine operators such as Yahoo!, Excite, and Lycos.[21]

1998

The first article from 1998 which featured the CDT was part of the "Privacy in the Digital Age Series" that appeared in March in the *Washington Post.*[22,23] This essay examined the way consumers are fighting back against corporate invasions of their privacy. A group of privacy experts had been consulted on what the public should do to safeguard their privacy.[24] For Janlori Goldman, fighting back against privacy erosion begins with chiding sales clerks who ask for personal information: "You don't say 'hello,' you don't say, 'how are you?'—you just ask for my zip code. I don't want that kind of relationship with you. I just want to buy my shirt."[25] She also urged consumers to review their credit reports before an important transaction (i.e., check the document before credit comes into play such as when purchasing property) so that incorrect information can be emended beforehand.

On the eve of FCC's hearing on the implementation of CALEA, the *San Francisco Chronicle* published an article laying out the context of the issue and explaining what it would mean to ordinary citizens if the FBI obtained its wish of reprogramming "the computers in the

telephone system to get types of surveillance they never could before."[26] At the hearing, Attorney General Janet Reno is expected to
ask the Commission to ensure that law enforcement agents have the
technical ability to know when a person under investigation re-
ceives voice mail, and where he or she is when using a cell phone.
Tom Abate reported that a group of civil libertarians led by the CDT
would present a counter proposal asking the FCC to reject the FBI's
wiretapping wish list as an invasion of privacy. With the October implementation looming, the FCC had to weigh giving LEAs the technological tools to monitor suspected criminals against the fear they
might abuse such technique and become dangerous themselves. To
conclude his article, Abate suggested that anyone interested in
learning more about the civil libertarian and FBI views on wiretapping should consult the CDT's web page http://www.cdt. org/
digitele.

On 5 June, the *Washington Post* reported that the FTC had urged
Congress to approve a law protecting the privacy of children online
as a result of the Commission's study.[27] FTC Chairman, Robert Pitof-
sky, said he and other commissioners had requested a new law because "consumer surveys tell us that Americans have serious concerns about the way online marketers protect personal information
in general and the privacy of children's personal information in particular."[28] For the study, the FTC examined 1,400 websites and found
that only 14 percent provided notice about how they collect information, and only 2 percent had comprehensive policies that allow
consumers to choose what data can be extracted and ensure the security of the data. Eighty-nine percent of the 212 children's sites in
the survey gathered personal data from minors, but only about 50
percent of them disclosed that they collect such information, and
fewer than 1 in 10 sites sought parental input. O'Harrow solicited
the opinions of privacy advocates on this matter. EPIC praised the
FTC report, saying that legislation was long overdue. The Direct
Marketing Association opposed the proposal on the grounds that
parents do not want government intervention. The CDT was leery
that Congress might politicize the Internet.

In "Making the Web Work for You" which appeared in the "Technology Bonus Section" of *USA Today*, Leslie Miller sought suggestions from three privacy advocates on how to reduce the risk of online privacy invasions.[29] David Sobel of EPIC suggested that people
look for the website's privacy policy before registering to use serv-

ices. Also, the public should veer on the side of anonymity. He gave an example of two sites that offer the same information (news, air-fares, etc.), but one asks for personal information and the other does not. People should choose the latter in this scenario. Kathryn Mont-gomery of the Center for Media Education suggested that adults teach children that privacy is something that belongs to them, and that they should not allow others to con them into giving it away for "free" gifts or other perks. Deirdre Mulligan advocated clearing the computer's memory cache which contains details of which web-pages someone has viewed to facilitate faster web browsing. One should also be aware that privacy-enhancing tools are readily avail-able to the public such as Pretty Good Privacy, the anonymizer, and anonymous remailers.

On the same day that the FTC released a "Dirty Dozen" list of the top 12 companies that engaged in consumer fraud by way of unso-licited mail, an article in the 14 July edition of the *Wall Street Journal* discussed a proposal that was to be delivered to the FTC the same day concerning "spam" put forth by a group of technology compa-nies and consumer groups.[30] The group which consisted of the likes of Microsoft, IBM, AOL, and the CDT recommended a program of industry self-regulation to control unsolicited, commercial e-mail combined with some oversight by the FTC. Additionally, the group urged the FTC and the DoJ to clarify their legal jurisdiction over such activity by taking test cases to court; that technology compa-nies develop filtering software to help users screen their e-mail; and that commercial e-mail companies develop a self-regulatory system that allows Internet users to choose whether or not to receive com-mercial mailings. Deirdre Mulligan explained that the proposal rep-resents a "healthy consensus" on the issue and a coming of age for the Internet industry. "Rather than saying that technology alone can take care of this problem, we are acknowledging that government has a role to play as well as technology and self-regulation."[31] How-ever, the author of the article thought that the recommendations may have come too late as Congress was already considering legis-lation to outlaw spamming altogether, and several states already have devised laws against such practice.

Linda Tripp's tapes of her conversations with Monica Lewinsky, the White House intern's book purchases, and a sailor's profile on AOL in 1998 triggered questions about exactly how much personal information can the government and others obtain about citizens.

Leslie Miller of *USA Today* suggested testing one's knowledge with the CDT's new quiz on their privacy website (http://www.cd.org /privacy/quiz). She previewed several questions available on the quiz, and recommended that the public examine the CDT's other privacy resources, including its top 10 ways to protect one's online privacy, while they are at the site.[32]

Dan Gillmor's article concerning the additional power Congress had bestowed on LEAs appeared in both the *St. Louis Post-Dispatch* and the *Denver Post* on the same day.[33] The reporter seemed outraged about how a few members of Congress, pressured by the FBI and indifferent to privacy concerns, sneaked the "roving wiretap" provision into law without any debate on its merits the week of 12 October.[34] Gillmor enlisted James Dempsey's help in explaining why the law was "a genuine blow to some fundamental notions of privacy and liberty":

> The law gives law enforcement additional power to tap: your phone, your computer, and your cell phone. After President Clinton signs this bill, you won't have to be a criminal suspect anymore to be wire-tapped. You won't even have to know the suspect. If someone already under surveillance visits your home or business, any communications device there will be subject to wiretapping, too—even if the suspect doesn't intend to use it. . . . Roving wiretaps have been allowed for more than a decade, but under extremely limited circumstances. . . . The new law drastically expands what is allowable . . . by loosening standards for obtaining these taps, and by expanding the reach to include all nearby communications.[35]

According to Gillmor, "contrary to the FBI's spinmeistering, which is nearly indistinguishable from outright lying, this is a dramatic expansion of today's wiretapping law. And it shreds one of the few remaining protections under the Constitution's Fourth Amendment, which once upon a time shielded us from unreasonable searches and seizures."

On the topic of electronic eavesdropping, things seemed to be going in LEA's favor, for on 22 October, the *Wall Street Journal* announced that the FCC's proposal would allow law enforcement officers with court orders to access the content of conference calls, including information on all participants.[36] Also, an officer could obtain information about when a party places another caller on hold, joins another conversation, or drops a caller from the line. The FCC proposal would also require phone companies to make available data on callers who are transferred to a suspect's phone via a call-waiting system; information on the time and length of calls, including segments of conference calls; and information about a call's destination, even when a calling-card number or toll-free service is used. The proposed rules have met with objections by privacy advocates. John Simons quoted James Dempsey as an example: "By putting this in, the commission has destroyed the balance in the law—the balance among the interests of law enforcement and the public's privacy. On all of the issues that mattered, the commission ruled against privacy."

1999

The first article in 1999 that featured the CDT appeared in the *Times-Picayune* on 27 February.[37] The account relates the CDT-led effort in persuading the FTC to prohibit the sale of Intel Pentium III processors due to the company's "unfair and deceptive trade practices" and the ramifications from the chip's tracking feature. It was reported that the CDT's complaint also asked the Commission to ban computer manufacturers from selling machines with the chips unless the technology has been disabled. However, there was no mention of how computer makers could specifically satisfy the CDT's concerns.

The next article announced a new report from the CDT on how well federal agency websites are protecting American's online privacy which was released the same day as the article was published.[38] As a matter of fact, the report came on the heels of two events, the first being the appointment of Peter Swire, formerly a law professor at Ohio State University, as the first "chief counsel of privacy" in March, and a privacy study by AT&T Laboratories released the same week as the CDT's report.[39,40] According to the CDT study, not all federal websites practice what the administration preaches.[41] Only one-third of the websites reviewed publish a link to a "privacy notice" or privacy policy on their home page. Out of that one-third, only half of them had notices that could be found with a few clicks of the mouse. The Department of Health and Human Services, for example, had no clear policy stated. The Department of Veteran Affairs showed information on its site that it collected from visitors' cookies, which in turn, could be used to identify some visitors to the site. The CIA's site had no posted privacy policy; instead, it included a "consent to monitoring policy" that reads, "Government may monitor and audit the usage of this system, and all persons are hereby notified that use of this system constitutes consent to monitoring and auditing." However, the site did not go on to explain the kind of monitoring in which it engages. As Ari Schwartz pointed out, "posting the privacy notices just gets us to the point where the agencies say, 'Yes we agree privacy is an issue.' Next we can look at the actual content of the policies."[42]

In the aftermath of the 27 March release of the crippling Melissa e-mail virus, the 7 April hoax concerning the fictitious e-posting that PairGain Technologies had been taken over by another company, and the 29 April unleashing of another computer virus called the Chernobyl, the *Denver Post* printed an article about how Internet users leave digital footprints behind in cyberspace which others can use to trace a document back to the original sender. Bruce Meyerson quoted Ari Schwartz to explain how these digital footprints work and why the public should be concerned about this capability:

> The same technology that tracks individuals is used to solve crimes and vice versa. It's melded into one kind of surveillance technology which could lead to an erosion of privacy. . . . We could go around society with tattoos on our forehead and cameras everywhere, but most people wouldn't like that. But that's what these serial numbers do. . . . Law enforcement has a lot of tools out there to find out who these people are. We want them to find crooks. But when we make technology, do we want technology that brands individuals, that puts our serial numbers everywhere we visit? There has to be some sense of anonymity online.[43]

In the national and world business news in brief section of the 28 July edition of the *Times-Picayune,* there was a paragraph concerning the CDT's plea to Congress to pass laws to force compliance with FTC guidelines. According to Deirdre Mulligan, the lack of privacy protection on the Internet contributes to a pervasive "unease that someone's watching you."[44] This urging led Senator Conrad Burns (R-MT) to introduce the "Online Privacy Protection Act of 1999" (S. 809), a bill that would require website operators to post privacy policies on their pages and allow customers to instruct those operators not to share their personal information.

The 2000 presidential campaign is considered the first truly wired election with every candidate hosting a website. These are not only fonts of press releases, but they also act as focal points for organizing volunteers and soliciting campaign contributions. In view of this, the CDT expanded on its study on privacy policies on federal agencies' websites and examined the pages of the 11 leading presidential candidates. The criteria used were (1) whether the sites displayed some kind of privacy policy, and (2) whether those policies were easy to find. Again, the effectiveness of the policies was not evaluated. The *Washington Post* reported that the Center found that most of the presidential contenders were not giving enough prominence to privacy issues on their webpages.[45] According to Ari Schwartz, "many of the candidates have discussed the importance of privacy for the future. But their actions within their own campaign speak louder than their words." Only Vice President Al Gore and Senator John McCain (R-AR) received a grade "A." Governor George W. Bush, Elizabeth Dole, and Dan Quayle were among those who failed the Center's privacy test. Nonetheless, Marc Rotenberg of EPIC noted that he did not think "the issue is about whether candidates are posting privacy policies on their web site." He thinks the "issue is whether candidates will back legislation to protect the privacy issues of American voters."[46]

In September, the *Los Angeles Times* reported on the CDT's privacy survey from which the Center concluded that less than 10 percent of websites were abiding by the FTC's guidelines that call for disclosure of privacy policies to consumers, and about 87 percent of web users were concerned about threats to their personal privacy whilst online. Seventy-three percent of users were uneasy about giving out their credit card numbers over the web.[47]

The CDT was used to elaborate on the context of a study conducted by Robert Ellis Smith's *Privacy Journal* in a *Houston Chronicle* article published on 5 October.[48] The study was an attempt to assess which states were upholding citizens' privacy and which were not. The states were ranked with the first tier including those that offer the best privacy protection, and the fifth tier the least. The results were as follows:

- *Tier 1*: California, Connecticut, Florida, Hawaii, Illinois, Massachusetts, Minnesota, New York, Rhode Island, Wisconsin.

- *Tier 2:* Alaska, Arizona, Colorado, Georgia, Maine, Maryland, Montana, Nevada, Ohio, Oklahoma, Oregon, Utah, Virginia, Washington.
- *Tier 3:* Indiana, Michigan, New Jersey, New Mexico, Pennsylvania.
- *Tier 4:* Alabama, Arkansas, Delaware, District of Columbia, Iowa, Kansas, Kentucky, Louisiana, Mississippi, Nebraska, New Hampshire, North Carolina, South Dakota, Tennessee, Vermont, West Virginia, Wyoming.
- *Tier 5:* Idaho, Missouri, South Carolina, Texas.

The only comment the CDT made in this article was that "as public concern over privacy has risen, states are trying to address these issues in distinct and novel ways."[49]

The final article of 1999 concerning the CDT appeared in *USA Today's* news digest, "Briefly. . . ."[50] The snippet alerted readers about CDT's Operation Opt-Out page, which was created as the Doubleclick saga unfolded.

2000

As of writing, only five articles could be found in the database from this year. The context of the first article was a decision handed down by the Supreme Court on 12 January. The Justices ruled that Congress is free to prevent states from selling a driver's name, home addresses, telephone number, social security number, medical and disability information, vehicle descriptions, and registration and title information on vehicles collected by motor vehicle departments. The *Reno vs. Condon* decision turned down South Carolina's challenge to the federal Driver Privacy Protection Act of 1994 which was enacted after actress Rebecca Schaeffer was murdered by a stalker who had obtained her address from California motor vehicles records. South Carolina argued that the law was an infringement on state power, but the Supreme Court voted unanimously that the law does not require a state to take any action or to assist in its law enforcement.[51] In Richard Willing's article, James Dempsey's quote that the ruling "has significant implications," that it "removes the constitutional question about whether Congress can set privacy regulations [for] the computer world," and that the court had shown "it understands that we live in an information economy" was used to sum up the proponents' feelings. Whereas, Gregg Leslie, acting director of the Reporters Committee for Freedom of the Press, characterized the opponents' opinion: "the court wrongly supported Congress' sweeping decision to keep reporters from viewing drivers' license information even though the data could serve the public interest."[52]

Articles from February through March involving the CDT were written in the context of the uproar that Doubleclick's tracking practices created. Deirdre Mulligan was quoted for the purposes of explaining online profiling and how it affects Internet users:

> The profiling activities of advertising networks, such as Doubleclick, which currently commands approximately 60 percent of market share, are the leading edge of a growing industry built upon the widespread tracking and monitoring of individuals' online behavior. The increasingly pervasive use of surreptitious monitoring systems breeds consumer distrust and undermines consumers' efforts to protect their privacy by depriving them of control over their personal information.[53]

Articles published in the *New York Times* on 7 February and the *Washington Post* on 15 March briefly mentioned the CDT in terms of its weapon for retaliation against the online advertising giant (i.e., Operation Opt-Out campaign [http://opt-out.cdt.org]).[54,55] Other measures were mentioned in Glenn R. Simpson and Andrea Petersen's article that appeared in the *Wall Street Journal* on 1 March (i.e., warning Doubleclick's partner Kozmo.com about how titles of videos rented by its customers were being shipped to Doubleclick; and a letter to the FTC explaining why the Commission should investigate Doubleclick's practices).[56]

TELEVISION

Staff at the CDT have appeared on four television programs, and the Center was mentioned in one. Three of the physical appearances had been on *CNN The World Today* (1996, 1997, and 1999) and the other was on *CBS This Morning* (1999). The single mention of the organization was as a news headline on *CBS This Morning* (1999). Below is a description of the CDT's television appearances.

1996

The topic of *CNN The World Today* on 15 September was privacy and the Internet with Lexis-Nexis' database, P-tracks, forming the focus of discussion. P-tracks is akin to an electronic-White Pages whose content includes a person's name, present address, telephone number, month and year of birth, and up to two prior addresses.[57] This database serves Lexis-Nexis' clients who are predominantly law firms, large businesses, and the government, and will be primarily used to locate individuals such as witnesses to accidents, heirs under estates, beneficiaries, and litigants. Deirdre Mulligan had been invited to present the views of privacy advocates, and Steven Emmert, corporate counsel for Lexis-Nexis, had been invited to defend his company's product.

Kathleen Kennedy, the program's anchor, began by asking Mulligan "What is the big fuss about P-tracks?" The privacy advocate replied that while the information included in the database may not be unusual, and that the service may not be unique, Lexis-Nexis had tapped into a deep-seated public sentiment that this type of information should not be bought or sold, nor should it be so easily available. In other words, the public seemed very concerned about the ease of access to data about them. Kennedy then turned the conversation to Emmert by asking, "Isn't personal information already out there on the Internet?" To which the corporate counsel agreed and clarified that the information on Lexis-Nexis is not on the Internet, and that even though dates of birth are not included in the White Pages, only the month and year of birth appear on P-tracks. Kennedy returned to Mulligan and inquired if this centralization of data was dangerous. Mulligan explained that there is both risk to individuals from a security point of view, as well as just the inherent feeling that regardless of whether or not they are going to be physically harmed or stalked, people's privacy is being invaded. They have given up information in order to obtain a driver's license, for example, and all of a sudden, this information is being made available without their consent or knowledge to anyone willing to pay the price. That, to many, is in itself the harm, according to Mulligan. People should be able to maintain some control over sensitive data about themselves.

The program ended with a question-and-answer session with the two guests and members of the public. A caller from Virginia asked Mulligan if she was aware that most personal data are already available in courthouse records, if the CDT is at all involved in limiting the information that a citizen could obtain from a county courthouse, and if Mulligan really felt that P-tracks is more dangerous because it is readily available over a computer as opposed to taking a trip to the courthouse. Mulligan replied that she thought there was an increased concern that once information used to be available just at the local courthouse or the local Department of Motor Vehicles (DMV) office, and while there is a concern about who is going down there and accessing the information and what they might be using it for, the concern is far greater when that information is available at the touch of a button from anywhere across the country via the Internet.

1997

On the same day that the National Research Council's (NRC) report was released, Janlori Goldman, and John Glaser of Partners HealthCare Systems were invited on *CNN Today* to discuss the report's findings as well as the ramifications of medical records being increasingly computerized.[58] In Goldman's opinion, the problem of medical records privacy is extensive, and the NRC's conclusion—that medical records are vulnerable to misuse and abuse, and that the problem is very real in the United States, but yet there is no federal law or national policy to protect such information—did not differ from those of other studies that had been produced in the last 20 years.[59] When Bill Hemmer, the show's anchor, asked Goldman what evidence she had for this, she replied that with the transition to managed care, the traditional doctor-patient relationship (where people entrust sensitive information to their physician) collapsed. Insurance companies and self-insured companies, too, compounded the problem. As a result, people withhold information because they no longer feel comfortable telling their doctors everything; they may lie to their doctors; they may be afraid to submit claims; or worse, they may not even seek treatment for fear their privacy will be compromised.

Glaser pointed out that there are, nonetheless, advantages in using information technology to improve the quality of healthcare such as centralizing data and assisting in diagnoses and treatments, etc. Having said that, he agreed with Goldman that technology does, indeed, raise some issues, one being that while there is a variety of technical mechanisms that one can use to improve the security of computerized records, they are not uniformly adopted amongst healthcare providers of payer organizations. Therefore, this avenue needs to be more aggressively pursued. Second, there is also a variety of organization mechanisms that ensure people are educated about confidentiality, informed consent, etc., that have not been rigorously employed.

In the last 30 seconds of the program, Goldman was asked to describe what she would like to see Congress do in terms of medical records privacy protection. She said:

> What would make me very happy is if Congress acts to pass a law that gives people the right to see their own medical records, a right to control who can see them, strong enforcement mechanisms, and remedies. Senator Leahy, Senator Jeffords, and members of the House have been very interested in passing this legislation and we need everyone to come together.

1999

On 20 August, the *Washington Post* reported that the DoJ would ask Congress to approve secret searches of personal computers of crime suspects and that the Justice Department was looking into technological means to unscramble encrypted computer files. James Dempsey was invited on *CNN Today* to discuss this development.[60] When asked what he thought about this, he said:

> Well, we think this is a pretty outrageous proposal. What had been, up until now, a somewhat esoteric debate about scrambling technology and encryption and export controls has now really come down to a question of the sanctity of the home. The Justice Department is going to ask Congress for authority to secretly break into people's homes with a court order, but without any knowledge of the homeowner to search their computers for passwords and encryption keys so that the government at some future point can read any information on that computer.

Natalie Allen, the anchor, pointed out that the government has justified the proposal by saying that these would be suspects only and that it would help them solve child pornography, drug trafficking, terrorism, and other crimes. Dempsey agreed that these wrongdoings deserve a serious and concerted federal law enforcement effort. Nevertheless, he still objected to the notion that the government has to break into one's house secretly to seize evidence of crime:

> We believe that the traditional constitutional principles are adequate for cyberspace. If the government has a court order, they come, they knock on your door, if you don't answer, they can break the door down, but they have to serve that order to you, give you notice, so that you know what is being done to you.

When asked how he thought the proposal would be received by Congress, Dempsey predicted that it would face considerable opposition. He worried "about the ability of the Justice Department to exploit some tragic accident, a terrorist attack or some other crisis, and try to jam this through."

In the wake of the publication of a study sponsored by several online firms that found an increasing number of websites now warn customers how private information they provide online will be used, and the fact that Congress was examining a number of Internet privacy laws, Deirdre Mulligan was invited on *CBS This Morning* to discuss Internet privacy laws.[61] In Mulligan's opinion, while privacy policies are a start, more needs to be done to protect online privacy:

> both the industry through a number of very laudatory, self-regulatory efforts and the Federal Trade Commission and the administration, have kind of set out a gold standard. And they've said, "We need you to tell consumers these things, and we need those policies to actually give consumers real control over their data." And there have to be real resolution mechanisms and real redress for consumers that get harmed.

When asked what kind of recommendations she would like to see the FTC make to Congress, Mulligan said that policy makers, both in the White House and up on the Hill, need to take a more active role to develop some legal framework in which we can really ensure that privacy is protected all across the web, and not just in the safe zones.

The final television appearance of the CDT was on 28 July. It was not an in-person interview like the ones above, but the CDT was mentioned as a news item on *CBS This Morning's Business News and*

Stock Report.[62] Thalia Assuras, the program's cohost, reported that the Center was calling on Congress to pass regulations to protect online privacy of individuals. The organization argued that few website operators were abiding by federal guidelines to protect personal information of online users. Some lawmakers rebutted that it was too early to place such regulations on the still-developing Internet industry.

RADIO

The CDT had been mentioned on six radio programs between 1995 and 2000. Five out of the six times had been on National Public Radio's (NPR) *All Things Considered* where the CDT staff had been quoted in news items.[63] One out of six had been on NPR's *Talk of the Nation*. This was the only occurrence of a solo-interview-cum-question-and-answer session with the CDT as opposed to stories in the news. Below is a description of these radio programs.

1999

In the 18 February edition of the *Washington Post,* a story appeared about how the Secret Service provided $1.5 million toward the development of a system that uses driver license photos to prevent fraud.[64] Image Data, based in Nashua, NH, bought the rights to use state drivers' license photos as part of this pilot program to prevent fraud. Members can check the identity of people cashing checks by calling up an e-driver's license photo on a small computer screen. South Carolina was being used as a test bed for the rest of the nation to see if this national database would succeed in fraud prevention, and possibly in the collection of other data in which the Secret Service may be interested. The revelation outraged state officials who claimed they were not informed about the federal funding when they agreed to provide the pictures. Thus, South Carolina and Colorado officials were fighting to revoke Image Data's contract; and Florida's deal was put on hold.

Deirdre Mulligan was asked to comment on the situation on NPR's *All Things Considered.*[65] She said that the government should have learned its lesson from the routine abuse of Social Security Numbers (e.g., federal banking authorities' "Know Your Customer" program, which called for banks to monitor the habits of customers in an effort to uncover money laundering, and its support of including Social Security Numbers on every driver's license):

> That if you put something out there and there are no limits on how it's used, we find out that it gets used in every system that can possibly capture it, and that, in fact, it becomes one of the key tools of people who want to engage in fraud.

On the eve of the House vote on H. R. 10, a bill that would overhaul the nation's banking laws, NPR ran a story on the bill and its ramifications on bank consumer privacy.[66] The banking reform bill aimed to modernize the U.S. banking industry by allowing financial institutions to offer new services, including the sale of securities and insurance. The issue at hand is that as banks are allowed to move into new businesses, they will be able to develop massive consumer databases which could be used to invade consumers' privacy. Mulligan was asked to comment on the bill, about which she said that up until then, there had been a wall of regulation between the insurance, securities and banking industries, and that wall helped slow the exchange of information about consumers.

Privacy groups thought they had won some limited protections. In June, one House committee approved language that said banks had to give consumers a choice about whether their information could be moved to a third party. That language would also have stopped a bank from sharing information with its own subsidiary. However, the banking industry argued that these kinds of restrictions could defeat the whole point of the bill. As Ed Yingling of the American Bankers Association said:

> You couldn't have your checks printed because they couldn't give your account number to the check printer to get the check printed. You couldn't have a credit card that gives you mileage or something like that, because they cannot communicate back and forth between the airline and the credit card company to share that information. Or you couldn't look across a consumer's account and say, "My goodness, something funny's going on there. I bet somebody's stolen their credit card."

The banking industry was willing to let consumers stop banks from selling information to other companies, but they insisted that they have to be able to move information to their own subsidiaries. Whichever bill passes in the House, it is likely to include some privacy language, but privacy groups think the ultimate impact of these provisions is unclear because they presume that the industry can sell information unless consumers say no. Mulligan said that that confuses consumers and gives banks the upper hand:

> Because if an institution wants you to say yes, they're going to make it easy. If they're giving you the opportunity to say no, there's probably less of an incentive for them to make it really easy for you to do so.

2000

Deirdre Mulligan appeared as a guest on *Talk of the Nation* on 10 January in an hour-long discussion on consumer privacy with a focus on how the public deals with unwanted calls, direct mail, spam, and so forth.[67] Most of this program consisted of callers describing their personal strategies, but Mike Shuster, the host, specifically asked Mulligan, as the privacy expert, what one can do to stop or limit telemarketers. Mulligan suggested registering for the Direct Marketing Association's "Phone Preference Service" and noted that there are states that have implemented their own laws. She also explained that if you asked the telemarketer not to call again and he or she does, you have the right to sue the company. If you are providing information, ask why it is needed, what they are going to do with it, if they are going to give it to third parties, if they will sell it, and ask them not to do any of that with your information. Should a commercial caller not identify him-/herself and announce that it is a sales call, you can report the incident to the state attorney general, Consumer Protection Division, or a Bureau of Consumer Affairs.

On 12 January, *All Things Considered* reported on the Supreme Court ruling that upheld a federal ban on states selling personal information from drivers' licenses.[68] James Dempsey was asked to comment on the decision for the program:

> The Supreme Court held that personally identifying information is a thing, an interstate commerce, that can be regulated by Congress like any other commodity. And this is going to have very important implications for other ongoing privacy debates over medical records privacy, financial privacy, and e-commerce.

In anticipation of the Clinton Administration reducing export restrictions on encryption software, Alan Davidson was asked to speak on behalf of privacy advocates who have long opposed American encryption policy on the basis that it was ineffective:

> The good news is that consumers all over the world are going to have access to, really, the strongest encryption built into products that they use every day—web browsers, e-mail programs, popular encryption programs. . . . The bad news is that if you want to send encryption outside of the United States, you're still gonna need to hire a lawyer to do it [because products being shipped to other governments still face administration review].[69]

In December 1999, Northwest Airlines canceled more than 300 flights, claiming its Teamster flight attendants had staged a sick-out which grounded the planes. Northwest sued the following February, alleging that two employees had instigated the job action because both personnel hosted personal websites which contained message boards for coworkers. Anonymous postings on the site called for a sick-out which is illegal under federal labor laws. The airline wanted to find out who had sent the messages. The two employees reproduced documents related to the lawsuit as requested, but Northwest was still not satisfied, insisting that more incriminating evidence existed. That was when they sought an order to seize the relevant computers, and a judge ordered the two employees to turn over their personal computers to a supposedly neutral third-party, Ernst & Young, who are accountants for the airline. Dempsey believed that the case went awry when the computers were seized. As he said on *Morning Edition:*

> We have offline rules for resolving these kinds of discovery disputes. They do not involve rummaging through a person's entire life just because they're involved in a lawsuit.[70]

On 2 March, *All Things Considered* reported that Doubleclick had decided to postpone its plan to link Internet users' surfing habits with their names and addresses.[71] The practice had come under attack from privacy advocates including the CDT who claimed that the system deceived consumers because "when people go to sites that used Doubleclick advertising, they do not know that they're handing information over to Doubleclick."[72] Reporter Larry Abramson believed that "this victory is likely to embolden the privacy groups that took Doubleclick on in the first place because these groups have been urging regulators to apply existing privacy laws more aggressively." Industry had warned that if the government stepped in, it could stifle e-commerce, especially since advertising is paying for many of the free sites on the Internet. However, Ari Schwartz argued that consumers can get targeted ads without giving up their privacy:

> Personalization is one of the great things that has been happening on the web and in the Internet revolution. Things that are being personalized towards—for individuals, that should continue. The question is just whether it is tied back to personally identifiable information.

Conclusion

In addressing RQ 2, "How has the CDT been perceived by the American public as reflected in the mass media?", the media tends to see the CDT in four different capacities. First, they view the Center as an authority so as to provide commentary and explanations on various privacy issues. For example, James Dempsey commenting on the Supreme Court's decision in upholding the federal ban on states selling personal information from DMVs on *All Things Considered: Supreme Court Ruling;* on FCC's proposal to allow LEAs with court orders to access contents of and other information about telephone calls in Simons, "FCC Wants Wireless Companies"; and the *Reno vs. Condon* decision in Willing, "High Court Protects Drivers' License Data." Second, the media regards the CDT as an educator on privacy issues as seen in Deirdre Mulligan's explanations on Internet privacy laws (*CBS This Morning: Deirdre Mulligan*), and the privacy ramifications of databases such as P-tracks (*CNN The World Today: Advocates Warn of Dangers*). Third, the media considers the Center as a leader in promoting privacy awareness via projects such as its privacy website www.13x.com/cgi-bin/cdt/snoop.pl (Bray, "They Know Who You Are," and Schwartz, "Cybercookies Eat Away"); its privacy quiz (Miller, "Just Between You and Me"); and its examination of privacy policies on websites of online services ("On-line Companies' Policies"), presidential candidates (Schwartz," "Privacy Loses in Web Bids"), and federal agencies

(Schwartz, "Privacy Policy vs. Practice"). Last, the media perceives the CDT as a defender of the public's right to privacy as seen in CDT's complaint to the FCC about Intel's Pentium III chip ("Group Objects to New Pentium Chip"), its plea to Congress to pass laws to force compliance with FTC guidelines ("Bottom Line—National and World Business News"), its fight against online profiling (Oldenburg, "Consummate Consumer"; Simpson and Petersen, "Alta Vista, Kozmo Distance Themselves"; and Tedeschi, "Critics Press Legal Assault").

In the next chapter, the focus will shift to the funders' perceptions on the CDT in terms of its work on Internet privacy, as opposed to the public's perceptions on the organization as was examined in this chapter.

NOTES

1. So that the positions of the CDT staff do not have to be given throughout the chapter, the following is a list of the staff mentioned in the articles along with their titles: James Dempsey (Senior Staff Counsel), Janlori Goldman (Deputy Director, 1995–1997), Deirdre Mulligan (Staff Counsel), Ari Schwartz (Policy Analyst), and Danny Weitzner (Deputy Director, 1997–1998).
2. Dinah Zeiger, "Internet Watchers Split Over Policies," *Denver Post,* 22 January 1995, H.05.
3. Zeiger, "Internet Watchers Split Over Policies."
4. Zeiger, "Internet Watchers Split Over Policies."
5. Leslie Miller, "On the Internet, Virtually No Privacy," *USA Today,* 30 May 1996, 06 D.
6. Janlori Goldman, quoted in Miller, "On the Internet."
7. Janlori Goldman, quoted in Miller, "On the Internet."
8. Janlori Goldman, quoted in Miller, "On the Internet."
9. "On-line Companies' Policies," *USA Today,* 30 May 1996, 06 D.
10. Janlori Goldman, quoted in "On-line Companies' Policies."
11. Kara Swisher, "As Internet Grows, So Do Interests of Trade Groups," *Washington Post,* 17 June 1996, F12.
12. Hiawatha Bray, "They Know Who You Are: Surfing the Internet Reveals a Lot More than One Might Want—Including E-Mail," *Boston Globe,* 4 July 1996, 32.
13. John Schwartz, "Cybercookies Eat Away at Privacy/Software for Web Strips Anonymity," *Houston Chronicle,* 7 July 1996, 5. It should be noted that originally this article appeared in Washington Post, 24 June 1996, F19.
14. Janlori Goldman, quoted in Schwartz, "Cybercookies."
15. Miller, "On the Internet."
16. Deirdre Mulligan, quoted in Bray, "They Know Who You Are."
17. Bray, "They Know Who You Are."

18. Ramon G. McLeod, "Computer Privacy Could Be Casualty of War on Terrorism/Government Wants Keys to Codes," *San Francisco Chronicle,* 21 August 1996, A5.

19. Danny Weitzner, quoted in McLeod, "Computer Privacy."

20. Elizabeth Corcoran, "House Committee Approves Bill to Relax Curbs on Encryption," *Washington Post,* 15 May 1997, E01.

21. Elizabeth Corcoran, "Clinton Vows to Work on Web Smut Safeguards," *Washington Post,* 17 July 1997, C03.

22. The series included an essay on new data warehouses that have an unprecedented ability to compile personal facts about ordinary people for marketers and others; and the debate on the proper use of electronic versions of public government records that have become an increasingly valuable source of information for businesses.

23. John Schwartz and Robert O'Harrow, "Databases Start to Fuel Consumer Ire: Series: Eye at the Keyhole: Privacy in the Digital Age Series Number 3/3," *Washington Post,* 10 March 1998, A1.

24. The experts included Don Goldhammer, a computer network administrator at the University of Chicago; Leonard P. Levine, a computer science professor at the University of Wisconsin-Milwaukee; Harold Burzstajn, a psychiatrist at Harvard University; Lance Cottrell, president of Anonymizer, Inc.; Robert Ellis Smith, publisher of *Privacy Times;* Richard Sobel, a researcher at Harvard University Law School; and Marc Rotenberg, director of EPIC.

25. Schwartz and O'Harrow, "Databases Start to Fuel Consumer Ire."

26. James X. Dempsey, quoted in Tom Abate, "Showdown Over New Wiretaps," *San Francisco Chronicle,* 26 March 1998, E3.

27. Robert O'Harrow, "FTC Urges Online Privacy Law for Minors," *Washington Post,* 5 June 1998, D02.

28. O'Harrow, "FTC Urges Online Privacy Law."

29. Leslie Miller, "For Now Privacy Protection is Up to You," *USA Today,* 16 June 1998, 11E.

30. John Simons, "Various Firms, Groups to Offer Ways to Curb Unsolicited E-Mail on Internet," *Wall Street Journal,* 14 July 1998, B6.

31. Simons, "Various Firms, Groups to Offer Ways."

32. Leslie Miller, "Just Between You and Me, Someone Could Be Listening," *USA Today,* 19 August 1998, 05D.

33. Dan Gillmor, "New Wiretap Law 'Attacks' Civil Liberties," *Denver Post,* 19 October 1998, E-09; "Sneak Attack on Liberty Means You Now Can Be Wiretapped," *St Louis Post-Dispatch,* 19 October 1998, 14.

34. The House and the Senate separately passed "intelligence authorization" legislation which is a routine annual bill detailing Congress' expectations for various intelligence services including the Central Intelligence Agency (CIA), National Security Agency (NSA), etc., for the coming year. Differences between the two bills led to a conference committee in which members of both houses reconciled their differences, returned the amended bill to both chambers for a final vote before going to the president. In this case, members of the conference committee added something that had not been in either versions of the bill: the roving wiretap provision. The provision was not in the original bills because neither the House nor the Senate cared for the provision on

its own. Therefore, when the legislation went back to the floors of the House and Senate, it was no longer subject to amendment, according to Congressional rules. The full bodies had to either pass the entire bill or reject it altogether. Both houses chose to pass the bill.

35. Gillmor, "New Wiretap Law."

36. John Simons, "FCC Wants Wireless Companies to Modify Networks to Help Police Tap Internet," *Wall Street Journal,* 23 October 1998, A16.

37. "Group Objects to New Pentium Chip: Complaint to FTC Cites Privacy Fears," *Times-Picayune,* 27 February 1999, 3C.

38. John Schwartz, "Privacy Policy vs. Practice: Group Finds Contrast in Agency Web Sites," *Washington Post,* 16 April 1999, A27.

39. During the week of 5 April 1999, Peter Swire addressed the annual Computers, Freedom, and Privacy Conference and pledged to use the power of the Office of Management and Budget (OMB) to push federal agencies across the board to strengthen their privacy policies. The CDT sent its report to Swire with a request that he make good on his promise and work to bring all federal websites into compliance with such standards as the Platform for Privacy Preferences (a set of technical guidelines for privacy protection being developed by the World Wide Web Consortium) ("Briefly. . . Privacy Opt-Out," *USA Today,* 17 November 1999, 07D; and Schwartz, "Privacy Policy vs. Practice").

40. The AT&T study revealed that people are reluctant to provide personal and financial information online. When asked to reveal personal information in return for obtaining brochures about their interests, 28 percent of those surveyed said they would be more likely to provide it if the site had a privacy policy. Forty-eight percent said they would be more likely to provide it if privacy laws prevented the site from using the information for any purpose other than processing the request (Schwartz, "Privacy Policy vs. Practice").

41. It must be noted that the CDT survey looked only at the presence of a policy, but did not explore deeper questions of whether those policies are effective in protecting privacy (Schwartz, "Privacy Policy vs. Practice").

42. Schwartz, "Privacy Policy vs. Practice."

43. Bruce Meyerson, "Hackers Leave Web Trail: 'Net Footprints Aid Virus Sleuths," *Denver Post,* 1 May 1999, C–03.

44. "Bottom Line: National and World Business News: Internet Privacy Urge in Study," *Times-Picayune,* 28 July 1999, C3.

45. John Schwartz, "Privacy Loses in Web Bids: Many Campaign Sites Fail to Disclose Privacy," *Washington Post,* 2 September 1999, A37.

46. Schwartz, "Privacy Loses in Web Bids."

47. "Study Looks at Online Privacy," *Los Angeles Times,* 19 September 1999, 9.

48. David L. Wilson, "State Takes Lead in Privacy Protection/California at Top, Texas at Bottom of List," *Houston Chronicle,* 5 October 1999, 2.

49. Deirdre Mulligan, quoted in Wilson, "State Takes Lead."

50. "Briefly. . . Privacy Opt-Out," *USA Today,* 17 November 1999, 07D.

51. It is interesting to note that this decision, based on the Constitution's interstate commerce clause, runs counter to recent rulings restricting Congress' power over states.

52. Richard Willing, "High Court Protects Drivers' License Data—Ruling Could Affect Online Privacy," *USA Today,* 13 January 2000, 01A.

53. "Companies Make Big Bucks Profiling Browsers," *Detroit News*, 17 February 2000, C3.

54. Bob Tedeschi, "Critics Press Legal Assault on Tracking of Web Users," *New York Times*, 7 February 2000, C1.

55. Don Oldenburg, "Consummate Consumer: The Online Opt-Out Option," *Washington Post*, 1 March 2000, C04.

56. Glenn R. Simpson and Andrea Petersen, "Alta Vista, Kozmo Distance Themselves from Doubleclick Over Privacy Worries," *Wall Street Journal*, 1 March 2000, A3.

57. CNN, *The World Today: Advocates Warn of Dangers of Internet Data*, 19 September 1996, available from Lexis-Nexis (26 March 2000).

58. CNN, *CNN Today: The Computerization of Medical Records Breed Questions of Privacy*, 5 March 1997, available from Lexis-Nexis (26 March 2000).

59. As Janlori Goldman said on *CNN Today: The Computerization of Medical Records:*

People are vulnerable for a variety of reasons. They are vulnerable because they can be discriminated against in the workplace even though there is a law that prevents it. There is no law that prevents an employer from seeing your medical record. People are denied insurance time and again. People see their medical records and they can be embarrassed. There can be stigma attached. And people have lost control and are continuing to lose control over the most personal sensitive information about them.

60. CNN, *CNN Today: Dempsey: "The Traditional Constitutional Principles are Adequate for Cyberspace,"* 20 August 1999, available from Lexis-Nexis (26 March 2000).

61. CBS, *CBS This Morning: Deirdre Mulligan, Center for Democracy and Technology, Discusses Internet Privacy Laws*, 13 May 1999, available from Lexis-Nexis (26 March 2000).

62. CBS, *CBS This Morning: Business News and Stock Report*, 28 July 1999, available from Lexis-Nexis (26 March 2000).

63. In addition to Deirdre Mulligan and James Dempsey, Alan Davidson, CDT staff counsel, can also be heard on radio programs.

64. Robert O'Harrow and Liz Heyden, "U.S. Helped Fund Photo Database of Driver IDs: Firm's Plan Seen as Way to Fight Identity Crimes," *Washington Post*, 18 February 1999, A01.

65. NPR, *All Things Considered: Hour 2: Several States Angered Over Funding Given by the Federal Government to a Private Company Using Driver's License Photos for Fraud Protection*, 18 February 1999, available from Lexis-Nexis (26 March 2000).

66. NPR, *All Things Considered: Privacy Groups Struggling to Make Sure New Banking Reform Bill Includes Privacy Protections for Bank Consumers*, 30 June 1999, available from Lexis-Nexis (26 March 2000).

67. NPR, *Talk of the Nation: How to Deal with Telemarketers and Unwanted Direct Mail and E-mail*, 10 January 2000, available from Lexis-Nexis (26 March 2000).

68. NPR, *All Things Considered: Supreme Court Ruling that Forbids States to Disclose Information on People's Drivers Licenses*, 12 January 2000, available from Lexis-Nexis (26 March 2000).

69. NPR, *Morning Edition: Clinton Administration Reduces Barriers to Exporting Encryption Software*, 13 January 2000, available from Lexis-Nexis (26 March 2000).

70. NPR, *Morning Edition: Lawsuit Brought by Northwest Airlines Against Several of Its Employees Now Raising Concerns Over Privacy Issues*, 24 February 2000, available from Lexis-Nexis (26 March 2000).

71. NPR, *All Things Considered: Online Advertising Company Doubleclick Pulls Back from Its Plans to Link Names and Addresses to the Surfing Habits of People Who Visit Web Sites*, 2 March 2000, available from Lexis-Nexis (26 March 2000).

72. Ari Schwartz, quoted in NPR, *All Things Considered: Online Advertising Company.*

7

Funders' Perceptions of the Center for Democracy and Technology

CHARACTERISTICS OF RESPONDENTS

Fifty-nine organizations had been listed as funders of the CDT in the Center's annual reports from 1996 to 2000.[1] These funders can be classified into nine categories according to their line of work: (1) coalitions and trade associations (30.5 percent); (2) foundations (15.1 percent); (3) communications companies (11.9 percent); (4) network/Internet service providers (11.9 percent); (5) software manufacturers (10.2 percent); (6) financial institutions (8.5 percent); (7) computer manufacturers (5.1 percent); (8) the entertainment industry (5.1 percent); and (9) marketing firms (1.7 percent). Of those 19 funders who responded, 42.1 percent were coalitions/trade associations, 21.1 percent were communications companies, 15.8 percent were financial institutions, 15.8 percent were software manufacturers, and 5.3 percent were foundations.[2]

This chapter will provide an examination of the funders' responses to each question of the questionnaire.

Response to Question 1: "In your estimate, how much impact has the Center for Democracy and Technology (CDT) had on the following legislation?"[3]

The majority of funders (68.4 percent) replied don't know to the Antislamming Amendments Act. The next most frequent response was split between little or no impact and some or much impact at nearly 16 percent each.

Two laws that do not deal with online privacy per se had been included in the questionnaire because it was thought that the funders would associate the CDT more with these legislations. One such is the Child Online Protection Act (COPA). It is significant that respondents unanimously indicated that they thought the CDT had some or much impact on this particular legislation. This is not surprising as COPA evolved from the Communications Decency Act (CDA) which is considered one of CDT's achievements, if not the most significant.

In the case of the Communications Assistance for Law Enforcement Act (CALEA), two-thirds of the funders answered some or much impact (68.4 percent). The next highest response was don't know at nearly 27 percent. Almost 6 percent thought the CDT had little or no impact in this area. It is worthy of note that those who perceived the CDT to have the least influence on this legislation were predominantly trade associations. Since the focus of CALEA is outside their areas of concern, it is not surprising that they answered the way they did.

No funder thought the CDT had little or no impact on the Security and Freedom through Encryption (SAFE) Act. A sizeable majority (84.2 percent) thought the CDT had some or much impact on the Act. Of the remaining respondents who answered don't know (15.8 percent), it is somewhat surprising that one of them, although an association, nevertheless deals with financial matters: presumably a funder associated with the financial world would be familiar with SAFE since online banking uses encryption.

The Telecommunications Competition and Consumer Protection Act was the second strictly nononline privacy legislation included in the questionnaire. Clearly, the respondents were less familiar with this legislation: a little more than half answered don't know (52.6 percent). Slightly over one-third thought the CDT had some or much impact (36.8 percent), and one-tenth answered little or no impact

(10.5 percent). It had been anticipated that all funders would choose some or much impact for this legislation, but it did not happen most likely because the respondents did not realize that the CDA is a part of the Telecommunications Competition and Consumer Protection Act. Had the legislation been rephrased as Telecommunications Competition and Consumer Protection Act (which includes the Communications Decency Act) or simply, Communications Decency Act, in the questionnaire, the answers may well have been similar to that of COPA since CDA and COPA are very similar in intent.

Just as with the telecommunications legislations above (i.e., Anti-slamming Amendments Act and Telecommunications Competition and Consumer Protection Act), a high number of respondents (57.9 percent) did not know of the Wireless Communications and Public Safety Act.[4] A little over one-third selected some or much impact, and just 5 percent answered little or no impact. When the telecommunications-related legislations are examined as a group, a pattern emerged: most of the funders who selected don't know tended to have done so for all three Acts. Also, it is interesting to note that funders who lacked knowledge in the CDT's impact on these legislations are financial institutions, associations, and computer-related companies.

Three funders offered legislations not covered in the questionnaire in the *Other* category. One funder wrote that the CDT had much impact on COPA and the CDA. COPA had featured in the questionnaire, but for unknown reasons the funder listed it again and chose a different level of impact for this legislation. As for the CDA, it was, in fact, listed in Question 1, but under the legislation's formal title: Telecommunications Competition and Consumer Protection Act. The second funder replied that the CDT had much impact on "cybersecurity and privacy bills," but did not provide specific legislations as examples. The third respondent thought that the Center had some impact on "broadband access legislation" which was not included in the questionnaire due to its irrelevance to the survey's topic of online privacy.

Response to Question 2: "In your estimate, how much impact has the CDT had with the following projects?"

For the *Digital Democracy Project*, approximately the same percentage of respondents indicated some or much impact as don't

Table 7.1 Perceptions of the Impact of CDT on Legislative Acts

	Antislamming Amendments Act	Child Online Protection Act (COPA)	Communications Assistance for Law Enforcement Act (CALEA)	Security and Freedom through Encryption (SAFE) Act	Telecommunications Competition and Consumer Protection Act	Wireless Communication and Public Safety Act
Much impact	0%	53%	79%	63%	33%	38%
Some impact	50%	47%	14%	38%	44%	50%
Little impact	50%	0%	7%	0%	22%	13%
No impact	0%	0%	0%	0%	0%	0%
TOTAL	100%	100%	100%	101%	99%	101%
N ratings of impact	6	19	14	16	9	8
Number of "don't know" responses	13	0	5	3	10	11

Table 7.2 Perceptions of the Impact of CDT on Other Legislative Acts Not Listed in Questionnaire

Other Legislative Acts Suggested by Funders	Level of Impact
COPA and CDA	Much impact
Cybersecurity and privacy bills	Much impact
Broadband access legislation	Some impact

know at nearly 48 percent each, whereas only about 5 percent thought the CDT had little or no impact with this project. No relationship could be determined between the line of work to which the funder belongs and which of the two groups of impact it chose. For example, funders from the communications industry whom one would assume to have better knowledge of this project than, say, financial institutions, did not tend to indicate some or much impact, nor did noncommunications funders tend to respond that they didn't know for this question.

Regarding CDT's involvement in *Doubleclick,* about 10 percent of the funders chose little or no impact. Slightly over 50 percent thought the CDT had some or much impact, while a little over one-third did not know about this project. These results seem to support the view that *Doubleclick* was one of the CDT's major results in the area of Internet privacy.

In terms of *GetNetWise*, again, the majority of funders (nearly 58 percent) thought the Center had some or much impact. A little less than one-third (31.6 percent) answered don't know, and only 10 percent chose little or no impact. These percentages were expected since funders who chose some or much impact are also the CDT's partners in *GetNetWise*. Conversely, those who chose the other levels of impact are not associated with the project.

Most funders answered don't know (nearly 48 percent) for *Get-PrivacyWise*, followed by some or much impact (nearly 37 percent), and little or no impact (nearly 16 percent). The percentage for don't know seems to be in line with the fact that *GetPrivacyWise* caters to the individual Internet user, thus, organizations were not expected to be all that familiar with this project.

As for the *Privacy Watchdog Campaign*, the majority of funders selected don't know (52.6 percent), followed by little or no impact (26.3 percent), and some or much impact (21.1 percent). Like *GetPrivacyWise*, the *Privacy Watchdog Campaign* is geared toward individuals rather than organizations. Therefore, the high percentage of funders selecting don't know was expected.

For the *Other* category, one funder wrote that the CDT had "some impact" on "Platform for Privacy Preferences" (P3P).[6]

Response to Question 3: "In your estimate, how effective has the CDT been in the pursuit of the following?"[7]

Over three-quarters of the funders thought that the CDT had been effective or very effective in *Raising privacy awareness*, followed by not effective or somewhat effective (nearly 16 percent), and don't know (about 5 percent).

When it came to *Conceptualizing privacy policies*, over two-thirds of the respondents considered the CDT to have been effective or very effective, with the rest selecting not effective or somewhat effective (31.6 percent). It is significant that no funder chose don't know for this pursuit. The data indicate that all funders were aware of this component of the CDT's mission. In other words, the CDT has made some sort of an impact on its funders with this pursuit.

Table 7.3 Perceptions of the Impact of CDT with Projects

	Digital Democracy Project	"Doubleclick"/ anti-online profiling campaign	GetNetWise	GetPrivacyWise	Privacy Watchdog Campaign
Much impact	20%	33%	46%	10%	11%
Some impact	70%	50%	39%	60%	33%
Little impact	10%	8%	15%	30%	56%
No impact	0%	8%	0%	0%	0%
TOTAL	100%	99%	100%	100%	100%
N ratings of impact	10	12	13	10	9
Number of "don't know" responses	9	7	6	9	10

Table 7.4 Perceptions of the Impact of CDT with Projects Not Listed in Questionnaire

Project	Level of Impact
Platform for Privacy Preferences (P3P)	Some impact

Regarding the CDT's effectiveness in *Educating the public in privacy issues,* about 47 percent thought the Center had not been effective or somewhat effective, and about 41 percent considered the organization to have been effective or very effective. Nearly 11 percent responded don't know for this question.

As for *Developing privacy policies,* the majority (52.6 percent) answered not effective or somewhat effective, followed by effective or very effective (42.1 percent). A small minority (5.3 percent) selected don't know. Evidently, the funders thought the CDT was somewhat better at conceiving privacy policies rather than bringing them to fruition. On the one hand, this is slightly surprising considering that "developing" and "conceptualizing" policies both feature in the CDT's mission statement and that presumably the two activities go hand in hand:

Our mission is to conceptualize, develop, and implement public policies to preserve and enhance free expression, privacy, open access, and
other democratic values in the new and increasingly integrated communication medium [i.e., the Internet].

On the other hand, it is understandable that the funders deemed
the CDT to be less effective in developing policies for a couple of
reasons. First, from examining various documents pertaining to the
CDT, it seems that the Center works with, upon request, any member of Congress interested in privacy legislation, but the organization does not appear to submit unsolicited and fully developed privacy policies to legislators in hope that Congress would adopt them.
Therefore, the legislature is ultimately in the driver's seat for developing privacy policies and the CDT is available to educate, recommend, and support such bills. Second, even if the CDT did submit
unsolicited privacy policies that it had drawn up, it would be rather
difficult for a funder to know about the Center's involvement in developing such things unless the funder has worked alongside the
CDT in this activity.

In *Developing privacy-enhancing tools*, most funders considered the
CDT to have been effective or very effective (47.4 percent), followed
by an equal percentage who responded either don't know or not effective or somewhat effective (26.3 percent each). The comparatively
high figure for effective or very effective was somewhat unexpected
considering that funders who would know the most about this (i.e.,
software manufacturers) constitute a mere 15.8 percent of the total
respondents to this questionnaire. Funders who answered not effective or somewhat effective were consistent with the assumption that
noncomputer-related organizations would perceive the CDT to be
less effective in developing privacy-enhancing tools than computer-
related funders. Even though the funders who indicated don't know
were mostly software makers or communications companies, and
therefore, assumed to be knowledgeable in the development of privacy-enhancing tools, these particular software companies do not
create products for Internet usage (e.g., browsers), and the communications companies may not support total privacy since they are ac-
countable to other customers as well as LEAs. For example, if a
client complains of fraudulent e-mail advertisements, privacy-enhancing tools might hamper communications companies' and LEA's

investigations into who is responsible for such crime. It should also be noted that developing privacy-enhancing tools solicited the highest percentage of don't know answers out of all the pursuits in Question 3. When considered in conjunction with the press coverage on the CDT, it does not come as a surprise since the newspaper articles examined in Chapter 6 did not discuss the Center's role in developing privacy-enhancing tools in any way.

A minority of funders (21.1 percent) was of the opinion that the CDT had not been effective or only somewhat effective in *Monitoring the implementation of privacy laws;* even fewer answered don't know (10.5 percent). Most respondents (57.4 percent) considered the Center to have been effective or very effective in this area.

Five funders offered *Other* comments for Question 3. One wrote that the CDT had been very effective in "drawing together key representatives of high-tech industries, government and nonprofit, public interest community for meaningful dialogues on a wide range of contentious public policy issues." Another remarked that the Center had been very effective in providing "balanced comments to the press on privacy issues." The third funder thought that the CDT had been very effective in "First Amendment issues" and that "they have one of the best websites in town for the federal issues they cover." The fourth funder commented that the Center had been very effective in the "cryptography issue." The last was of the opinion that the Center had been very effective in "inside the beltway advocacy."

CONCLUSION

By calculating the total percentages for the three groups of impact (i.e., (1) no or little impact; (2) some or much impact; and (3) don't know) it seems that most funders (57 percent) perceived the CDT to have had some or much impact on all six privacy legislations listed in Question 1. The category with the next highest percentage was don't know (36.8 percent), followed by little or no impact (6.1 percent).

In terms of the CDT's impact with its own projects and activities, the funders were equally divided between don't know and some or much impact (43.2 percent each). As for the pursuits set forth in the CDT's mission (i.e., raising privacy awareness, conceptualizing pri-

Table 7.5 Perceptions of the Effectiveness of CDT in Pursuits Set Forth in Its Mission

	Raising privacy awareness	Conceptua- lizing privacy policies	Conceptua- lizing privacy policies	Conceptua- lizing privacy policies	Conceptua- lizing privacy policies	Monitoring the implementation of privacy laws
Very effective	33%	26%	12%	11%	21%	53%
Effective	50%	42%	35%	33%	43%	24%
Somewhat effective	17%	26%	41%	39%	21%	18%
Not effective	0%	5%	12%	17%	14%	6%
TOTAL	100%	99%	100%	100%	99%	101%
N ratings of pursuits	18	19	17	18	14	17
Number of "don't know" responses	1	0	2	1	5	2

Table 7.6 Perceptions of the Effectiveness of CDT in Pursuits Set Forth in Its Mission Not Listed in Questionnaire

Pursuits	Level of Effectiveness
"Drawing together key Representatives of high-tech industries, government and nonprofit, public interest community for meaningful dialogues on a wide range of contentious public policy issues."	Very effective
"Providing balanced comments to the press on privacy issues."	Very effective
"First Amendment issues and "one of the best websites in town for the federal issues they cover."	Very effective
"Cryptography issues."	Very effective
"Inside the beltway advocacy."	Very effective

vacy polices, educating the public in privacy issues, developing privacy policies, developing privacy-enhancing tools, and monitoring the implementation of privacy laws), most funders considered the Center to have been effective or very effective (nearly 58 percent), followed by little or no effect (nearly 33 percent), and don't know (nearly 10 percent).

Table 7.7 Perceptions of the Impact of CDT for Each Question in the Questionnaire

	Question 1 (privacy legislation)	Question 2 (CDT activities and projects)	Question 3 (CDT pursuits)
Some or much impact/ effective or very effective	90%	76%	64%
Little or no impact/ effective or somewhat effective	10%	24%	36%
TOTAL	100%	100%	100%
N ratings for questions	72	54	103

When combining the percentages of the impact groups for all three questions—where not effective or somewhat effective in Question 3 is similar to no or little impact in Questions 1 and 2; effective or very effective is similar to some or much impact; and so forth—the funders' overall perception is that the CDT has had at least some, if not much, impact in their work (53.3 percent), followed by don't know (29.1 percent), and little or no impact (17.6 percent). Based on this, the answer to RQ 3, "What has been the social impact of the CDT according to its funders?", is that most funders from this small group of respondents perceived the CDT to have had some or much impact in terms of its work on Internet privacy.

NOTES

1. See "Population Studied" section in appendix A for a complete list of CDT's funders.
2. Percentages reported may not add up to exactly 100 percent due to rounding.
3. Legislation and projects listed in Questions 1 and 2, respectively, in the questionnaire were gleaned from the CDT's annual reports from 1996 to 2000. For a glossary of these legislations and projects, see appendix F.
4. Even though CALEA can be considered as a telecommunications-related legislation, it was created for the benefit of law enforcement agencies, rather than consumers as in the Antislamming Amendments Act and Telecommunications Competition and Consumer Protection Act.

5. N ratings for Tables 7.1, 7.3, 7.5, and 7.7 exclude all "don't know" responses. Therefore, N ratings in these cases include only respondents who answered "no impact/not effective," "little impact/somewhat effective," "some impact/effective," or "much impact/very effective."

6. The CDT's Internet Privacy Working Group (IPWG) is developing a fair information practices language that MIT's World Wide Web Consortium (W3C) will translate into web browser readable code. Thus, the tool will enable website operators and Internet users to negotiate over how and to what extent personal information will be collected and used on the Internet.

7. The pursuits listed in Question 3 were derived from mission-type statements in the CDT's annual reports from 1996 to 2000.

8

Conclusions

The first half of this book discussed the various aspects of privacy: the emergence of privacy as an issue in the United States; the definitions, characteristics, criteria, and functions of privacy; the ownership of personal data; and the means of protecting one's privacy. The second half of this book endeavored to investigate the social impact of the Center for Democracy and Technology's work on Internet privacy. Below is a summary of the research findings followed by some suggestions for future research.

FINDINGS

RQ 1: What have been the major results of the CDT in terms of its work on Internet privacy?

The Communications Assistance for Law Enforcement Act (CALEA), the Communications Decency Act (CDA), Doubleclick, and Intel Pentium III constituted the major results of the Center for Democracy and Technology. These events are considered as major accomplishments for four reasons: (1) there are numerous materials—generated both by the Center as well as the media—that can be found pertaining to these episodes; (2) the CDT was one of the leaders, if not *the* leader in these fights for the public's right to privacy;

(3) the Center proved victorious in the outcomes of these events; and (4) the organization employed a variety of strategies in order to win these battles (e.g., litigation; social activism in the form of online petitions, electronic newsletters, and online campaigns; relaying the public's concerns over breaches of privacy to legislators, federal agencies, and the technology industry via letters, reports, policy analyses, and formal complaints); and the formation of coalitions so that the voices of civil libertarians can be heard loudly and clearly as one.

RQ 2: How has the CDT been perceived by the American public as reflected in the mass media?

Judging from the newspaper articles and broadcast transcripts examined for this study, the media tended to view the CDT in four different capacities. First of all, it considered the Center as an authority who could provide balanced and intelligent commentaries and explanations on privacy-related issues. Second, not only did the media regard the CDT as a sage in these matters, but also as an educator in this field. Third, the media saw the organization as a promoter of privacy awareness. Last, the media perceived the CDT as a defender of the public's right to privacy.

RQ 3: What has been the social impact of the CDT according to its funders?

When the percentages for the three groups of impact (i.e., no or little impact; some or much impact; and don't know) for all questions in the questionnaire were combined, it was found that the majority of funders perceived the CDT to have had some or much impact in its work on Internet privacy. Even though no sampling had been performed (in other words, the entire population of funders was surveyed) and only one-third of the population responded, the results of this questionnaire can be generalized to the universe of CDT funders: the respondents were representative of the population in that these funders belonged to five out of the nine organizational categories (i.e., coalitions/trade associations, communications companies, financial institutions, software manufacturers, and foundations) and that the proportion of respondents belonging to these categories was similar to that of the population with the exception of foundations. For those categories that were not represented by the respondents (i.e., network/Internet service providers, computer manufacturers, the entertainment industry, and marketing firms), they can be ignored since they were in the minority for the population. Nevertheless, suggestions for improvement on this part of the study will be made in the following section.

SUGGESTIONS FOR FUTURE RESEARCH

Suggestions for future research will be described in two sections: (1) Suggestions for future research based on the framework of the present study, and (2) Suggestions for future research for extending the boundaries of the present study.

Suggestions for Future Research Based on the Framework of the Present Study

First, getting funders to respond to the questionnaire had been somewhat of a trial due to the fact that, in most cases, only one person in the whole of the funding organization had dealt with the CDT and these key informants were very often either the head of the branch office or of a major department within the organization. In other words, these subjects were extremely busy and under tremendous pressures with no one else to answer the questionnaire on their behalf. Thus, the future researcher may want to consider expanding the questionnaire population to include organizations that have participated in the CDT's working groups—particularly the Digital Privacy and Security Working Group and the Internet Privacy Working Group—but are not actual funders of the Center. It is assumed that more than one person from each organization participates in the working groups, thereby, increasing the odds of someone responding to the questionnaire.

Second, the future researcher should consider using experts groups to obtain perceptions on the CDT since depth had been sacrificed to breadth in the present questionnaire. Such experts groups might include CDT funders, members of the CDT's working groups, past and present CDT board members, representatives from the technology industry who neither fund nor participate in working groups, privacy advocates, civil libertarians, legislators, lobbyists, policy analysts, staff at government agencies such as the Federal

Communications Commission or the Federal Trade Commission, etc. Since no respondents complained about ambiguity in the questions, the queries could conceivably be used to trigger and steer some of the discussion in experts groups. At any rate, future questions about legislation—be it in a questionnaire or experts group—should be accompanied by a brief description of each piece of legislation such as in appendix F. This is to ensure that all respondents have the same basic knowledge of the legislation and that the subjects understand exactly to which legislation the researcher refers.

Last, the same study with a little modification can be conducted every 5 to 10 years in order to examine how public opinion on the CDT and the Center's own strategies for tackling privacy issues evolve over time.

Suggestions for Future Research to Extend the Boundaries of the Present Study

Since its inception, the CDT has been involved in international privacy issues. As the Center's work gains prominence outside of the United States, it would be interesting to compare American with foreign views on the organization using, for instance, content analysis of newspaper articles and transcripts of broadcast media programs, and/or surveys on those who had come into contact with the CDT.

Another type of comparison study that can be conducted in the future is one involving public interest groups in the United States that are concerned with Internet privacy (e.g., CDT, ACLU, EFF, EPIC, and PRC). Projects and/or cases—where the outcomes have been both successful or unsuccessful—in which all of these organizations had participated could form the basis of an investigation into how each of these civil liberties groups have dealt with the matter, and how effective or ineffective they are perceived to be by the public, and perhaps, by each other.

The last suggestion is to adopt methodologies from studies looking at policy network and policy design, and use these tools to conduct social impact studies beyond a single issue such as that in this book.

Appendix A

Methodology

DATA COLLECTION METHOD

A combination of historical research, survey, and content analysis was employed to determine the answers to the Research Questions (RQs): (RQ 1) What have been the major results of the CDT in terms of its work on Internet privacy?; (RQ 2) How has the CDT been perceived by the American public as reflected in the mass media?; and (RQ 3) What has been the social impact of the CDT according to its funders? Historical research provided a chronological assessment of the CDT's results. Content analysis uncovered possible patterns in past documented writings about the CDT. Survey revealed current opinions on the CDT's impact on American society. Thus, triangulation of data collection strategies enabled a more complete picture of what was being studied, as well as provided a way to cross-check data.

HISTORICAL RESEARCH

Historical research is the systematic collection and evaluation of data related to past occurrences in order to describe causes, effects, or trends of those events that may help explain present events and anticipate future ones.[1] This methodology tends to be considered as rather unscientific. Admittedly, the nature of historical research precludes exercise of many of the control procedures characteristic of other types of methodologies. However, if it is done correctly, historical research, too, involves systematic, objective data collection and analysis. To be considered well structured, historical research must include (1) the identification of a particular problem to be examined; (2) the assemblage of relevant literature to facilitate investigation of the problem; (3) the formation of hypotheses to tentatively explain the relationships between identified variables; (4) the comprehensive collection and organization of the available evidence; (5) the identification, selection, and analysis of the most valuable evidence, and the formation of conclusions from them; and (6) the articulation of these conclusions in narrative form.[2,3]

All sources of historical data must be subjected to rigorous scientific analysis to determine both their authenticity (external criticism) and their accuracy (internal criticism). External criticism issues include authorship, dating, forgery, translation, and copying accuracy.[4] In determining internal criticism, there are at least four factors that must be taken into account:

1. *The knowledge and competence of the author.* It must be determined whether the person who wrote the document is/was a competent person and a person in a position to be knowledgeable concerning what actually occurred.
2. *Time delay.* An important consideration is how much time is likely to have elapsed between the event's occurrence and the recording of the facts. Reports written while an event is taking place (e.g., minutes of meetings) or shortly after (e.g., diary entries) are likely to be more accurate than reports written some time after (e.g., as part of a memoir).
3. *Bias and motive of the author.* People often intentionally or unintentionally report or record incorrect information due to faulty recall, selective memory, personal leanings, or ulterior reasons.
4. *Consistency of data.* Each piece of evidence must be compared with all other pieces to determine the degree of agreement. If one observer's account drastically differs from the others', his or her testimony may be suspect. Thus, to a certain extent, by the very fact that they agree, sources may validate their accuracy.

Having reviewed, abstracted, and evaluated the data, the researcher must then organize and synthesize the findings. Synthesis poses another area of concern in historical research. In order to "blend evidence into an account that accurately describes historical events or solves historical problems," synthesis involves interpretation and issues of operative subjectivism whereby the researcher draws upon his or her power of "discrimination, imagination, and sophistication" to select source materials and evaluate their relevancy in order to tell the story.[5]

Materials Examined

Primary Sources

Primary source materials examined for RQ 1 included:

1. *Legal documents*—plaintiff's filings, defendant's filings, judicial rulings, etc.
2. *Government records*—transcripts of congressional hearings and testimonies, committee reports, and congressional bills
3. *Materials from the CDT's archive*

Secondary Sources

Secondary source materials examined were:

1. Newspapers
2. Transcripts of television and radio programs
3. General-interest periodicals (e.g., *Time, Newsweek, Newsday,* and *National Journal*)
4. Special-interest periodicals (e.g., *Wired, CNET & CNET Radio, Interactive Week, ZDNet, Industry Standard,* and *National Journal of Technology Daily*)
5. Scholarly journals from the disciplines of law, business, and public affairs

SURVEY

A survey is an instrument for collecting data from members of a population in order to determine the current status of that population with respect to one of more variables.[6] It may be used for descriptive, explanatory, and exploratory purposes, and is chiefly employed in studies that have individual people as the units of analysis.[7] The strengths of surveys lie in the fact that (1) they are useful in describing the characteristics of a large population; (2) they, particularly self-administered surveys, make very large samples feasible which, in turn, make the study's findings more generalizable; (3) many questions may be asked on a given topic, thus increasing the breadth of knowledge; and (4) unlike experimental design, which requires the researcher to commit in advance to a particular operational definition of a concept, surveys allow the development of operational definitions from actual observation. Vis à vis the weaknesses of surveys, first the researcher is dependent on the good graces of his or her subjects to answer the questionnaire. Second, related to this is the potential for low response rate (assuming subjects respond at all), which affects the generalizability of the research findings and the validity of the study. Third, standardized questionnaires often represent the least common denominators in assessing people's attitudes, orientations, circumstances, and experiences. Thus, surveys may result in the "fitting of round pegs in square holes."[8] Fourth, a survey can seldom deal with the *context* of social life even if it can furnish information in this area. For example, a survey researcher can rarely develop the feel for the total life situation in which respondents are thinking and behaving that a field researcher can. Fifth, surveys typically require that an initial study design remain unaltered throughout the course of data collection. Compare this rigidity with field research where one can become aware of an important new variable emerging from the phenomenon being studied, and begin making careful observations of it. Last, surveys are artificial, particularly when it comes to the realm of action. Surveys cannot measure social action; they can only collect self-reports of recalled past, prospective, or hypothetical action. Akin to this is the problem of whether the subject's recollection is accurate, and whether the subject is honest in his or her response.

Survey is generally weak on validity and strong on reliability. On the one hand, if we compare this methodology with that of field research, the artificiality of surveys puts a strain on validity. For example, people's opinions on issues are rarely as clear-cut as strongly agree, agree, disagree, or strongly disagree with a specific statement. In such a case, survey responses must be regarded as approximations along a spectrum of feelings.

On the other hand, by presenting all subjects with a standardized stimulus, a survey eliminates, to a large extent, unreliability in observations made by the researcher. Moreover, carefully crafted questions can also significantly reduce the subject's own unreliability.

Population Studied

Past and present funders of the CDT formed the population for the questionnaire. These funders comprised of the following organizations:

America Online, Inc.	National Cummings Foundation
American Association of Advertising Agencies	National Cable Television Association
American Express	Netcom On-Line Communication Services
American Financial Services Association	Netscape Communications Corporation
Apple Computer, Inc.	
Association of American Publishers	Newspaper Association of America
Association of National Advertisers	Novell, Inc.
AT&T	
AT&T Wireless	Pacific Telesis Group
	Pitney Bowes
Bell Atlantic	Prodigy, Inc.
Business Software Alliance	PSINet
Cellular Telecommunications Industry Association	Recording Industry Association of America
Citicorp Financial Services	RSA Data Security
Coalition for Encryption Reform	
Compuserve, Inc.	Software & Information Industry Association
Deer Creek Foundation	Software Publishers Association
Direct Marketing Association	Soros Foundation
Disney Worldwide Services, Inc.	Southwestern Bell Communications
Dun & Bradstreet	Spyglass, Inc.
	Sun Microsystems, Inc.

Electronic Messaging Association	Targetbase Marketing
Experian	Time Warner, Inc.
	TRW Information Services
Ford Foundation	
	US West, Inc.
Glen Eagles Foundation	US Telephone Association
John A. Hartford Foundation	
IBM Corporation	
IBM International Fund	
Information Technology	
Association of America	
Information Technology	
Industry Council	
Interactive Digital Software	
Association	
Lotus Development Corporation	
Markle Foundation	
MCA/Universal	
MCI Worldcom	
Microsoft Corporation	
Mindspring	

No sampling was conducted since the population is so small. The key informant at each of these organizations received a copy of the questionnaire.

The Questionnaire

For questionnaires, it has been argued that the advantages of open questions are that (1) they allow respondents to express themselves in their own words; (2) they do not suggest answers (i.e., they do not hint at how subjects should answer); (3) they avoid format effects; (4) they enable complex motivational influences and frames of reference to be identified; (5) they are necessary prerequisites for the proper development of sets of response options for closed questions; and (6) they assist in the interpretation of deviant responses to closed questions.[9] The pros of closed questions lie in the fact that (1) they produce less variable answers so that responses can be meaningfully compared; (2) they present a recognition (as opposed to a recall) task to respondents that makes it simpler for them to answer; and (3) they produce answers that are much easier to analyze in computerized form.[10,11] Bearing in mind these points and the fact that the research subjects are very busy people, all questions were closed for this study.

The questionnaire consisted of three questions.[12] Question 1 solicited the funders' perceptions on the CDT's effectiveness in various privacy legislation. Question 2 pertained to the extent to which the CDT has been effective in projects it has created to combat privacy invasion. The last question examined the effectiveness of the CDT in aspects of privacy legislation versus privacy advocacy and developing technological means for privacy protection.

Copies of the cover letter and questionnaire were sent to key informants for all CDT funders in August 2000.[13] In September 2000, follow-up letters and new copies of the questionnaire were sent to subjects who had not returned the materials.[14] Since the questionnaires were serialized with unique identification numbers, it was easy to know exactly which subjects had returned the questionnaire and which ones had not. Recipients of the follow-up letter were given another month to return the document. In October 2000, the questionnaires were administered over the telephone to those who still had not responded. According to Earl Babbie, "three mailings (an original and two follow-ups) seem the most efficient" and that "two or three weeks is a reasonable space between mailings."[15] The Survey Research Office at the University of Hawaii found that within two weeks after the first mailing, approximately 40 percent of the questionnaires are returned; within two weeks after the first follow-up, an additional 20 percent are received; and within two weeks of the third and final follow-up, an additional 10 percent are remitted.[16] Therefore, it seemed futile to extend the return date to much more than 8 weeks after the original mailing date due to the inverse relationship between the elapse of time and the number of returns.

CONTENT ANALYSIS

Content analysis is any technique for making inferences by objectively and systematically identifying specified characteristics of messages.[17,18] The strengths of this methodology are (1) economy, (2) safety, (3) ability to study processes over long periods of time, and (4) unobtrusiveness.[19] Content analysis is economical in terms of time and money: no special equipment or large research staff are required. It is safe in that unlike survey or experimental research where one may be forced to repeat the whole project if one discovers an error had been committed, in content analysis it is usually feasible to repeat a portion of the study. Moreover, one might be required to recode only a portion of one's data rather than to repeat the entire enterprise. Content analysis permits researchers to investigate processes that have occurred over a long period of time. For example, with content analysis one is able to study a phenomenon over several years whereas with experimental research, one is only able to obtain a snapshot of a phenomenon. By being unobtrusive, content analysis avoids observation bias such as the Hawthorne Effect. Having said this, content analysis is not without faults. One disadvantage is that it is limited to the examination of recorded communications that may originally be oral, written, or graphic, but must be recorded in some fashion to permit analysis. However, this is not a disadvantage in our case because it is precisely because of this characteristic that we will employ such methodology.

In terms of reliability, three types are pertinent to content analysis: (1) stability, (2) reproducibility, and (3) accuracy. Stability refers to the extent to which the results of content classification are invariant over time. It can be determined when the same content is coded more than once by the *same* coder. Inconsistencies in coding constitute unreliability, and may stem from such factors as ambiguities in coding rules and in the text, cognitive changes within the coder, and recording the wrong numeric code for a category. Because only one person is coding, stability is the weakest form of reliability. Reproducibility (a.k.a. intercoder reliability) refers to the extent to which content classification produces the same results when the same text is coded by *more than one coder*. Conflicting codings usually stem from cognitive differences among the coders, ambiguous coding instructions, or random recording errors. High reproducibility is a minimum standard for content analysis as stability measures the consistency of the individual coder's private understandings, whereas reproducibility measures the consistency of shared understandings (or meanings) held by multiple coders. Accuracy refers to the extent to which the classification of text corresponds to a standard or norm. This is the strongest form of reliability. Apart from the purpose of training, standard codings are infrequently established for texts. Therefore, researchers seldom use accuracy in reliability assessment.[20]

In terms of validity, the weakest form is face validity, which consists of the correspondence between the investigator's definition of concepts and his or her definitions of the categories that measure them. A category is said to have face validity when it appears to measure the construct that it is intended to measure. Face validity is considered the weakest because even if several expert judges concur, face validity rests on only a single variable; stronger forms of validity involve more than one variable. Much stronger validity can be obtained by comparing content-analytic data with some external criterion. Four types of external validity are pertinent: (1) construct validity, (2) hypothesis validity, (3) predictive validity, and (4) semantic validity. A measure has construct validity to the extent that it is correlated with some other measure of the same construct. Thus, it entails the generalizability of the construct across measures or methods. Hypothesis validity relies on the correspondence among variables and the correspondence between these relationships and theories. A measure has hypothesis validity if it "behaves" as anticipated in relationship to other variables. Predictive validity occurs when forecasts about events or conditions external to the study correspond to actual events or conditions; these may concern future, past, or concurrent events. Predictive validity is powerful because the inferences from data are generalized successfully beyond the study to situations not under the direct control of the researcher. Having said this, content-analytic data are rarely shown to have predictive validity. Semantic validity exists when persons familiar with the language and texts examine lists of words (or other units) placed in the same category and agree that these words have similar meanings or connotations. Such validity may seem an obvious requirement for valid content analysis, but many problems arise due to ambiguities in words and category definitions. For example, the word "mine" can be the process of extraction, the place in which this process occurs, or a possessive noun.[21]

Materials Analyzed

This study analyzed selected content from two sources: (1) newspapers, and (2) transcripts of television and radio programs.

Newspapers

National Newspapers was used to identify articles about the CDT's work on privacy. The database includes articles from 29 newspapers in the United States and worldwide and its coverage is from 1986 to the present.[22] On arrival at the database's search page, in the section that says "Enter a word or phrase," the search terms "Center for Democracy and Technology and privacy" as well as "Jerry Berman and privacy" were used for two separate searches. As for the "Date range," "Current (1998-present)" and "Backfile (1986–1997)" were selected (note that two separate searches were required for the database since only one date range can be searched at a time).

Transcripts of Television and Radio Programs

Transcripts of television and radio programs were obtained from the database *Lexis-Nexis* by clicking on the hyperlink for "News" and then "Transcripts" once we were at the Lexis-Nexis homepage. At the search page, "Center for Democracy and Technology" was used as the keyword for the first search, and "Jerry Berman" for the second. In the line that says "Narrow search with additional terms," "Privacy" was entered. Nothing was selected for the "Source" line. "1995" and "2000" were inserted in the "From" and "To" boxes, respectively, for the "Date." Since we were interested in the impact of the CDT on American society, only transcripts of programs aired on ABC, CBS, CNN, NBC, NPR, and PBS Newshour with Jim Lehrer were considered.

DATA SYNTHESIS FOR CONTENT ANALYSIS

Newspapers

Three categories/variables were examined: (1) mention of the CDT or one of its staff; (2) quotes from CDT staff; and (3) the context in which the CDT or its staff is mentioned. For the first variable, if the article mentioned the CDT as well as a staff member, it was counted as only one occurrence, as were multiple mentions within a single article. For the second variable, if the article included more than one quote, it, too, was counted as only one instance. Social impact for the first two variables was determined by the number of occurrences where the higher the number, the more impact the CDT has had on society. For the last variable, the contexts in which the CDT or its staff was mentioned were listed and categorized by themes should they be evident.

Transcripts of Television and Radio Programs

The contents of television and radio program transcripts were described specifically by, but not necessarily limited to, the number of interviews the CDT has given; the timing of these interviews in relation to what was happening on Capitol Hill (e.g., did the interview occur before a bill was introduced, at the hearing stage, after the bill has been passed or defeated, etc.?); and the context in which the CDT was mentioned on these programs (e.g., in a headline, in a feature interview, in a discussion with other experts, etc.). It was assumed that the sheer mention of the CDT on television and radio is indication enough of the organization's impact on American society.

DATA SYNTHESIS FOR RQs

For RQ 2 ("How has the CDT been perceived by the American public as reflected in the mass media?"), impact was inferred by calculating the number of times the CDT or its staff have been mentioned, and the number of times CDT staff have been quoted. It was assumed that the CDT or its staff was mentioned or quoted because their work was considered of some importance and that they were able to offer expert commentary on what topic/event the article or program was about. How the public regards the CDT was also inferred from the number of interviews the Center has given. However, it must be recognized that the number of interviews, quotes, and mentions do not necessarily indicate the degree or quality of the CDT's impact on society. Therefore, just the fact that the CDT had even been mentioned in the mass media is, itself, an indication of impact. The context of the interviews could also reveal public sentiment on the CDT. For instance, the CDT could be held in higher esteem if it was not just mentioned in connection with one of their projects, but that they had been asked to comment on, explain, or describe something within their realm of expertise, but with which they are not involved.

For RQ 3 ("What has been the social impact of the CDT according to its funders?"), impact was determined from the answers to the questionnaire. Percentages for each of the categories of impact and effectiveness (i.e., no impact/not effective, little impact/somewhat effective, some impact/effective, much impact/very effective, and don't know) for each legislation and CDT projects were reported.

Triangulation is "the use of multiple methods, data collection strategies, and/or data sources, in order to get a more complete picture and to cross-check information."[23] The purpose of combining three different methodologies for this dissertation was not so much to verify data, but to obtain a more complete view of what has been the social impact of the CDT. Historical research, content analysis, and survey complemented one another in that each compensated for what the other methodology failed to address. Historical research provided the background to the timing of when CDT's television and radio interviews occurred. This methodology also involved the examination of documents that were otherwise not covered by content analysis. It revealed past perceptions on the impact of the CDT whereas the survey provided current views on the Center's work. In compiling the questionnaire, the researcher had much more control over what data should be collected, compared with content analysis or historical research where the investigator had to obtain data from existing documents that may have been created for purposes somewhat different from that of the researcher. Also, by using a questionnaire, present perceptions of the CDT could be obtained from an altogether different population than that which might have composed the documents examined for historical research or content analysis. Even though content analysis in general is the means by which the researcher makes sense of the data from historical research and surveys, as a methodology, content analysis complemented historical research by involving somewhat different, more concrete, and more quantifiable criteria for determining the social impact of the CDT.

LIMITATIONS OF THE STUDY

There are five major limitations in the present study. The first is that the social impact of the Center for Democracy and Technology is based only on the organization's work on privacy. Therefore, the Center's impact (or lack thereof) cannot be generalized to the effectiveness of the CDT as a whole. The next limitation can be found in the population for the questionnaire. The population consisted of only CDT funders. These subjects are likely to have positive opinions on the organization since they fund it. Thus, their answers may be biased. The third major limitation of this study is the questionnaire itself. Ideally, all questions should have been open-ended, but due to constraints in time for both the subjects as well as the researcher, only closed questions were offered. Follow-up interviews and experts groups would probably have yielded more in-depth answers than closed questions, but again, time constraints and the geographic spread of the participants made these difficult to pursue. The fourth limitation is that this study focused only on federal events and not those that had occurred statewide, locally, or internationally. The final limitation of this study lies in the types of newspapers analyzed: (1) the publications indexed in National Newspapers may be seen by some people to have a liberal bias; (2) the database includes only newspapers from major cities in the United States. Even then, they are newspapers from only selected major cities. For instance, newspapers from Philadelphia, Dallas, Minneapolis-St. Paul, Miami, Cleveland, etc., are excluded; and (3) the smaller newspapers that feature in National Newspapers may not have their own staff to cover certain events, thus they borrow articles from the Associated Press or Reuters. Therefore, in all three cases, public opinion gleaned from these newspapers is not necessarily representative of the entire population of the United States.

In closing, the limitations listed above should not be considered as serious or detrimental to the validity of this study due to triangulation in the methodology. Moreover, these limitations can be redressed by future research in the same way that additional questions stemming from the results of this study can be addressed in subsequent investigations.

NOTES

1. L. R. Gay, *Educational Research: Competencies for Analysis and Application*, 5th ed. (Upper Saddle River, N. J.: Prentice-Hall, 1996), 185.
2. Charles H. Busha and Stephen P. Harter, *Research Methods in Librarianship: Techniques and Interpretation* (New York: Academic Press, 1980), 92.

3. Gay, *Educational Research,* 189.

4. Robert Jones Shafer, ed., *A Guide to Historical Method* (Homewood, Ill.: Dorsey, 1974), 25–26.

5. Shafer, *Historical Method,* 25–26.

6. Gay, *Educational Research,* 251.

7. Earl Babbie, *The Practice of Social Research,* 7th ed. (Belmont, Calif.: Wadsworth, 1995), 257.

8. Babbie, *Social Research,* 274.

9. William Foddy, *Constructing Questions for Interviews and Questionnaires: Theories and Practice* (Cambridge: Cambridge University Press, 1994), 128.

10. Foddy, *Constructing Questions,* 128.

11. For an evaluation of the assumptions underlying the use of open and closed questions, see Foddy, *Constructing Questions,* 129–152.

12. See appendix B.

13. See appendix C.

14. See appendix D.

15. Babbie, *Social Research,* 261.

16. Babbie, *Social Research,* 261.

17. Ole R. Holsti, *Content Analysis for the Social Sciences and Humanities* (Reading, Mass.: Addison-Wesley, 1969), 14.

18. Robert Philip Weber, *Basic Content Analysis,* 2nd ed. (Newbury Park, Calif.: Sage, 1990), 9.

19. Babbie, *Social Research,* 320–321.

20. Weber, *Basic Content Analysis,* 17.

21. Weber, *Basic Content Analysis,* 18–20.

22. For a list of newspapers indexed in *National Newspapers,* see appendix F.

23. Gay, *Educational Research,* 626.

Appendix B

Questionnaire

(UNIQUE ID #)

1. In your estimate, how much impact has the CDT had on the following legislation (circle your estimate for each legislation)?

Antislamming Amendments Act	no impact	little impact	some impact	much impact	don't know
Child Online Protection Act (COPA)	no impact	little impact	some impact	much impact	don't know
Communications Assistance for Law Enforcement Act (CALEA)	no impact	little impact	some impact	much impact	don't know
Security and Freedom Through Encryption (SAFE) Act	no impact	little impact	some impact	much impact	don't know
Telecommunications Competition and Consumer Protection Act	no impact	little impact	some impact	much impact	don't know

Wireless Communication and Public Safety Act	no impact	little impact	some impact	much impact	don't know

Other (specify) _____	no impact	little impact	some impact	much impact	don't know

2. In your estimate, how much impact has the CDT had with the following projects (circle your estimation for each project)?

Digital Democracy Project	no impact	little impact	some impact	much impact	don't know
Doubleclick/ anti-online profiling campaign	no impact	little impact	some impact	much impact	don't know
GetNetWise	no impact	little impact	some impact	much impact	don't know
GetPrivacyWise	no impact	little impact	some impact	much impact	don't know
Privacy Watchdog Campaign	no impact	little impact	some impact	much impact	don't know
Other (specify) _____	no impact	little impact	some impact	much impact	don't know

3. In your estimate, how effective has the CDT been in its pursuit of the following (circle your estimate for each)?

Raising privacy awareness	not effective	somewhat effective	effective	very effective	don't know
Conceptualizing privacy policies	not effective	somewhat effective	effective	very effective	don't know

Educating the public in privacy	not effective	somewhat effective	effective	very effective	don't know
Developing privacy policies	not effective	somewhat effective	effective	very effective	don't know
Developing privacy-enhancing tools	not effective	somewhat effective	effective	very effective	don't know
Monitoring the implementation privacy laws	not effective	somewhat effective	effective	very effective	don't know
Other (specify) _____	not effective	somewhat effective	effective	very effective	don't know

Appendix C
Questionnaire Cover Letter

Joyce Li
Department of Library
    and Information Science
School of Information Sciences
University of Pittsburgh
135 N. Bellefield Ave.
Pittsburgh, PA 15260
tel: (412) 885-6584
fax: (412) 885-6585
e-mail: joyceli@sis.pitt.edu

DATE

NAME OF SUBJECT
SUBJECT'S ADDRESS, etc.

Dear X:

I am a doctoral candidate in the Department of Library and Information Science at the University of Pittsburgh, and the topic of my dissertation is the Center for Democracy and Technology of which Jerry Berman is the executive director. According to the CDT's annual reports, your company has funded/is funding the Center. Key-informants for every CDT funder are being asked to provide information for an assessment of this public interest group.

You may be assured of complete confidentiality. The identification number on the questionnaire is only for the purposes of identifying nonrespondents, and if necessary, for answer clarification.

The questionnaire takes less than 5 minutes to complete. Every response is vital to the success of the survey: the survey report should represent the full range of perceptions of CDT funders.

Please return the questionnaire using the self-addressed stamped envelope, and feel free to contact me if you have any questions.

Thank you for your assistance,

Joyce Li

Appendix D

Questionnaire Follow-Up Letter

Joyce Li
Department of Library
    and Information Science
School of Information Sciences
University of Pittsburgh
135 N. Bellefield Ave.
Pittsburgh, PA 15260
tel: (412) 885-6584
fax: (412) 885-6585
e-mail: joyceli@sis.pitt.edu

DATE

NAME OF SUBJECT
SUBJECT'S ADDRESS, etc.

Dear X:

On (DATE), a questionnaire was sent to you. Perhaps you never received it or your response was lost in the mail on its way to Pittsburgh, but I would be very grateful if you would take a few minutes to complete the enclosed questionnaire.

Let me tell you a little bit about myself and my research. I am a doctoral candidate in the Department of Library and Information Science at the University of Pittsburgh, and the topic of my dissertation is the Center for Democracy and Technology of which Jerry Berman is the executive director. According to the CDT's annual reports, your company has funded/is funding the Center. Key-informants for every CDT funder are being asked to provide information for an assessment of this public interest group.

You may be assured of complete confidentiality. The identification number on the questionnaire is only for the purposes of identifying nonrespondents, and if necessary, for answer clarification.

The questionnaire takes less than 5 minutes to complete. Every response is vital to the success of the survey: the survey report should represent the full range of perceptions of CDT funders.

Please return the questionnaire using the self-addressed stamped envelope, and feel free to contact me if you have any questions.

Thank you for your assistance,

Joyce Li

Appendix E

Newspapers Indexed in National Newspapers

(f = available in full text)

Afro-American Red Star; Washington

American Banker; New York (f)

Amsterdam News; New York

Barron's; Chicopee (f)

Boston Globe; Boston (f)

Call & Post; State edition; Cleveland

Chicago Defender; Chicago

Chicago Tribune; Chicago (f)

Christian Science Monitor; Boston (f)

Denver Post; Denver (f)

Detroit News; Detroit (f)

Houston Chronicle; Houston (f)

Houston Post; Houston

Michigan Chronicle; Detroit

Muslim Journal; Chicago

New Journal & Guide; Norfolk

New York Times Book Review; New York   (f)

New York Times Magazine; New York   (f)

New York Times; Late Edition (East Coast); New York   (f)

San Francisco Chronicle; San Francisco   (f)

Sentinel; Los Angeles

St. Louis Post-Dispatch; St. Louis   (f)

The Atlanta Constitution; Atlanta   (f)

The Atlanta Journal and *The Atlanta Constitution;* Atlanta   (f)

The Atlanta Journal; Atlanta   (f)

The Detroit News and *Detroit Free Press;* Detroit

The Guardian; Manchester, UK   (f)

The Los Angeles Times; Record edition; Los Angeles   (f)

The Washington Post; Washington   (f)

Times-Picayune; New Orleans   (f)

USA Today; Arlington   (f)

Wall Street Journal; Eastern edition; New York   (f)

Appendix F

Glossary of Legislation and Center for Democracy and Technology Projects in Questions 1 and 2 in the Funders' Questionnaire

ANTISLAMMING AMENDMENTS ACT

The Antislamming Amendments Act (H. R. 3888 and S. 1618 introduced by Representative Billy Tauzin [R-LA] and Senator John McCain [R-AZ], respectively) amends the Communications Act of 1934 to improve the protection of consumers against "spamming" by telecommunications carriers, and for other purposes.

CHILD ONLINE PROTECTION ACT (COPA)

Also known as "CDA II" or the "Son of CDA," the Child Online Protection Act makes it a crime for anyone, by means of the World Wide Web, to make any communication for commercial purposes that is "harmful to minors," unless the person has restricted access by minors by requiring a credit card number. COPA imposes criminal and civil penalties of up to $50,000 per day for violations (for further information, see "CDA: Aftermath" in Chapter 5 of this book).

COMMUNICATIONS ASSISTANCE FOR
LAW ENFORCEMENT ACT (CALEA)

Also known as the "wiretapping" or "digital telephony" bill, Congress enacted the Communications Assistance for Law Enforcement Act in 1994. CALEA was intended to preserve, but not expand law enforcement wiretapping capabilities by requiring telephone companies to design their systems to ensure a certain basic level of government access. However, the FBI has tried to use the law to expand its capabilities by turning wireless phones into tracking devices, requiring phone companies to collect specific signaling information for the government's convenience, and allowing interception of packet communications without privacy protections (for further information, see "Communications Assistance for Law Enforcement Act" in Chapter 5 of this book).

DIGITAL DEMOCRACY PROJECT

The Center for Democracy and Technology is pioneering the use of the Internet to enhance citizen participation in the democratic process, and to ensure that the voice of Internet users is heard in critical public policy debates about the Internet. Some examples of the CDT's work in digital democracy are the online petition in support of Senator Patrick Leahy's opposition to the Communications Decency Act; National Day of Protest which generated more than 20,000 telephone calls, faxes, and e-mails to Congress in support of free speech on the Internet; "Black Thursday" where nearly 5,000 operators of the World Wide Web (WWW) turned their pages black to protest the CDA; the Citizens Internet Empowerment Coalition that challenged the CDA in the Supreme Court; the first ever cybercast of a Congressional hearing (26 June 1996 and 25 July 1996) which could be heard by Netizens around the world and where Netizens could submit comments on the hearings and participate in a simultaneous online discussion with congressional staff and encryption policy experts; the creation of the Congressional Internet

Caucus and the subsequent coordination of the Internet Caucus Advisory Committee which, in conjunction with the Caucus, sponsors and conducts educational events and seminars to educate Congress about Internet issues, convince more members to use the Internet, and find new ways to increase citizen access to Congress and its deliberations.

DOUBLECLICK/ANTI-ONLINE PROFILING CAMPAIGN

Doubleclick specializes in advertising on the World Wide Web. In June 1999, the company purchased Abacus, a mail catalog distributor. In January 2000, it was revealed that Doubleclick intended to merge online information with offline information. However, DoubleClick announced on 2 March 2000 that it would not proceed with its plans until government and industry have reached a consensus on privacy rules for the Internet. The move came after the CDT and other privacy advocates filed a Statement of Additional Facts and Grounds for Relief with the Federal Trade Commission noting that sensitive information including video titles, salaries, and search terms were being passed to DoubleClick (for more information, see "Doubleclick" in Chapter 5 of this book).

GETNETWISE

Developed by a coalition of Internet industry corporations (e.g., Alta Vista, America Online, AT&T, Dell, Excite@Home, IBM, Lycos, MCI Worldcom, Prodigy, PSINet, Verizon, and Yahoo!) and public interest organizations (e.g., Cyber Patrol, Internet Alliance, Internet Content Coalition, and Internet Content Rating Association), GetNetWise (http://www.getnetwise.org) is a web-centered resource that provides parents and other caretakers access to a wide range of tools to protect children from inappropriate online material. The website includes a searchable database of over 110 user empowerment products, consumer information explaining how these tools work, information on recognizing and reporting online problems, an online safety guide, and hyperlinks to good sites for kids and families.

GETPRIVACYWISE

GetPrivacyWise is a web resource created by the CDT that informs web surfers on ways to protect their privacy whilst online.

PRIVACY WATCHDOG CAMPAIGN

CDT's Privacy Watchdog site (http://watchdog.cdt.org) offers consumers a quick way to scan and analyze websites' privacy policies, or lack thereof, and tell these organizations what they think. To use the Watchdog, users answer a seven-question survey to analyze the privacy policies at the websites they regularly surf or shop. Based on the results submitted by these users, the CDT compiles a list of those sites with privacy policies and those without. The "Naughty and Nice" lists provide Internet users with basic information on the privacy practices of websites. The CDT continues to review privacy policies of these websites to assess whether they are meeting consumers' expectations of privacy and reflect time-honored standards for privacy protection.

SECURITY AND FREEDOM THROUGH
ENCRYPTION (SAFE) ACT

The Security and Freedom through Encryption Act (H. R. 850) introduced by Representatives Bob Goodlatte (R-VA) and Zoe Lofgren (D-CA), is intended to protect domestic use of encryption and dramatically ease export controls. Major provisions of SAFE are that it: (1) guarantees all Americans the freedom to use any type of encryption anywhere in the world, and allows the sale of any type of encryption domestically; (2) prohibits the government from requiring mandatory key recovery; (3) modernizes U.S. export controls to permit the export of generally available software and hardware if a product with comparable security is commercially available from foreign suppliers; (4) creates criminal penalties for the knowing and willful use of encryption to conceal evidence of a crime, but specifies that the use of encryption does not constitute probable cause of a crime; (5) calls upon the Attorney General to compile examples in which encryption has interfered with law enforcement; and (6) calls upon the President to convene an international conference to draft encryption policy agreement.

TELECOMMUNICATIONS COMPETITION AND CONSUMER PROTECTION ACT OF 1995

The Telecommunications Competition and Consumer Protection Act (S. 652), introduced by Senator Larry Pressler [R-SD] provides for a procompetitive, deregulatory national policy framework designed to accelerate private sector deployment of advanced telecommunications and information technologies and services to all Americans by opening all telecommunications markets to competition, and for other purposes. The Communications Decency Act (CDA) is Title V of this legislation.

WIRELESS COMMUNICATION AND PUBLIC SAFETY ACT OF 1998

H. R. 3844, the Wireless Communication and Public Safety Act introduced by Representative Billy Tauzin, R-LA, directs the Federal Communications Commission (FCC) and any agency or entity to which the FCC delegates such authority to designate 911 as the universal emergency telephone number within the United States for reporting an emergency to appropriate authorities and requesting assistance. The legislation applies such designation to both wireline and wireless telephone service and directs the FCC to provide appropriate transition periods for areas in which 911 is not currently an emergency number. The part which poses potential privacy problems is Section 10 which authorizes telecommunications carriers to provide call location information concerning a user of a commercial mobile service to emergency dispatch providers and emergency service personnel in order to respond to the user's call or to notify the user's immediate family in a life-threatening situation. H. R. 3844 authorizes such carriers to transmit crash information as part of the automatic crash notification system, and requires the customer's prior consent for disclosure to any other person.

Bibliography

Alderman, Ellen, and Caroline Kennedy. *The Right to Privacy.* New York: Vintage Books, 1997.

Altman, Irwin. *The Environment and Social Behavior: Privacy, Personal Space, Territory, and Crowding.* Monterey, Calif.: Brooks/Cole, 1975.

American Civil Liberties Union. *The American Civil Liberties Union: Freedom is Why We're Here.* New York: American Civil Liberties Union, 1999.

American Civil Liberties Union, et al. *More Privacy and Consumer Groups Urge FTC to Act Immediately to Prevent Harm to Consumer Privacy.* 5 March 1991. http://www.cdt.org/privacy/issues/pentium3/990305intel.moregroups.shtml (23 Aug. 2000).

———. *American Civil Liberties Union vs. Reno II,* U.S. D. C., E. D. Penn., Case No. 98–5591. 22 October 1998. http://www.techlawjournal.com/courts/copa/19981022.htm (14 Aug. 2000).

———. *Privacy Advocates' Letter to Intel on Pentium III.* 28 January 1999. http://www.cdt.org/privacy/issues/pentium3/990128intel. letter.shtml (23 Aug. 2000).

Amidon, Paige. "Widening Privacy Concerns." *Online* (July 1992): 64–67.

Anderson, Diane, and Keith Perine. "Marketing the Doubleclick Way." *Industry Standard.* 25 July 2000. http://thestandard.com/article/display/0,1151,12400,00.html (25 July 2000).

Angelica, Amara D. "Identity Crisis: The Pentium III's Serial Number Feature is the Latest Flash Point in the Debate Over Privacy." *TechWeek.* 8 February 1999. http://www.techweek.com/articles/2-8-99/privacy.htm (26 Aug. 2000).

Associated Press Online, 23 June 2000.

Association of American Publishers, et al. *Amici Curiae, in Support of Plaintiffs.* 11 January 1999. http://www.cdt.org/speech/copa /990111amicus.html (14 Aug. 2000).

―――. *Amicus Brief: Child Online Protection Act* (COPA). 1 September 1999. http://www.cdt.org/speech/copa/990901amicus. shtml (14 Aug. 2000).

Atlanta Journal, 4 May 1999.

Baarslag, Karl. *Robbery by Mail: The Story of the U.S. Postal Inspectors.* New York: Farrar & Rinehart, 1938.

Babbie, Earl. *The Practice of Social Research.* 7th ed. Belmont, Calif.: Wadsworth, 1995.

Bailey, George W. S. *Privacy and the Mental. Amsterdam: Rodopi,* 1979.

Bakel, Rogier van. "How Good People Helped to Make a Bad Law." *Wired.* Archive 4.02 1996. http://www.wired.com/wired /archive/4.02/digitel_pr.html (18 July 2000).

Barlow, John Perry. *A Not Terribly Brief History of the Electronic Frontier Foundation.* 8 November 1990. http://www.eff.org/pub /Misc/EFF/history.eff (21 Sept. 2000).

Bates, Alan P. "Privacy—A Useful Concept?" *Social Forces* 42 (1964): 429–434.

Bazelon, David L. "Probing Privacy." *Gonzaga Law Review* 12 (1977): 587–619.

BBBOnline. *How the BBBOnline Privacy Program Works.* 2001. http://www.bbbonline.org/privacy/how.asp (19 Aug. 2001).

Benn, Stanley I. "Privacy, Freedom and Respect for Persons." In *Privacy,* ed. J. Roland Pennock and John W. Chapman. New York: Atherton, 1971.

Berman, Jerry, and Daniel Weitzner. *CDT Analysis of Senate Passed Exon/Coats Communications Decency Act.* 1995. http://www.cdt. org/publications/pp190620.html (16 Aug. 2000).

Berman, Jerry, et al. *Analysis of Proposed Revision of Exon CDA.* 1995. http://www.cdt.org/publications/pp140526.html (16 Aug. 2000).

Bersheid, Ellen. "Privacy: A Hidden Variable in Experimental Social Psychology." *Journal of Social Issues* 33 (1977): 85–101.

Bezanson, Randall P. "The Right to Privacy Revisited: Privacy, News, and Social Change, 1890–1990." *California Law Review* 80 (1992): 1133–75.

Biden, Joseph. *Comprehensive Counter Terrorism Act of 1991.* 24 January 1991. http://thomas.loc.gov/cgi-bin/bdquery/D?d102:1:. /temp/~bdtnWx:@@@L/bss/d102query.html (23 Sept. 2000).

Bloomberg News, 29 January 1999.

Bloustein, Edward J. "Privacy as an Aspect of Human Dignity: An Answer to Dean Prosser." In *Philosophical Dimensions of Privacy: An Anthology,* ed. Ferdinand David Schoeman. Cambridge: Cambridge University Press, 1984.

Bok, Sisela. *Secrets: On the Ethics of Concealment and Revelation.* New York: Pantheon, 1982.

Borgatta, E. F., and H. J. Meyer, eds. *Sociological Theory: Present-Day Sociology From the Past.* New York: Knopf, 1956.

Boston Globe, 4 July 1996–3 March 2000.

Bradford, William. *History of Plymouth Plantation, 1620–1627.* Boston: Massachusetts Historical Society, 1912.

Branscomb, Anne Wells. *Who Owns Information? From Privacy to Public Access.* New York: Basic Books, 1994.

Busha, Charles H., and Stephen P. Harter. *Research Methods in Librarianship: Techniques and Interpretation.* New York: Academic Press, 1980.

Cate, Fred H. *Privacy in the Information Age.* Washington, D.C.: Brookings Institute Press, 1997.

Cavoukian, Ann, and Don Tapscott. *Who Knows: Safeguarding Your Privacy in a Networked World.* New York: MacGraw-Hill, 1996.

CBS. *CBS This Morning: Deirdre Mulligan, Center for Democracy and Technology, Discusses Internet Privacy Laws.* 13 May 1999. Available from *Lexis-Nexis* (26 Mar. 2000).

———. *CBS This Morning: Business News and Stock Report.* 28 July 1999. Available from *Lexis-Nexis* (26 Mar. 2000).

Cellular Telecommunications Industry Association, et al. *Communications Assistance for Law Enforcement Act (CALEA): Industry and Privacy Advocates Response to FBI Implementation Plan.* 29 April 1997. http://www.cdt.org/digi_tel/970429_resp_over.html (22 Aug. 2000).

Cellular Telecommunications Industry Association, and Center for Democracy and Technology. *Petition for Review.* 22 November 1999. http://www.cdt.org/digi_tel/appeal/appeal.shtml (15 Aug. 2000).

Center for Democracy and Technology. *CDT Policy Post 3/24/95, Number 6.* 24 March 1995. http://www.cdt.org/publications /pp060323.html (16 Aug.2000).

―――. *CDT Policy Post 3/30/95, Number 7.* 30 March 1995. http://www.cdt.org/publications/pp070330.html (16 Aug. 2000).

―――. *CDT Policy Post 4/7/95, Number 8.* 7 April 1995. http://www.cdt.org/publications/pp080407.html (16 Aug. 2000).

―――. *CDT Policy Post 5/26/95, Number 14.* 26 May 1995. http://www.cdt.org/publications/pp140526.html (16 Aug. 2000).

―――. *CDT Policy Post 6/6/95, Number 16.* 6 June 1995. http://www.cdt.org/publications/pp160606.html (16 Aug. 2000).

―――. *CDT Policy Post 6/14/95, Number 18.* 14 June 1995. http://www.cdt.org/publications/pp180614.html (16 Aug. 2000).

―――. *CDT Policy Post 6/21/95, Number 20.* 21 June 1995. http://www.cdt.org/publications/pp200621.html (16 Aug. 2000).

―――. *CDT Policy Post 12/1/95, Number 30.* 1 December 1995. http://www.cdt.org/publications/pp301201.html (16 Aug. 2000).

―――. *CDT Policy Post 12/4/95, Number 31.* 4 December 1995. http://www.cdt.org/publications/pp311204.html (16 Aug. 2000).

―――. *CDT Policy Post 12/6/95, Number 32.* 6 December 1995. http://www.cdt.org/publications/pp321206.html (16 Aug. 2000).

―――. *House Approves New Unconstitutional Indecency Statute.* 1995. http://www.cdt.org/speech/cda/950804hsecrim.html (19 Aug. 2000).

―――. *CDT Policy Post 1/4/96, Number 33.* 4 January 1996. http://www.cdt.org/publications/pp33010496.html (16 Aug. 2000).

―――. *CDT Policy Post 2/1/96, Volume 2, Number 5.* 1 February 1996. http://www.cdt.org/publications/pp_2.5.html (16 Aug. 2000).

———. *CDT Policy Post 2/8/96, Volume 2, Number 6.* 8 February 1996. http://www.cdt.org/publications/pp_2.6.html (16 Aug. 2000).

———. *CDT Policy Post 3/1/96, Volume 2, Number 8.* 1 March 1996. http://www.cdt.org/publications/pp_2.8.html (16 Aug. 2000).

———. *CDT Policy Post 3/14/96, Volume 2, Number 10.* 14 March 1996. http://www.cdt.org/publications/pp_2.10.html (16 Aug. 2000).

———. *Comments on the FBI's Second CALEA Capacity Notice.* 18 February 1997. http://www.cdt.org/digi_tel/970218_comments. html (22 Aug. 2000).

———. *Petition for Rulemaking Under Sections 107 and 109 of the Communications Assistance for Law Enforcement Act.* 26 March 1998. http://www.cdt.org/digi_tel/980426_fcc_calea.html (22 Aug. 2000).

———. *Comments of the Center for Democracy and Technology in the Matter of Communications Assistance for Law Enforcement Act: Extension of October 1998 Compliance Date.* 2 April 1998. http://www.cdt.org/digi_tel/cdtcomments.html (22 Aug. 2000).

———. *Comments of the Center for Democracy and Technology in the Matter of Communications Assistance for Law Enforcement Act.* 20 April 1998. http://www.cdt.org/digi_tel/calea052098.html (15 Aug. 2000).

———. *Reply Comments of the Center for Democracy and Technology in the Matter of Communications Assistance for Law Enforcement Act.* 12 June 1998. http://www.cdt.org/digi_tel/cdtreplycom.html (15 Aug. 2000).

———. *Constitutional Analysis of the Oxley Bill—The Child Online Protection Act (H. R. 3783).* 1998. http://www.cdt.org/speech /copa/980924constitutional.html (16 Aug. 2000).

———. *Reply Comments of the Center for Democracy and Technology.* 27 January 1999. http://www.cdt.org/digi_tel/cdtreply012799. shtml (22 Aug. 2000).

———. *CDT Asks Equipment Manufacturers How They Plan to Implement the ID Feature.* 16 February 1999. http://www.cdt.org /privacy/issues/pentium3/990216oem.letter.shtml (23 Aug. 2000).

———. *CDT Policy Post 8/31/99, Volume 5, Number 21.* 31 August 1999. http://www.cdt.org/publications/pp_5.21.html (22 Aug. 2000).

———. *Equipment Manufacturer's Default Settings on the Intel Pentium III PSN*. 1999. http://www.cdt.org/privacy/issues /pentium3/990414OEM.shtml (23 Aug. 2000).

———. *CDT Principles*. 2000a. http://www.cdt.org/mission /principles.shtml (24 Jan. 2000).

———. *Chapter Three: Existing Federal Privacy Laws*. 2000b. http://www.cdt.org/privacy/guide/protect/laws.html (17 Aug. 2001).

———. *COPA Commission*. 2000c. http://www.cdt.org/speech /copa/commission.html (14 Aug. 2000).

———. *FCC Wiretap Decision Challenged*. 2000d. http://www.cdt. org/digi_tel/appeal (15 Aug. 2000).

———. *Getting Started: Top Ten Ways to Protect Privacy Online*. 2000e. http://www.cdt.org/privacy/guide/basic/topten.html (17 Aug. 2001).

———. *Summary of CDT Activities 1999—Work Plan 2000*. 2000f. http://www.cdt.org/mission/activities2000.html (5 Oct. 2000).

———. *Supporting CDT*. 2000g. http://www.cdt.org/mission /supporters.shtml (24 Jan. 2000).

———. *Survey*. 2000h. http://www.cdt.org/privacy/survey /findings/cdtbody.html (29 Jan. 2000).

———. *CDT.org Resource Library: Privacy: Tools: Categories*. 2001. http://www.cdt.org/resourcelibrary/Privacy/Tools (17 Aug. 2001).

Center for Democracy and Technology, Electronic Frontier Foundation, and Computer Professionals for Social Responsibility. *Comments of the Center for Democracy and Technology, Electronic Frontier Foundation, and Computer Professionals for Social Responsibility*. 12 December 1997. http://www.cdt.org/digi_tel /971212_nprm_comments.htm (22 Aug. 2000).

Center for Democracy and Technology, and Computer Professionals for Social Responsibility. *Reply Comments of the Center for Democracy and Technology, and Computer Professionals for Social Responsibility Regarding Implementation of the Communications Assistance for Law Enforcement Act* (CALEA). 11 February 1998. http://www. cdt.org/digi_tel/980211_fcc.html (22 Aug. 2000).

Chapin, F. S. "Some Housing Factors Related to Mental Hygiene." *Journal of Social Issues* 7 (1951): 164–171.

Citizens Internet Empowerment Coalition. *Citizens Internet Empowerment Coalition Trial Bulletin Update No. 15, October 31, 1996.* 31 October 1996. http://www.ciec.org/bulletins/bulletin_15.html (9 Aug. 2000).

———. *Brief for Appellants.* 1997a. http://www.ciec.org/SC_appeal /970121_DOJ_brief.html (9 Aug. 2000).

———. *U.S. Supreme Court Rules on Communications Decency Act: Reactions from Plaintiffs and Attorneys.* 1997b. http://www.ciec.org /SC_appeal/970626_CIEC.shtml (20 Aug. 2000).

Cleaver, Cathy. *Court Reaffirms Government's Interest in Protecting Children from Porn, But Strikes CDA As Too Broad.* 1997. http://www.ciec/org/SC_appeal/970626_FRC.html (20 Aug. 2000).

CNN. *The World Today: Advocates Warn of Dangers of Internet Data.* 19 September 1996. Available from *Lexis-Nexis* (26 Mar. 2000).

———. *CNN Today: The Computerization of Medical Records Breed Questions of Privacy.* 5 March 1997. Available from *Lexis-Nexis* (26 Mar. 2000).

———. *CNN Today: Dempsey: "The Traditional Constitutional Principles are Adequate for Cyberspace."* 20 August 1999. Available from *Lexis-Nexis* (26 Mar. 2000).

CNet News.com, 11 February 1999–28 April 2000.

CPA WebTrust. *About WebTrust.* 2001. http://www.cpawebtrust. org/factsheet.htm (1 Sept. 2001).

Cranor, Lorrie Faith, Joseph Reagle, and Mark S. Ackerman. *Beyond Concern: Understanding Net Users' Attitudes About Online Privacy.* 1999. http://www.research.att.com/library/trs/TRS/99/99.4 /99.4.3/report.htm (28 Jan. 2000).

Crespi, Irving. *Public Opinion, Polls, and Democracy.* Boulder, Colo.: Westview, 1989.

Davis, Robert C. "Confidentiality and the Census, 1790–1929." In United States Department of Health, Education, and Welfare, *Records, Computers, and the Rights of Citizens.* Washington, D.C.: Government Printing Office, 1973. Quoted in David J. Seipp, *The Right of Privacy in American History* (Cambridge: Harvard University Program on Information Resources Policy, 1978), 23.

Decew, Judith W. "Defending the 'Private' in Constitutional Policy." *Journal of Value and Inquiry* 21 (1987): 171–184.

Dempsey, James X. *Status Report on the Communications Assistance for Law Enforcement Act (CALEA): FBI Seeks to Impose Surveillance Mandates on Telephone System: Balanced Objectives of 1994 Law Frustrated.* 1999. http://ww.cdt.org/digi_tel/status.html (22 Aug. 2000).

Denver Post, 22 January 1995–1 May 1999.

Detroit News, 19 October 1998–17 February 2000.

Doubleclick. *Doubleclick Press Kit.* 1996–2000a. http://www. doubleclick.com:8080/company_info/press_kit (10 Aug. 2000).

———. *Doubleclick Privacy Statement.* 1996–2000b. http://www. doubleclick.com:8080/privacy_policy (10 Aug. 2000).

"Draft Bill Would Give FCC Role in Regulating On-Line Speech." *Communications Daily.* 1 June 1995. http://www.cdt.org/speech /cda/950601cd.html (16 Aug. 2000).

Eckerson, Wayne. "Privacy Suit Forces Users to Examine E-mail Policies: Case against Epson Raising Troubling Questions." *Network World* 17 (17 September 1990): 1–2.

Edney, J. J., and M. A. Buda. "Distinguishing Territoriality and Privacy: Two Studies." *Human Ecology* 4 (1976): 283–296.

Electronic Frontier Foundation. *New Foundation Established to Encourage Computer-Based Communications Policies.* 10 July 1990. http://www.eff.org/pub/Misc/EFF/Historical/eff_founded. announce (21 Sept. 2000).

———. *Berman to Head New EFF Washington Office.* 15 January 1992. http://www.eff.org/pub/Misc/EFF/Historical/eff_dc_ office.announce (21 Sept. 2000).

———. *About the Electronic Frontier Foundation.* 1996. http://www.eff.org/pub/Misc/EFF/about.eff (21 Sept. 2000).

Electronic Privacy Information Center. *About EPIC.* n. d. http://www.epic.org (15 Aug. 2001).

Elgesem, Dag. "Privacy, Respect for Persons, and Risk." In *Philosophical Perspectives on Computer-Mediated Communication,* ed. Charles Ess. Albany: State University of New York Press, 1996.

Emmerson, Thomas. *The System of Freedom of Expression.* New York: Random House, 1970.

Ennis, Bruce, et al. *ALA Plaintiff's Memorandum of Law in Support of Their Motion for a Preliminary Injunction.* 1996. http://www.ciec.org/trial/injunction_brief.html (19 Aug. 2000).

Ess, Charles, ed. *Philosophical Perspectives on Computer-Mediated Communication.* Albany: State University of New York Press, 1996.

Etzioni, Amitai. *The Limits of Privacy.* New York: Basic Books, 1999.

Eysenck, Hans Jurgen, and Sybil B. J. Eysenck. *Personality Structure and Measurement.* London: Routledge & Kegan Paul, 1969.

Feingold, Russ. *Feingold Applauds Supreme Court Decision Striking Down Unconstitutional Internet Censorship Law.* 1997. http://www. ciec.org/SC_appeal/970626_Feingold.html (20 Aug. 2000).

Fischer, C. T. "Toward the Structure of Privacy: Implications for Psychological Assessment." In *Duquesne Studies in Phenomenological Psychology,* ed. A. Giorgi, W. G. Fischer, and R. von Eckartsberg. Pittsburgh, Penn.: Duquesne University Press, 1971.

Flaherty, David. *Privacy in Colonial New England.* Charlottesville: University Press of Virginia, 1967.

———. *Protecting Privacy in Surveillance Societies.* Chapel Hill: University of North Carolina Press, 1989.

Foddy, William. *Constructing Questions for Interviews and Questionnaires: Theory and Practice in Social Research.* Cambridge: Cambridge University Press, 1994.

Foddy, W. H., and W. R. Finighan. "The Concept of Privacy from a Symbolic Interaction Perspective." *Journal for the Theory of Social Behavior* 10 (1981): 1–17.

Freeh, Louis. *Prepared Statement of Louis J. Freeh, Director, Federal Bureau of Investigation, Before the House Committee on the Judiciary Subcommittee on Crime.* 20 March 1995. Available from Congressional Universe (20 Mar. 1995).

Fried, Charles. *An Anatomy of Values: Problems of Personal and Social Choice.* Cambridge: Harvard University Press, 1970.

Fries, John, and Thomas Carpenter. *The Two Trials of John Fries On an Indictment for Treason.* Philadelphia: William Wallis Woodward, 1800. Quoted in David J. Seipp, *The Right to Privacy in American History* (Cambridge: Harvard University Program on Information Resources Policy, 1978), 19.

Gales, Joseph, comp. "Census of the Union." *Annals of the Congress of the United States.* Washington, D.C.: Globe Office, 1865–1873. Quoted in David J. Seipp, *The Right to Privacy in American History* (Cambridge: Harvard University Program on Information Resources Policy, 1978), 18.

Gandy, Oscar. *The Panoptic Sort: A Political Economy of Personal Information.* Boulder, Colo.: Westview, 1993.

Gans, David, and Ken Goffman. *Mitch Kapor and John Barlow Interview.* 5 August 1990. http://www.eff.org/pub/Misc/Publications /John_Pe.../barlow_and_kapor_in_wired.interview (21 Sept. 2000).

Gavison, Ruth. "Privacy and the Limits of Law." In *Philosophical Dimensions of Privacy: An Anthology,* ed. Ferdinand David Schoeman. Cambridge: Cambridge University Press, 1984.

Gay, L. R. *Educational Research: Competencies for Analysis and Application.* 5th ed. Upper Saddle River, N.J.: Prentice-Hall, 1996.

Geisinger, Patrick. *RSA Data Security Conference and Expo '99: "A Billion Trusted Computers."* 20 January 1999. http://www.intel. com/pressroom/archive/speeches/pg012099.htm (23 Aug. 2000).

Gellman, Robert. "Privacy." In *Federal Information Policies in the 1990s: Views and Perspectives,* ed. Peter Hernon, Charles McClure, and Harold C. Relyea. Norwood, N.J.: Ablex, 1996.

Gerstein, Robert S. "Intimacy and Privacy." In *Philosophical Dimensions of Privacy: An Anthology,* ed. Ferdinand David Schoeman. Cambridge: Cambridge University Press, 1984.

Gingrich, Newt. *Interview with David Frost, PBS 5/31/95.* 1995. http://www.cdt.org/speech/cda/950531gingrich_exon.html (16 Aug. 2000).

Glasser, Ira. *Visions of Liberty: The Bill of Rights for All Americans.* New York: Arcade, 1991.

Goode, Stephen. *The Right to Privacy.* New York: Franklin Watts, 1983.

Gorelick, Jamie S. *Text of DoJ Letter to Senator Exon.* 26 June 1996. http://www.ciec.org/SC_appeal/DOJ_Exon_ltr.html (18 Aug. 2000).

Graphics, Visualization & Usability Center. *Graphics, Visualization & Usability Center's 8th WWW User Survey.* 1997. http://www.gvu.gatech.edu/user_survey?survey-1997–10 (29 Jan. 2000).

Grassley, Charles. *Protection of Children from Computer Pornography Act of 1995.* 1995. http://thomas.loc.gov/cgi-bin/query/c?c104:. /temp/~c104p7KJK (18 Aug. 2000).

Greenleaf, Simon. *A Treatise on the Law of Evidence.* 3d ed. Boston: Little & Brown, 1846. Quoted in David J. Seipp, *The Right to Privacy in American History* (Cambridge: Harvard University Program on Information Resources Policy, 1978), 12.

Gross, Hyman. "Privacy and Autonomy." In *Privacy*, ed. J. Roland Pennock and John W. Chapman. New York: Atherton, 1971.

Halmos, Paul. *Solitude and Privacy: A Study of Social Isolation, Its Causes and Therapy*. London: Routledge & Kegan Paul, 1952.

Harris, Louis, and Equifax. *Health Information Privacy Survey 1993*. Atlanta, Georgia: Equifax, Inc., 1993.

Harris, Louis, and Alan Westin. *Harris-Equifax Consumer Privacy Survey 1992*. Atlanta, Georgia: Equifax, Inc., 1992.

———. "BW/Harris Poll: Online Insecurity." *Business Week*. 1998a. http://www.businessweek.com/1998/11/b3569107.htm (29 Jan. 2000).

———. *E-commerce & Privacy: What Net Users Want*. Hackensack, N.J.: Privacy & American Business, 1998b.

Hernon, Peter, Charles McClure, and Harold C. Relyea, eds. *Federal Information Policies in the 1990s: Views and Perspectives*. Norwood, N.J.: Ablex, 1996.

Holsti, Ole R. *Content Analysis for the Social Sciences and Humanities*. Reading, Mass.: Addison-Wesley, 1969.

Houston Chronicle, 7 July 1996–10 May 1999.

Hubbard, Gardiner G. "Our Post Office." *Atlantic Monthly* 35 (1875): 97–104. Quoted in David J. Seipp, *The Right to Privacy in American History* (Cambridge: Harvard University Program on Information Resources Policy, 1978), 9.

Intel. *Find Your New Intel Processor Powered PC at These Manufacturers' Web Sites*. 2000a. http://www.intel.com/home/buynow/maker.htm (23 Aug. 2000).

———. *Pentium III Processors: Processor Serial Number Control Utility*. 2000b. http://support.intel.com/support/processors/pentiumiii/snum.htm (23 Aug. 2000).

———. *Pentium III Processors: Processor Serial Number Questions and Answers*. 2000c. http://support.intel.com/support/processors/pentiumiii/psqa.htm (23 Aug. 2000).

Internet Working Group. *Letter to Senators Pressler, Exon, and the Senate Commerce Committee*. 9 February 1995. http://www.cdt.org/publications/pp30302.html (18 Aug. 2000).

———. *Child Protection and Parental Empowerment in Interactive Media*. 9 November 1995. http://ww.cdt.org/speech/cda/951109_iwg_ltr.html (18 Aug. 2000).

Introna, Lucas D. "Privacy and the Computer: Why We Need Privacy in the Information Society." *Metaphilosophy* 28 (1997): 259–275.

Ittelson, William H., et al. *An Introduction to Environmental Psychology*. New York: Holt, Rinehart and Winston, 1974.

Kapor, Mitch, and John Perry Barlow. *Across the Electronic Frontier*. 10 July 1990. http://www.eff.org/pub/Misc/EFF/electronic_ frontier.rff (20 Sept. 2000).

Kapor, Mitch, et al. *Major Changes at the Electronic Frontier Foundation*. 13 January 1993. http://www.eff.org/pub/Misc/EFF /Historical/major_changes.announce (21 Sept. 2000).

Katz, James E., and Annette R. Tassone. "Public Opinion Trends: Privacy and Information Technology." *Public Opinion Quarterly* 54 (1990): 125–144.

Kelvin, Peter. "A Social-Psychological Examination of Privacy." *British Journal of Social and Clinical Psychology* 12 (1973): 248–261.

Lardner, James. "Intel Even More Inside." *U.S. News Online*. 8 February 1999. http://www.usnews.com/usnews/issue/990208 /8inte.htm (26 Aug. 2000).

Leahy, Patrick. *Senate Floor Statement of Senator Leahy on Censoring Cyberspace*. 30 March 1995. http://www.cdt.org/publications /pp070330.html (16 Aug. 2000).

———. *Child Protection, User Empowerment, and Free Expression in Interactive Media Study Bill (S. 714)*. 7 April 1995. http://thomas. loc.gov/cgi_bin/query/C?c104:./temp?~c104JwzSa3 (18 Aug. 2000).

———. *Statement on Supreme Court's Decision Declaring Unconstitutional the Communications Decency Act*. 1997. http://www. ciec.org/SC_appeal/970626_Leahy.html (20 Aug. 2000).

Linowes, David F. *Privacy in America: Is Your Private Life in the Public Eye?* Urbana: University of Illinois Press, 1989.

Lofgren, Zoe. *Congresswoman Lofgren Urges Sensible Solution Not "Knee Jerk" Posturing*. 1997. http://www.ciec.org/SC_appeal /970626_Lofgren.html (20 Aug. 2000).

Los Angeles Times, 19 September 1999.

Maines, Jepsen Ronald D., M. Kendall Brown, and Enough is Enough. *Amici Curiae Brief*. 1997. http://www.ciec/org/SC_appeal /970121_EIE_brief.html (9 Aug. 2000).

Marcus, Kent. *Department of Justice's Letter to Senator Patrick Leahy Regarding the Communications Decency Act*. 13 May 1995. http://www.cdt.org/speech/cda/950503doj_ltr.html (18 Aug. 2000).

Margulis, Stephen T. "Conceptions of Privacy: Current Status and Next Steps." *Journal of Social Issues* 33 (1997): 5–21.

Markey, Edward. *Markey Reaction to Online Censorship Ruling.* 1997. http://www.ciec.org/SC_appeal/970626_Markey.html (20 Aug. 2000).

Marshall, Nancy J. "Dimensions of Privacy Preferences." *Multivariate Behavioral Research* 9 (1974): 255–271.

Massachusetts Historical Society. *Collections,* 3d serv., v. 7. Quoted in David J. Seipp, *The Right to Privacy in American History* (Cambridge: Harvard University Program on Information Resources Policy, 1978), 8.

McCandish, Stanton. *EFF's Top 12 Ways to Protect Your Online Privacy.* 2001. http://www.eff.org/Privacy?eff_privacy_top_12.html (17 Aug. 2001).

McCloskey, H. J. "Privacy and the Right to Privacy." *Philosophy* 55 (1980): 17–38.

McGinley, Phyllis. *Province of the Heart.* New York: Viking, 1959.

McLean, Deckle. *Privacy and Its Invasion.* Westport, Conn.: Praeger, 1995.

Meeks, Brock N. "Berman's Bailout." *Wired.* Archive 3.03 1995. htp://www.wired.com/wired/archive/3.03/eworld.html?pg= 8 (6 Aug. 2000).

Merriam, W. R. "The Evolution of American Census-Taking." *Century* 65 (1903): 831–842. Quoted in David J. Seipp, *The Right to Privacy in American History* (Cambridge: Harvard University Program on Information Resources Policy, 1978), 19.

Miller, Seumas. "Privacy, Data Bases, and Computers." *Journal of Information Ethics* 7 (1998): 42–48.

Mulligan, Deirdre K., et al. In the *Matter of Doubleclick: Statement of Additional Facts and Grounds for Relief.* Washington, D.C.: n. p., 2000.

Murphy, Paul L. ed. *Criminal Procedure.* New York: Garland, 1990.

———. *Free Press.* New York: Garland, 1990.

———. *Free Speech.* New York: Garland, 1990.

———. *Religious Freedom: Separation and Free Exercise.* New York: Garland, 1990.

———. *The Right to Privacy and the Ninth Amendment.* New York: Garland, 1990.

————. *Rights to Assembly, Petition, Arms and Just Compensation.* New York: Garland, 1990.

Murray, Patricia. *Murray Outlines Plan to Protect Children from Material on Internet.* 1997. http://www.ciec.org/SC_appeal /970626_Murray.html (20 Aug. 2000).

Nadler, Jerrold. *Representative Nadler Hails U.S. Supreme Court Decision Striking Down the "Communications Decency Act."* 1997. http:///www.ciec.org/SC_appeal/970626_Nadler.html (20 Aug. 2000).

Newell, Patricia Brierley. "Perspectives on Privacy." *Journal of Environmental Psychology* 15 (1995): 87–104.

New York Times, 19 July 1875–7 February 2000.

NPR. *All Things Considered: Hour 2: Several States Angered Over Funding Given by the Federal Government to a Private Company Using Driver's License Photos for Fraud Protection.* 18 February 1999. Available from *Lexis-Nexis* (26 Mar. 2000).

————. *All Things Considered: Privacy Groups Struggling to Make Sure New Banking Reform Bill Includes Privacy Protections for Banking Customers.* 30 June 1999. Available from *Lexis-Nexis* (26 Mar. 2000).

————. *Talk of the Nation: How to Deal with Telemarketers and Unwanted Direct Mail and Email.* 10 January 2000. Available from *Lexis-Nexis* (26 Mar. 2000).

————. *All Things Considered: Supreme Court Ruling that Forbids States to Disclose Information on People's Drivers Licenses.* 12 January 2000. Available from *Lexis-Nexis* (26 Mar. 2000).

————. *Morning Edition: Clinton Administration Reduces Barriers to Exporting Encryption Software.* 13 January 2000. Available from *Lexis-Nexis* (26 Mar. 2000).

————. *Morning Edition: Lawsuit Brought by Northwest Airlines Against Several of Its Employees Now Raising Concerns Over Privacy Issues.* 24 February 2000. Available from *Lexis-Nexis* (26 Mar. 2000).

————. *All Things Considered: Online Advertising Company Doubleclick Pulls Back from Its Plan to Link Names and Addresses to the Surfing Habits of People Who Visit Web Sites.* 2 March 2000. Available from *Lexis-Nexis* (26 Mar. 2000).

O'Connor, Kevin. *Statement from Kevin O'Connor, CEO of Doubleclick.* 2000. http://www.doubleclick.com.../company_info /press_kit /pr.00.03.02.htm (10 Aug. 2000).

O'Connor, Sandra Day, and William Rehnquist. *Concurrence by Justice O'Connor and Chief Justice Rehnquist: Janet Reno, Attorney General of the United States, et al., Appellants vs. American Civil Liberties Union,* et al. 1997. http://www.ciec.org/SC_appeal/concurrence.shtml (20 Aug. 2000).

Olsen, Donald J. "Victorian London: Specialization, Segregation, and Privacy." *Victorian Studies* 17 (1974): 265–278.

Oxley, Michael. *Child Online Protection Act (H. R. 3738 IH).* 30 April 1998. http://thomas.loc.gov/cgi-bin/query/D?c105:1:./temp/~c105zg1WJj (16 Aug. 2000).

Parent, W. A. "Recent Work on the Concept of Privacy." *American Philosophical Quarterly* 20 (1983): 341–355.

Pastalan, Leon A. "Privacy as an Expression of Human Territoriality." In *Spatial Behavior of Older People,* ed. Leon A. Pastalan and Daniel H. Carson. Ann Arbor: University of Michigan Press, 1975.

Pastalan, Leon A., and Daniel H. Carson, eds. *Spatial Behavior of Older People.* Ann Arbor: University of Michigan Press, 1975.

PBS. "Focus—Sex in Cyberspace?" *MacNeil/Lehrer News Hour.* 22 June 1995. http://www.cdt.org/speech/cda/950622macneil_lehrer.html (16 Aug. 2000).

Pedersen, Darhl M. "Dimensions of Privacy." *Perceptual and Motor Skills* 48 (1979): 1291–97.

Pennock, J. Roland, and John W. Chapman, eds. *Privacy.* New York: Atherton, 1971.

Perrson, Christian. "Pentium III Serial Number is Soft Switchable After All." *Heise Online.* 22 February 1999. http://www.heise.de/ct/english/99/05/news1 (23 Aug. 2000).

Privacy Rights Clearinghouse. *More About the Privacy Right Clearinghouse.* n. d. http://www.privacyrights.org/about_us.htm (15 Aug. 2001).

———. *Privacy in Cyberspace: Rule of the Road for the Information Superhighway.* 2001. http://www.privacyrights.org/fs/fs18-cyb.htm (17 Aug. 2001).

Quittner, Joshua. "The Merry Pranksters Go to Washington." *Wired.* Archive 2.06 1994. http://www.wired.com/wired/archive/2.06/eff_pr.html (26 July 2000).

Rachels, James. "Why Privacy is Important." In *Philosophical Dimensions of Privacy: An Anthology,* ed. Ferdinand David Schoeman. Cambridge: Cambridge University Press, 1984.

Reed, Lowell. *Text of Judge Lowell Reed's Opinion.* 1 February 1999. http://www.cdt.org/speech/copa/990201ACLUvsRENOdecision. shtml (14 Aug. 2000).

Regan, Priscilla M. *Legislating Privacy: Technology, Social Values, and Public Policy.* Chapel Hill: University of North Carolina Press, 1995.

Reich, Charles A. *The Greening of America: How the Youth Revolution is Trying to Make America Livable.* New York: Random House, 1970.

Reno, Janet. *ACLU vs. RENO: Notice of Appeal.* 31 March 1999. http://www.cdt.org/speech/copa/990331appealdocument.gif (14 Aug. 2000).

Reuters, 29 April 1999.

Roberts, Bill. "Intel Reconsiders Plan for Security Feature." *Internet World.* 1 February 1999. http://www.internetworld.c...int/1999 /02/01/news/19990201-intel.html (23 Aug. 2000).

Rogers, Michael, and Norman Oder. "Congress Passes Coats' 'CDA II'." *Library Journal* 123 (1998): 13.

Rotenberg, Marc. "In Support of a Data Protection Board in the United States." *Government Information Quarterly* 8 (1991): 79–83.

Rule, James B. *The Politics of Privacy.* New York: Elsevier, 1980.

Salton, Gerard. "A Progress Report on Information Privacy and Data Security." *Journal of the American Society for Information Science* 31 (1980): 75–83.

San Francisco Chronicle, 21 August 1996–26 March 1998.

Schoeman, Ferdinand David. "Privacy: Philosophical Dimensions." *American Philosophical Quarterly* 21 (1984): 199–213.

———. "Privacy: Philosophical Dimensions of the Literature." In *Philosophical Dimensions of Privacy: An Anthology,* ed. Ferdinand David Schoeman. Cambridge: Cambridge University Press, 1984.

Schoeman, Ferdinand David, ed. *Philosophical Dimensions of Privacy: An Anthology.* Cambridge: Cambridge University Press, 1984.

Schwartz, Barry. "The Social Psychology of Privacy." *American Journal of Sociology* 73 (1968): 741–752.

Schwartz, Ephraim, and Dan Briody. "Intel's Pentium Security Woes Continue." *InfoWorld Electric.* 10 March 1999. http://www. infoworld.com/cgi_bin/displayStory.p1?990310.wepsn.htm (23 Aug. 2000).

Seipp, David J. *The Right to Privacy in American History.* Cambridge: Harvard University Program on Information Resources Policy, 1978.

Shafer, Robert Jones, ed. *A Guide to Historical Method*. Homewood, Ill.: Dorsey, 1974.

Shils, Edward. "Privacy: Its Constitution and Vicissitudes." *Law & Contemporary Problems* 31 (1966): 281–306.

Simmel, George. "Knowledge and Ignorance." In *Sociological Theory: Present-Day Sociology from the Past*, ed. E. F. Borgatta, and H. J. Meyer. New York: Knopf, 1956.

Slough, M. C. "The Roots of Privacy." In *Privacy, Freedom and Responsibility*. Springfield, Ill.: Charles C. Thomas, 1969.

Sloviter, Dolores K., Ronald L. Buckwater, and Stewart Dalzell. *Adjudication on Motions for Preliminary Injunction*. 1996. http://www.ciec.org/decision_PA/decision_text.html (19 Aug. 2000).

Smith, Janna Malamud. *Private Matters*. Reading, Mass.: Addison-Wesley, 1997.

Smith, Martha Montague. "Information Ethics." *Annual Review of Information Science and Technology* 32 (1997): 339–366.

Smith, Stephen A. "Communication and the Constitution in Cyberspace." *Communication Education* 43 (1994): 87–101.

Stevens, John Paul. *Supreme Court Opinion: Janet Reno, Attorney General of the United States, et al., Appellants vs. American Civil Liberties Union, et al., on Appeal from the United States District Court for the Eastern District of Pennsylvania*. 1997. http://www.ciec.org /SC_appeal/opinion.shtml (20 Aug. 2000).

Stewart, Sandra. "Whatever Happened to the EFF?" *Industry Standard* (20 March 2000): 156–172.

Stiles, Michael R., et al. *Defendants' Notice of Appeal*. 1996. http://www.ciec.org/SC_appeal/DOJ_notice.html (9 Aug. 2000).

St. Louis Post-Dispatch, 19 October 1998.

St. Mery, Moreau de. *American Journey, 1793–1798*. Trans. Kenneth Roberts and Anna M. Roberts. Garden City, N.Y.: Doubleday, 1947.

Stone, Henry. "The Census of 1880." *Lippincott's* 22 (1978): 108–113. Quoted in David J. Seipp, *The Right to Privacy in America History* (Cambridge: Harvard University Program on Information Resources Policy, 1978), 20.

Stratford, Jean Slemmons, and Juri Stratford. "Computerized and Network Government Information." *Journal of Government Information: An International Review of Policy, Issues and Resources* 25 (1998): 299–303.

Strum, Philippa. *Privacy: The Debate in the United States Since 1945.* Fort Worth, Tex.: Harcourt Brace College Publishers, 1998.

Sullivan, Eamonn. "Web Laws: Less is Definitely More." *PC Week* (8 July 1996): 57.

Tatel, David S. *USTA, et al. vs. FCC: Court Opinion.* 15 August 2000. http://pacer.cade.uscourts.gov/common/opinions/200008/99-1442a.txt (23 Aug. 2000).

Times-Picayune, 27 February 1999–28 July 1999.

TRUSTe. *Building Trust Online: TRUSTe, Privacy and Self-Governance.* n. d. http://www.truste.org/about/truste/index.html (19 Aug. 2001).

Tuerkheimer, Frank M. "The Understandings of Privacy Protection." *Communications of the ACM* 36 (1993): 69–73.

United States Federal Bureau of Investigation. *Electronic Surveillance—Report on the FBI's Publication of the Second Notice of Capacity.* 14 January 1997. http://www.cdt.org/digi_tel/970114fbi1.html (22 Aug. 2000).

———. *Communications Assistance for Law Enforcement Act (CALEA) Implementation Plan.* 3 March 1997. http://www.cdt.org/digi_tel/CALEA_plan.html (22 Aug. 2000).

———. *Reply Comments of the FBI Regarding Implementation of the Communications Assistance for Law Enforcement Act* (CALEA). 11 February 1998. http://www.cdt.org/digi_tel/CALEA_FBI_Reply_980211.html (22 Aug. 2000).

United States Telephone Association, Cellular Telecommunications Industry Association, and Center for Democracy and Technology. *USTA/CTIA/CDT vs. FCC Brief.* 20 January 2000. http://www.cdt.org/digi_tel/appeal/000120cdt-ctia-ustabrief.shtml (15 Aug. 2000).

———. *CTIA/CDT/USTA vs. FCC Reply Brief.* 4 April 2000. http://www.cdt.org./digi_tel/appeal/000404cdt-ctia-ustareply.shtml (15 Aug. 2000).

USA Today, 30 May 1996–13 January 2000.

Velecky, L. C. "The Concept of Privacy." In *Privacy,* ed. John B. Young. Chichester, UK: Wiley, 1978.

Voters Telecommunications Watch. *Campaign to Stop the U.S. Communications Decency Act (S. 314/H. R. 1004).* 17 March 1995. http://www.cdt.org/speech/cda/950317s314campaign.html (16 Aug. 2000).

———. *The Petition is CLOSED.* 5 October 1995. http://www.cdt.org/speech/cda/951005petition.html (16 Aug. 2000).

———. *Petition to Help Senator Leahy Fight the Communications Decency Act and to Prevent the Federal Government from Regulating Online Speech.* 5 October 1995. http://www.cdt.org/speech/cda /951005petition.html (16 Aug. 2000).

———. *Press Release on National Day of Protest from the Net.* 13 December 1995. http://www.cdt.org/speech/cda/951213protest_ pr.html (16 Aug. 2000).

———. *Campaign to Stop the Unconstitutional Communications Decency Act.* 1 January 1996. http://www.cdt.org/speech/cda /960101protest_alert.html (16 Aug. 2000).

———. *Campaign to Stop the Unconstitutional Communications Decency Act. January 31, 1996 (Expires February 29, 1996).* 31 January 1996. http://www.cdt.org/speech/cda/960131alert.html (16 Aug. 2000).

———. *Join Hundreds and Thousands of Other Internet Users in 48 Hours of Protest After President Clinton Signs the Bill That Will Censor the Internet.* 3 February 1996. http://www.cdt.org/speech /cda/960203_48hrs_alert.html (19 Aug. 2000).

Wacks, Raymond. *Personal Information: Privacy and the Law.* Oxford: Clarendon, 1989.

Wall Street Journal, 14 July 1998–1 March 2000.

Ware, Willis H. "The New Faces of Privacy." *Information Society* 9 (1993): 195–211.

Warren, Carol, and Barbara Laslett. "Privacy and Secrecy: A Conceptual Comparison." *Journal of Social Issues* 33 (1977): 43–51.

Washington Post, 17 June 1996–15 March 2000.

Weber, Robert Philip. *Basic Content Analysis.* 2d ed. Newbury Park, Calif.: Sage, 1990.

Weinstein, Michael A. "The Uses of Privacy in the Good Life." In *Privacy,* ed. J. Roland Pennock and John W. Chapman. New York: Atherton, 1971.

Weiss, Avrum Geurin. "Privacy and Intimacy: Apart and a Part." *Journal of Humanistic Psychology* 27 (1987): 118–125.

Westin, Alan F. *Privacy and Freedom.* New York: Atheneum, 1967.

White, Rick. *An Open Letter to the Internet Community.* 4 December 1995. http://www.cdt.org/speech/cda/951204white_ltr.html (18 Aug. 2000).

Bibliography

————. *White Praises Supreme Court for Realizing Potential of the Internet*. 1997. http://www.ciec.org/SC_appeal/970626_White.html (20 Aug. 2000).

Wired News, 27 April 2000.

Wright, Carroll D., and William C. Hunt. *The History and Growth of the United States Census*, Prepared for the Senate Committee on the Census. Washington, D.C.: Government Printing Office, 1900. Quoted in David J. Seipp, *The Right to Privacy in American History* (Cambridge: Harvard University Program on Information Resources Policy, 1978), 19.

Young, John B. *Privacy*. Chichester, UK: Wiley, 1978.

ZDNet News, 26 January 1999–27 April 2000.

Name Index

Italic page numbers indicate figures.

Name Index

Subject Index

Italic page numbers indicate figures.

About the Author

Joyce H-S Li was born in Hong Kong and has lived in Asia, Europe, the Middle East, and North America. She obtained a B.M. from Ohio University, an M.L.S. from Indiana University, and a Ph.D. from the University of Pittsburgh.

Dr. Li is the author of several online and print journal articles in the field of Information Ethics. She has contributed a number of entries to Macmillan's *Computer Sciences* encyclopedia. *The Center for Democracy and Technology and Internet Privacy in the U.S.* is her first monographic publication.

55−